YUGOSLAVIA'S ETHNIC NIGHTMARE

YUGOSLAVIA'S ETHNIC NIGHTMARE

The Inside Story of Europe's Unfolding Ordeal

Edited by
JASMINKA UDOVIČKI & JAMES RIDGEWAY

Lawrence Hill Books

Library of Congress Cataloging-in-Publication Data

Yugoslavia's ethnic nightmare : the inside story of Europe's unfolding
    ordeal / edited by Jasminka Udovički and James Ridgeway.—1st ed.
        p.   cm.
    Includes bibliographical references and index.
    ISBN 1-55652-215-0 (cloth).—ISBN 1-55652-216-9 (paper)
    1. Yugoslavia—History.   2. Yugoslav War, 1991–   .   I. Udovički,
Jasminka, 1945–   .   II. Ridgeway, James, 1936–   .
DR1246.Y84   1995
949.702′4—dc20   94-42717
                                                                      CIP

Chapters 2 through 9 were translated from the Serbo-Croatian
by Karolina Udovički
All rights reserved
Printed in the United States of America
First edition
Published by Lawrence Hill Books, New York, New York
An imprint of Chicago Review Press, Incorporated
814 North Franklin Street
Chicago, Illinois 60610

For the civilian victims of this war—Muslim,
Croatian, and Serb
And for all those who, in agony,
found themselves in arms
against their will

Acknowledgments

The editors are indebted to Hubert Hohn, Leslie Everett, Dusan Kaljensic, and Herbert Krohn for their generous technical help and for assistance in obtaining some rare historical sources.

The publisher wishes to recognize two individuals for their noteworthy contributions to this book: Thanks to Stephen Schwartz, staff writer of the *San Francisco Chronicle,* for illuminating part of the final draft of this work with his extensive knowledge of the Balkans and his editorial assistance, and thanks to copyeditor Barbara Flanagan for bringing her exceptional editorial insight and meticulous attention to detail to bear on this project from its inception.

Contents

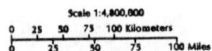

Introduction

James Ridgeway and Jasminka Udovički

At the beginning of the 1990s, a terrible series of events, signaling a crisis in Europe deeper and more troubling than any since World War II, began to unfold in southeastern Europe. The country of Yugoslavia disintegrated. Threats of war and calls for secession by the former Yugoslav republics led to the collapse of the state and to horrific fighting, of a cruelty unseen in Europe for generations.

The scale and sadism of the atrocities that rapidly began to succeed each other so shocked the world public that it was, at least at the beginning, rendered numb and apparently incapable of response. The situation was, most commentators said, a matter of deep ethnic hatred: mainly, of delayed revenge by Serbian patriots for their victimization by Croat fascists in World War II.

As the fighting continued and reached new levels of savagery, spreading from Slovenia through Croatia into Bosnia-Hercegovina, the World War II paradigm of Serbian antifascism came to be reversed. The question was not that of crimes committed fifty years ago, but of those immediately reported and even viewed on the world's television screens: "ethnic cleansing," internments and deportations, massacres, mass rapes, wholesale cultural vandalism. A debate ensued: Was it genocide? Was it as bad as Nazism or in some ways even worse? That and related issues were never adequately addressed and quickly gave way to further imponderables—namely, what can or should the world, Europe, the United States, do about it?

For the victims—Muslims, Christians, and Jews, adults and

1

children, men and women, the strong and active along with the handicapped and helpless, the successful and affluent along with the impoverished and disadvantaged—who remained after Yugoslavia suddenly became a former country, such topics were, of course, interesting, but somewhat dry when compared with daily reality. In the regions devastated by war, it was as if the sky had literally fallen and the world was literally ending.

Across the breathtakingly beautiful landscape, in communities where people had lived together for generations, sadistic monsters appeared whose imaginations—perhaps reflecting the violence increasingly present in global popular culture—had been led to the edge of utter inhumanity, and then pushed beyond the edge. Trained soldiers, irregular combatants, political and ethnic fanatics, and mere criminals broke down the doors of countless dwellings, torturing, killing, kidnapping their peaceful occupants, looting and leveling property.

The toll on the cultural heritage of the former Yugoslavia was the least noticed by the rest of the world. The borders of the state encompassed not only classical Roman ruins, splendid Orthodox Christian monasteries, and the magnificent Venetian-style cities of Dalmatia, but also the greatest array of mosques and other Ottoman structures in Europe and the genuinely unique remains of the fascinating culture of premodern Bosnia-Hercegovina, represented by *stecci*, or gravestones, a resource that existed to the same extent nowhere else.

The balance sheet of three years' fighting, in cultural terms, included hundreds of mosques, Catholic and Orthodox churches, monasteries, and related buildings destroyed or seriously damaged. Some of the most famous and remarkable mosques, in such cities as Banja Luka, Bijeljina, and Visegrad, were leveled altogether. In Sarajevo, the wanton attack on a single building, the National Library of Bosnia-Hercegovina, obliterated thousands of precious manuscripts, wiping out centuries of cultural memory and achievement.

There was yet another cultural price to pay in the degeneration of intellectual and public discourse. A few well-known former dissidents who, in valiant struggle for civil rights under Tito, had gained the support of international human rights groups and the respect of foreign intellectuals suddenly emerged as the most bizarre, extreme, and in the case of one even murderous nationalist agitators. The forms of such advocacy became increasingly pathological, with yesterday's most outspoken proponents of liberalism embracing doctrines that could only be called fascist. Nationalist politicians pranced across the political stage, now made credible by the guns in their hands and the number of followers willing to kill and maim for them.

The immediate human cost was yet greater. Refugees clogged the roads and streets of Croatia, Serbia, and Bosnia-Hercegovina, spilling over into Slovenia, Hungary, Germany and Austria, Italy, and other countries farther away. Even families whose members remained alive were torn apart, some of them losing touch with each other for long stretches of time, if not forever. Ghastly wounds and the heroic efforts of foreign doctors became a feature of television reporting. But who could put a price on the suffering of children who watched their parents, siblings, relatives, and peers gratuitously tortured and killed? Who could predict the effects of such horror in another twenty years? Most important, what did it mean for the rest of the world? Would it spread elsewhere? Was it contagious?

The latter anxieties are shared by many in Western Europe, the United States, and other places, but have yet to be widely addressed or even formulated. Perhaps the prospect is indeed too frightening to be put into words. Certainly, many of the pundits and predictable theorists who have so long dominated Western discussion of international relations have remained confused or silent in the face of the crisis.

It has been the intention of the editors and authors of this book, as well as of its publisher, to provide a view of events that led up to the present Yugoslav nightmare, to unravel the complexities of the Balkan crisis, and to point to some of the far-reaching consequences of the most catastrophic event in Europe since the Holocaust from the standpoint of journalists of former Yugoslavia—all of them strongly opposed to the war. Their testimony presents to the American reader an account that evades repetition of the commonly cited clichés about the subject.

The current war in former Yugoslavia broke out against a background of sea change in Europe, framed on one side by the collapse of the Soviet Union and the Eastern bloc and on the other by the movement for unification of Western Europe. The genocidal war in Yugoslavia that horrifies the world is in part a reflection of these changes and a clue to possible future currents.

The demise of Yugoslavia was not unexpected. In December 1990 the *New York Times* carried the news of a Central Intelligence Agency report predicting that Yugoslavia would fall apart in eighteen months because of ethnic tensions and political infighting among the republics. The report warned that civil war was possible. One month later, in January 1991, at the Conference for Security and Cooperation in Europe (CSCE) meeting in Prague, the British first formally raised the possibility that Yugoslavia could disintegrate during the year.

No one paid much attention. By then the United States had four hundred thousand troops deployed across the Persian Gulf. Among them were American heavy armor redeployed from Germany, where they had been permanently poised to defend Western Europe against a Soviet attack. Events in the Gulf from the initial attack on Baghdad on January 16 to the war's aftermath would consume the attention of the United States and the Western alliance over the next six months.

Policymakers in both the United States and Europe had speculated for some years on whether Yugoslavia could survive Tito. As time went on, the prospect of the country's continued existence seemed more and more uncertain. Slovenia and Croatia, seeking greater economic prosperity, were increasingly raising the possibility of autonomy, if not independence. The new Serbian leader, Slobodan Milosevic, was replacing communism with hysterical nationalism. Yet in the American government no one wanted to deal with another conflict. Despite all the brave talk in Washington about fighting several wars at once, the Pentagon was taken up with the war in Iraq. There was little interest in Yugoslavia.

NATO was as preoccupied as the United States and, as for the Europeans, the CSCE was too new to have any serious bearing on what was to happen. The countries of Western Europe were immersed in the debate over the terms of a united Europe, and the solution to the problems of Yugoslavia was seen only as a function of this larger movement. As it turned out, the unification of Europe would be far more difficult to achieve than anyone expected, at least from a reading of the American press.

The possible rewards of unification were clear. For the European powers, German economic advantage was easier to swallow in the context of a unified Europe. For Germany itself, unification meant a full rehabilitation at last. For the first time since World War II, Germany no longer had to be embarrassed by its past or its economic power. Finally, the time had come for Germany to exercise leadership. Yugoslavia was turned into a testing ground for the strength of Germany versus France and the rest of Europe.

The United States was content to let the Europeans go through the motions of asserting themselves over the breakup of Yugoslavia. How could the United States lose? A common European defense, the Bush administration feared, could only hurt and possibly cripple NATO. But if the Europeans failed to solve Yugoslavia's problems, their lack of unity would enhance NATO's standing and hence that of the United States behind NATO. And if Europe succeeded, then the United States would not have had to get involved.

The American government's position smacked of the self-congratulatory attitude that had come to characterize its foreign policy after the collapse of the Berlin Wall. The United States had driven NATO for forty years and, with the disintegration of the Soviet Union, was more than ever the main geopolitical player in Europe and the world. As Bush was fond of pointing out, there was only one superpower left at the close of this American century, and the United States was it. His administration was especially disingenuous over Yugoslavia: not only had the United States prided itself on its long-standing influence and success in maintaining Yugoslavia as a counterweight within the Communist bloc against the Soviet Union, but, more to the point, the Bush administration's top diplomats had years of firsthand experience in Yugoslavia. Lawrence Eagleburger, the under secretary of state when the war broke out and secretary of state at its peak, had been ambassador to Yugoslavia under Tito, as had Brent Scowcroft, Bush's national security adviser.

The United States and European powers took the disintegration of Yugoslavia rather lightly at first and miscalculated its costs. The case of Yugoslavia meant more than the breakup of a complex federation. Submerged beneath the political map of Yugoslavia, a country roughly the size of Pennsylvania, there existed other, uncharted maps. These were established by a history of alliances and conflicts, of resentment and reconciliation in a collection of eighteen national minorities and six distinct nationalities, dispersed in six republics and two autonomous provinces and practicing four religions: Catholic, Orthodox, Muslim, and Jewish. The submerged maps were to determine how Yugoslavia would fall apart, because those maps had a much longer history than the current modern overlay. But the international community saw none of this.

The essential misconception concerned the principle of "self-determination"—the right of each region, or nation, to rule itself—adopted as the key to efforts to defuse the tensions. But applied to Yugoslavia, a country where the regions seeking self-determination were made up of completely intermixed populations of diverse nationalities, the concept of self-determination turned out to be not only absurd but perilous.

In Slovenia, for example, with an overwhelming Slovene majority, self-determination was a logical value. But Slovenia was the only one among the Yugoslav republics and autonomous provinces in which this was true. All the rest had populations made up of diverse national communities. Croatia has a large Serbian minority; Bosnia-Hercegovina is composed of three major ethnic communities, Bosnian Muslim, Serb, and Croat, none of which constitutes an actual majority; Montenegro and Macedonia have restive Albanian minorities; Serbia proper had a considerable Muslim population in its southern Sanjak region; the province of Vojvodina was dominated in recent years by Serbs but had large Hungarian and Croatian populations; and the province of Kosova,* although with an Albanian majority, included a significant and militant Serbian minority.

As soon as the principle of self-determination was allowed to guide the search for solutions, the question "Who gets what in former Yugoslavia?" became central. The country was falling apart, and the heirs of what remained of Yugoslavia had to divide the inheritance. Each national group had its own claims, asserting either some historical or some demographic right to the same area

---

*The spelling most commonly used is *Kosovo,* but the publisher has elected to use the standard Albanian spelling, which is also now used by many news-gathering organizations.

as other groups. If the international community did not understand the implications, the Serbian President Slobodan Milosevic and the Croatian President Franjo Tudjman understood perfectly. They knew that the appeal to self-determination opened up a unique opportunity for territorial expansion for the stronger parties. Territorial expansion is the true objective of the Yugoslav war. Virulent nationalism, carefully engineered and brought to a pitch first by the Serb and later by the Croat leadership, was the vehicle to make the war happen.

But the foreign powers were still thinking in terms of old cold war strategies and solutions. During the spring and early summer of 1991, the United States waffled over what to do in Yugoslavia. As time went on, Western governments came to view the breakup of Yugoslavia as a precedent for what was beginning to happen in the Soviet Union, and they became more and more sensitive about their approach to handling it. Lord Owen, the British diplomat who together with Cyrus Vance would seek to negotiate a settlement for the war in Bosnia in 1992, noted later, "An essential interest, once the war started, was that the newly established U.S.-Russian partnership over Iraq in the [UN] Security Council could be maintained over Yugoslavia and that the Russian Federation would see it as in their interest to curb the gross excesses of Serb nationalism, for a dangerous national fervor was breaking out all over Europe."

At the outset, the United States did not want to encourage a breakup of Yugoslavia, fearing it might in turn lead to a breakup of the Soviet Union, which might be violent and raise questions about nuclear weapons in the Soviet republics. In addition, Bush's main foreign policy advisers may have misjudged the situation in Yugoslavia, precisely because of their lengthy cordial experience with people like Slobodan Milosevic and others. After all, they had known such people ten to fifteen years earlier as good business or diplomatic partners. The Bush team may have had too much faith that Yugoslav leaders would not act on their extreme nationalist ideology.

Why did NATO not intervene militarily straightaway? Why did the United States, Britain, and France not treat Yugoslavia in the same way they treated the Gulf? Lord Owen commented on the contradictions plaguing the international community in its approach to Yugoslavia. "Could the Europeans in NATO—for after all this is primarily a European problem—have acted militarily without the U.S.?" he asked. "Regrettably, the answer is no. The Germans were excluded militarily . . . [as was Italy]. Turkey and Greece were also mutually excluded. So for France and Britain to fill the gap they would have had to put substantial ground forces into what they felt was a civil war far more complex than was or could be presented on TV. . . . The only military involvement France and Britain would countenance was the vital humanitarian role they began with Spain in the autumn of 1992 and a commitment to help implement any peace plan genuinely agreed between all three parties."

There were military reasons as well. Intervening in wooded mountains and deep valleys was quite different from attacking across flat desert. Tito had built Yugoslavia into a fortress to withstand an attack from the Soviet Union and the West. The Serbs were well armed and had a defense in depth. And what no one acknowledged was that the countries of the former Eastern bloc, desperate for foreign exchange, were doing just as they had done under the Soviet Union: selling arms to whoever would buy. East Germany, Czechoslovakia, Hungary, and Poland all found eager customers in Yugoslavia.

Beneath the banner of unification, the Western Europeans were divided over Yugoslavia. The Germans felt they had historic ties to Croatia and an affinity for Slovenia. German diplomats argued that granting independence for Croatia and Slovenia would deter full-scale civil war in Yugoslavia, at the worst resulting in a limited war over territory between rump Yugoslavia and the two breakaway states. Others within the European community thought that independence for Slovenia and Croatia would precipitate war. The French especially were greatly opposed to the breakup for that reason, as well as for the German interest and influence the French feared in the region. German business interests had rushed east gobbling up businesses, forging new alliances, and sinking millions of dollars into new investments in Czechoslovakia, Hungary, Poland, and they were eagerly eyeing Yugoslavia's skilled labor, as were the Americans, Swiss, and Austrians.

When six months of fighting between Croatia, which wanted out of Yugoslavia, and Serbia, which wanted to preserve Yugoslavia, ended in late 1991, European diplomats thought the conflict had been contained and viewed its management as something of a success, the horror of the war's devastation and its atrocities notwithstanding. The war had not spread, and the alliances created in the Gulf remained in place.

It is widely assumed that behind the scenes in Maastricht—where in December 1991 the European nations met to set the major foundation stone of European unity—the continental powers agreed on the future course in Yugoslavia. According to American diplomats, the Germans insisted on Croatia's independence. The French, fearful of German expansion eastward, wanted a firm agreement on a united Europe that would protect them. In the end the European nations agreed to set up a commission to handle demands for independence by Croatia and other states. But the Germans, feeling confident they had the upper hand in the issue, unilaterally recognized Croatia in early January, before the commission could meet. The rest of Europe and the United States followed suit. After all, Western diplomats argued, trying to appease themselves as much as the rest of the world, Croatia and Slovenia have proved they were democratic—haven't they held free elections in 1990?

So the West made another fatal error. Caught up in one of those old cold war dichotomies, it framed the conflict in Yugoslavia as a conflict between democracy, championed by Croatia and Slovenia, and old-fashioned communism, represented by Serbia, where free elections had not taken place. The dichotomous view was politically and intellectually evasive and ignored the facts. The Yugoslav conflict was in fact a conflict between two conceptions of strident ultranationalism, one propounded by the Serbian regime, the other by the Croatian, and had little to do with either communism or democracy. Free elections or not, Croatia under Franjo Tudjman sought to establish not a Western-style democracy but rather an authoritarian, nationalistic state entirely indifferent to the issue crucial for Yugoslavia: the rights of minority ethnic groups in the republics and provinces. Europe and the United States, including their major media, took pains not to notice.

As the positions on the war were argued behind the scenes, and with the United States engaged in nondiplomacy, the phony propaganda war began. Having scarcely understood Yugoslavia as being, in the best of times, anything more than a pleasing socialist tourist spa, the Western powers sought the root cause of the war in ethnicity, in particular in a suddenly exploding recognition of ethnic identity. According to this interpretation, communism had long provided a sort of hermetic seal on the ethnic identities that purportedly drive the South Slavs. Once the Berlin Wall came down and communism fell, these long-pent-up emotions based on ethnicity burst out.

This interpretation met just about everyone's needs. It offered a pleasing explanation to the West, especially the United States, gloating in its triumph over the Soviet Union. It showed that far from building a brighter world, the Communists had suppressed the human condition, which the United States championed. The arrogance of the United States filled the newspapers, providing an ideological gloss on the horrible images that appeared on the screen every night.

The glib assumption in the West has been that the war in Yugoslavia was some sort of "ethnic" conflict. Yet for at least the last fifty years, the peoples of former Yugoslavia were referring to themselves not as "ethnic groups" but as "nations," a concept that the Western media find hard to comprehend. In one sense "ethnic group" and "nation" are similar terms. Both apply to communities tied by blood, language, customs, worship, and a shared sense of history as well as a collective memory. But "nation" implies in addition a state to which the nation belongs and the "ethnic group" does not. The distinction stems from the nineteenth century, when nation-states were first formed in Europe. The "real" nations—France, Britain, Germany, Italy—were, according to Western nineteenth-century political vocabulary, the "historical nations." They had old and well-established empires; they each had a language cultivated not only by their cultured elites but also by their diplomatic emissaries and bureaucrats; and they had political institutions guaranteeing their sovereignty as nations. Other proud trappings also distinguished their nationhood: booming industrial zones, expanding markets, railways, grand theaters, magnificent department stores, telephones, and social graces—the commodity in short supply among the "ethnic" non-Westerners. In short, in the nineteenth-century Western consciousness, historical nations embodied progress. As Eric Hobsbawm has shown, Western liberal bourgeoisie took all that into account and established the "threshold principle" for awarding the status of nation: size was the determining factor. "Great" meant that all this progress could be comfortably contained within a single common polity, a single nation-state.

"Small" was the opposite. Yet between 1830 and 1880, a number of smaller nations also emerged to claim their space as nation-states on the map of Europe, among them Serbia alongside Greece, Bulgaria, Romania, and then Poland, Czechoslovakia, and Belgium. The term invented to mark a distinction between the smaller nations and the "real," "great" nations was the newly forged German word for "statelets." Highbrow politicians called them with a grin *Kleinstaaterei*. The word implied something absurdly minuscule for its alleged ambitions: a state that was basically a joke.

After 1880, the "threshold principle" was abandoned, and after World War I the Wilsonian principle of national self-determination helped create a Europe with twenty-six states. Thus, despite the ironic grin of the "real" nations, Balkan peoples too became "nations." At the end of the twentieth century, the grin is still there: in the 1990s the peoples of former Yugoslavia were once again called "ethnic groups."

This is important not only because the terminology is wrong but also because the misnomer hides from view an important part of historical reality, especially in the Balkans. The status of a nation had a significant political and social consequence for the relationships between the newly born "nations" and the "national minorities," smaller groups of a different ethnic origin living in the newly formed Balkan states. The regimes representing those states started treating their national minorities with the same contempt Slavic peoples had suffered under Austria-Hungary, the empire A. J. P. Thompson called "the greatest prison-house of nations." Some of those regimes, notably Serbia, adopted yet another criterion implicitly regarded by the great powers as a token of nationhood: the "proven capacity for conquest." In trying to restore its medieval state, Serbia entered the Balkan Wars in 1912–1913. It behaved as all the great nations always have: promoting its own interests through any means available and neglecting the interests of those smaller and weaker than itself. Becoming a "nation" had a great deal to do with Serbia's expansionism.

The current war is the continuation of Serbia's nation building according to the nineteenth-century model of territorial expansion and the twentieth-century model of national "self-determination"—both Western conceptions. The Western solution to this sort of war? A full-throated national self-identity, built on democratic elections. This has been the steady message exported from the United States over the last decade, most especially as it was beamed into Central and Latin America as a counter to Communist ideology. Communism, according to the propaganda, had suppressed discussion of ethnicity. What the Western media failed to say was that in Yugoslavia communism had suppressed ultranationalism. And ultranationalism let loose, not ethnic identity, was the prime cause of the war.

The World War II memories of fratricide, a war cause often cited in the Western media, indeed played an important part in the most recent march toward war in Yugoslavia. The unexamined assumption was that somehow World War II memories would have been less relevant elsewhere in Europe under analogous circumstances. Yet in Yugoslavia, as in other European countries, the memories were still alive, but the emotions underlying the memories had by and large been laid to rest. This was perhaps the greatest achievement of Tito's Yugoslavia. To start the war, therefore, those emotions had to be not only reawakened but exacerbated by half-truths and innuendo. Milosevic turned out to be the master conjurer, a latter-day Machiavelli of the kind that is born perhaps once in a couple of centuries.

The Western media reports talked about his stirring up the ancient ethnic hatreds but failed to notice that he was in fact infinitely more subtle and shrewd. Rather than addressing ethnicity directly, Milosevic addressed something much less abstract and closer to heart: his people's sense of fairness. He drew on their real grievances and then conjured up others that began to appear real only after endless repetition. His focus, however, had never been on ethnicity, but on national injury and injustice. The point was to awaken among the Serbs a sense of being, through no fault of their own, massively wronged by others, endangered wherever they lived as a minority outside of Serbia itself—in Kosova, Croatia, or Bosnia. The voice was shrill, warning of the possibility of physical peril and drawing parallels to the genocide of World War II. The appeal was not to ethnic hatred and revenge but to the innate need for elementary fairness: the Serbs have not deserved this. The appeal was also for righting the painful wrongs by claiming back the inalienable rights of the Serbs as a people—no more. Milosevic portrayed himself as their only true friend: of all Serbian politicians, he alone was committed to assisting the Serbs in regaining their pride and fighting for fairness. This approach worked infinitely better than the appeal to square some fictitious ancient accounts would have done, particularly because Milosevic was talking to the Serbs in Serbia not about their own experiences and grievances but about someone else's: those with whom most of his audience had little contact—the Serbs in Kosova, Croatia, and Bosnia. Their grievances were not verifiable through direct personal perceptions of the Serbian Serbs; the truth of Milosevic's claims could not be challenged without an uncomfortable sense of betrayal of one's own kin. Milosevic built his following on wildly exaggerated claims of injustice that had just enough basis in reality to bewilder, frighten, and make the danger appear vaguely but inexorably imminent.

Yet Western media stuck to "tribalism" as the explanation for the war. The Balkans were a dark, mysterious place in the Western view, a place inhabited by primitives governed, if ever, by old tribal codes beyond modern understanding, and perhaps best left alone. The tacit understanding was that Western Europeans knew best: they had tried to deal with these people for centuries, and without much success. The atrocities were unspeakable, especially those visited on the children, but what can be done in the face of such tribalism? When all was said and done, one must realize that the Balkans were a true no-man's-land. Something terrible had happened to the people who lived there. It was almost biological. The West certainly could not be blamed. It was safest to simply take a hygienic approach: deliver humanitarian aid, drop food from helicopters, help the wounded where one could.

In 1990 and 1991, when the disintegration of Yugoslavia, and with it war, became a clear possibility, the international community could have defused the crisis and pulled the rug out from under Milosevic in one way only: by insisting that any and every republic of Yugoslavia seeking secession and international recognition give demonstrable proof of firm guarantees of minority rights. That, and not the principle of self-determination of the republics, which ultimately guided the decision for the recognition of Slovenia and Croatia, should have formed the core of the comprehensive solution. Had Croatia been forced to guarantee its Serb population all minority rights and to stick by it, Milosevic's war design, whose ideology rested on the allegation of grave violations of those rights, would have suffered a serious blow. But the UN Security Council remained inactive for too long. No rules of peaceful disengagement of the republics of former Yugoslavia and no specific requirement for international recognition of the new states were ever defined. The 1991 recognition of Croatia, despite its flagrant violations of minority rights, further convinced the Serbs that Milosevic knew full well what he was talking about and that not only Kosova, Croatia, and Bosnia but the West as well conspired against Serbia.

A claim can be made that the inaction of the international community was at least in part conditioned by the lack of genuine commitment of the West to sustain Yugoslavia or—the other side of the same coin—by the West's eagerness to see communism finally and irrevocably dismantled in Europe. The disintegration of Yugoslavia implied, after all, also the dissolution of its specific, hybrid form of socialism, which since 1948 had set it apart from Communist Europe. Yugoslavia was not only the country that broke away from the Soviet Union but also the country where the standard of living was continuously rising, where people enjoyed considerable freedoms and could travel abroad whenever and wherever they wished. All in all, it was not a bad place to live. Had it survived, Yugoslav socialism might have remained a viable historical alternative—an irritant to the triumphant restoration of capitalism the world over.

To the European community and the United States, the prospect of the survival of Yugoslav socialism could not have looked too appealing, and they acted accordingly. The Western powers in 1990 withheld the support they promised to Ante Markovic, Yugoslavia's liberal socialist-reformist prime minister and the only politician at the time who stood firmly for a unified, antinationalist Yugoslavia. The future of Yugoslavia hung in the balance—as the CIA report of late 1990 also indicated. But Markovic was an enlightened socialist reformer, not a born-again anti-Bolshevik. With the defeat of Ante Markovic by the joint effort of Slobodan Milosevic and Franjo Tudjman, Yugoslav socialism was definitively crushed, and with it Yugoslavia. The West had done nothing to support Markovic. Instead, it supported the right of self-determination of the former republics. Within the republics, however, the minorities remained entirely unprotected. That was, and to this day is, true for the Kosova Albanians in Serbia, for the Hungarians and Croats in Vojvodina, and for the Serbs in Croatia. And it is true for every region in Bosnia where the Muslims, the Croats, or the Serbs are in the minority.

When, according to the principle of self-determination, the international community recognized the independence of Bosnia-Hercegovina on April 6, 1992, it did so in some gratuitous hope of preventing a total war between Serbia and Croatia over Bosnia. Yet what Bosnia received with the recognition of its right to self-determination was simulacra and nothing more: a state title, a flag, and independence. One could do nothing, least of all defend an entire population, with such chimeras. Instead of dissipating the deepening crisis, the recognition of Bosnia played into the hands of Milosevic and became a precipitating factor in the outbreak of the war.

Meanwhile, having granted Bosnia international recognition, the international community had committed itself to absolutely nothing. No safeguards whatsoever for peace were provided. For the coming two years, noises and motions to the contrary notwithstanding, the world sat and watched "their" tragedy, "their" genocide.

In bringing about the war and sustaining its momentum, Slobodan Milosevic and Franjo Tudjman were engaged in a dance of perfect enemies. In a strange dynamics, each of them, acting ruthlessly to promote his own objectives, made it possible for his archenemy to realize his objectives: the expansion of Serbia in the case of Milosevic, the independence of Croatia and inroads into Bosnia in the case of Tudjman. Meanwhile, the fate of Serbs outside Serbia—Milosevic's cabal and the axis he built his war effort around—had become the cause of untold suffering for Muslim, Croat, and Serb civilians alike.

And the roads crossing the magnificent country of Bosnia became "corridors" as Serbian warlords try to link the occupied territories and eventually join them to Serbia.

ONE

The Rise and Fall of the Balkan Idea

Jasminka Udovički

I t took almost a century, from the emergence of the South Slavic unification movement in the early nineteenth century to the end of World War I, to create Yugoslavia. It took only a few years to destroy it—or so it seemed. Visions of national liberation and modernization brought the South Slavs—the Yugo-Sloveni—excluding only the Bulgarians, together at last in 1919. Seventy years later a retrograde, mythical, antimodern vision tore them apart.

At the heart of their history lay the experience of plural ethnic communities fought over for hundreds of years by competing foreign rulers: Roman popes, Byzantine emperors, Hungarian and Habsburg kings, and Ottoman sultans. Their separate histories under domination from outside divided the South Slavs at the same time as it united them, through a shared desire to be rid of their overlords. After World War I the Yugoslav state was created on the basis of six Slavic nations: Slovenes, Croats, Serbs, Montenegrins, Macedonians, and Muslims (although the latter three groups were at that time effectively counted as Serbs). In addition, the country's population included two large non-Slav minorities, Albanian and Hungarian. The foundation of Yugoslavia reflected the long, slow collapse of the decadent empires, a process expressed in the work of intellectuals and political leaders throughout the nineteenth century and the first two decades of the twentieth. The best of these leaders hoped the bonds of a common Slav origin and close linguistic relations would prove stronger than differences in habits of heart and mind and ways of life imposed under foreign influence. The unification of the South Slavs into a single state, according to nineteenth-century advocates, offered the only way to overcome the alien powers and to secure the survival of small and economically disadvantaged nations in a harsh environment ruled by the great powers.

Today, separated from each other since 1991, by three years of artillery fire, sniping, and massacre, these nations seem even smaller, their environment even harsher and more unjust. Not because they occupy a volatile territory that is the object of foreign ambitions—they no longer do, although some refuse to believe it— but rather because the chaos of evil unleashed in Croatia in 1991 and subsequently in Bosnia seems to have drowned, perhaps forever, the noble vision of a common future, the kind of vision that so profoundly marked the previous century of their history.

To understand the South Slavs and their knotted existence together and apart is to grasp a contradiction. The genuine sense of kinship they shared as Slavs was, and is to this day, coupled with the rival sense of their particular, sub-Slavic identities as Slovenes, Croats, Bosnians, Serbs, Montenegrins, and Macedonians. Memories of long-past independence and glory, preserved in national folk songs, myths, and legends, were passed through generations as a support for communal faith in the future, during the darkest hours of oppression. Yet—and here lies the contradiction—the same resilience and pride in identity that helped each group endure half a millennium or more of bondage turned out to be the most formidable obstacle to their eventual unification.

In many cases South Slavic identity has rested on esoteric but tenacious traditions and claims of medieval statehood. Slovenia, which until 1991 never possessed a state, found any possibility of a medieval political identity erased by the Franks beginning in the eighth century. Croatia was constitutionally absorbed into the Hungarian realm four hundred years later. Serbia, which contended with Bulgaria for Macedonia, was overwhelmed in the fifteenth century by the Turks, who conquered Bosnia soon after.

Only two South Slavic entities remained semi-independent. On the Adriatic, Dubrovnik, also known as Ragusa, maintained itself as a city-state under the remote and light-handed suzerainty of Venetians, Hungarians, and Turks and flourished in its curious isolation. Montenegro (the "Black Mountain") was conquered late by the Turks (in 1699) but was too geographically inhospitable for them to exploit; no revenue could be squeezed out of its shepherds and free peasants, who inhabited mountains too high and too steep to govern. Montenegro also retained considerable self-rule—the source of its remarkable local tradition of independence and courage.

For the other states, the dream of eventual resurrection offered them their only basis for resistance, endurance, and hope. In the late 1980s, in a development wildly at odds with the times, such dreams were reborn along the fault-lines that separated the ethnic territories.

One such fault line, that separating Croats and Serbs, may be said to have originated before their arrival in the region, with the division of the Roman Empire in 395 A.D. between West and East along a line from Belgrade (the ancient Roman city of Singidunum) on the Danube to Scodra (now Shkodër) in northern Albania. The Croats settled north and west of the dividing line, the Serbs south and east. But the division was destined to worsen with the creation in 1578 of the so-called Military Frontier or Vojna Krajina, a zone extending in an arc from the district of Lika in Dalmatia, near the Adriatic coast, north and east through Slavonia and Hungary to the Iron Gates of the Danube. The Frontier, which remained in effect until 1881, was established by Ferdinand, the Holy Roman Emperor, who was elected king of Croatia, and his successor, Maximilian II, as a defense zone to protect Europe from further Turkish incursions.

The idea of the frontier was brilliant; instead of the Christian rulers being obligated to raise armies to respond to Ottoman attacks, local Christian colonists would inhabit and defend a Balkan buffer zone. With the establishment of the Military Frontier, Croatia was divided into "Civil Croatia," governed by the local ecclesiastical and aristocratic elite, and "Military Croatia," ruled from Vienna.

At the time the Military Frontier was set up, the terrain had been devastated and depopulated by the wars with the Turks. However, Croatian nobles protested the establishment of a separate frontier zone, which they saw as a violation of "Croat state right," the legal status that the "triune kingdom" of Croatia, Slavonia, and Dalmatia had claimed to preserve since its union with Hungary in 1102. That political tradition was expressed through an assembly of notables, the Croatian Sabor, that embodied the autonomy of the Croat elite even though the Croatian state had disappeared.

The barren nature of the Military Frontier was fortuitous for the Habsburgs. As an incentive for armed colonization of a no-man's-land susceptible to Turkish attack, the emperors offered good and productive soil, not to the Croats, but to the Serbs who had fled into Croatia before the Ottoman advance and the Vlachs, a mountain people speaking a Romance language. The Serbs, driven from their own native land, and hardy as the Vlachs, would, it was thought, make up a tenacious border force. In exchange for their service, they were granted title to the land, local autonomy, and freedom for the Orthodox faith.

The offer was hard to refuse. Free land was a privilege otherwise unimaginable for the newcomers. But the fear of war was constant, and Serb men found themselves under arms most of the time. Gradually, a rigid military mentality developed among them, encouraged and fostered by the imperial authorities. Inevitably, this produced resentment among the Croats, laying the basis for conflict between the two groups.

Considering themselves warriors, the Serbs felt responsible to the emperor alone and acted defiantly toward Croatian authorities. Needless to say, this outraged the Croat elite, whose land had been awarded to the Serbs without proper compensation. But distrust of the Serb newcomers in Croatia was not limited to the gentry; it grew everywhere. The Serbs' status as free peasants was a permanent irritant to the nobility. The Sabor passed laws prohibiting the Serbs from permanently residing or purchasing property in the towns. Landless Croat serfs resented the presence of Serbs, who, although of a different religious loyalty, came to enjoy privileges far exceeding those of Croat commoners. The Catholic church regarded Orthodox Serbs as schismatics.

Religious differences were compounded by cultural ones. The Krajina Serbs as well as those from then-Turkish Serbia itself were viewed as primitive semi-Orientals by Catholic Croats who considered themselves, with some reason, to be more culturally developed and who took pride in their efficiency as well as their law and order. The gentry of central Croatia emulated the splendor of the Hungarian and Austrian courts, while the Croat priests and writers in Venetian-ruled Dalmatia and Ottoman Bosnia, continuing long-established traditions, excelled in poetry, philosophy, and science. They were at home in Latin as well as in Croatian and in the Croat "recension" of church Slavonic. Literacy was more widespread in Croatia than in Serbia, and the birthrate lower; by the late nineteenth century, the sons and often the daughters of the landowning families, even those of moderate means, took piano lessons and studied at the University of Vienna and other foreign institutions.

By contrast, in Serbia land was customarily divided among the offspring after a father's death, thus becoming fragmented into smaller and smaller plots. In addition, thousands of Serbs had migrated en masse to the Vojvodina area of southern Hungary, fleeing the Ottomans and leaving much of Serbia uncultivated and unpopulated. Central Serbia, in particular, reverted to a wilderness of forest and brush. Few roads wound through the thick woodland.

"Like American frontiersmen," wrote one traveler, "the Serbian peasants regarded the surrounding forests as a nuisance to be rid of as soon as possible. . . . They set fire to vast stands in order to scatter corn seed between the charred stumps. Also, the manner of everyday life in the Morava Valley closely resembled that in the Ohio Valley—the same log cabins, home-made furniture, plain food but plenty of it, plum brandy in place of rum . . . and an abundance of malaria and other diseases which were treated with a combination of home remedies, barbers, and quacks."

In Croatia the wealth of the local nobility, although limited, added luster to the way of life to which Croatians aspired even if the peasantry lived in a manner far from being cultured and comfortable. No such luster existed in Serbia. To the Croats everything to the east of the Drina River appeared tainted by the lawlessness, corruption, and poor hygiene characteristic of "Asia." And the Krajina Serbs seemed to have brought that mentality into Croatia, along with the arms they carried openly.

These attitudes had a profound effect on the historic relations between the Croats and Serbs. The resentment of all strata of the Croat population and acceptance by none merely strengthened the internal cohesion and militance of the Krajina Serbs. Also strengthened was their belief that their real home was in Serbia. Nostalgia for the original homeland persisted well into the twentieth century, even though by then the Serbs were largely assimilated into Croatian society and the Military Frontier had ceased to exist. What was left, however, was a dream that somehow the Serbs in Croatia and in Serbia could be united once again, in the same state. It was that lingering dream that Slobodan Milosevic appealed to in 1990.

Had the Krajina never been settled in the way it was, tensions between the Croat and Serb communities might never have grown to the levels they reached. In the nineteenth century the Krajina Serbs began to press for special rights, which they hoped would strengthen them against what they felt to be Hungarian and Catholic pressure. At the end of the twentieth century Slobodan Milosevic re-created and expanded the concept of Krajina autonomy to the point of independence, which, as the world saw, led to war.

Another fault line between Croats and Serbs ran through Bosnia-Hercegovina. Populated by both Croats and Serbs beginning with the Slavic invasion of the Balkans in the seventh century, Bosnia was always in an ambiguous position. Byzantines, Serbs, Hungarians, and Croats ruled it in turn. Beginning in 1189, its ruler Ban Kulin wrought a certain independence from both Croats and Serbs for Bosnia, strengthened by his patronage of the independent "Bosnian church," whose members were frequently called "Bogomils" because of their similiarity to a dissident Bulgarian sect of that name.

The Bosnian church has been described as "dualistic," embracing a creed that saw the universe fought over between good and evil, with the devil ruling the world of human physical experience. It has also been equated with the Cathars, a sect of "perfected" religious ascetics much like the Bulgarian Bogomils, and even portrayed as semipagan and naturistic. In reality, very little of substance is known of the Bosnian church, except that it was condemned by both Catholic and Orthodox powers and was a pretext for brutal crusades aimed at its suppression.

In the end, all we can say is that the Bosnian church had an ecclesiastical structure different from that elsewhere in Christendom and that it expressed, if nothing else, a distinct Bosnian identity separate from that of the Catholic Croats and Orthodox Serbs.

The Turkish conquest in 1463 once again changed the identity of Bosnia as well as its religion. Thousands of Bosnians converted to Islam. It has long been held that the conversion took place en masse; in any event, it frequently reflected a transfer of independent loyalties by the adherents of the Bosnian church to the creed of Muhammad as a means of reinforcing their difference from their Catholic and Orthodox neighbors.

Equally important, however, Islamization, while not imposed on the population, brought with it social advantages and rewards. The serfs willing to convert were granted freedom; feudal landowners refusing to convert ran the risk of losing first their privileges and then the land itself. Finally, Christians and Jews were taxed more heavily than Muslims. All these were logical reasons for conversion, and many Bosnians certainly did convert. But many also did not. The conversions generated a specific, Muslim-dominated social hierarchy; the landowning and administrative classes were overwhelmingly Muslim. Given such a situation, both Serbs, who were in the majority, and Croats, who were in the minority, felt a considerable identity with the countries that carried their names.

For the Christian peasants, suppressed and heavily taxed, life was bitter. As the Ottoman Empire began its long descent through the eighteenth and nineteenth centuries, ever heavier taxes were levied on the empire's peasant population. The Bosnian serfs were among the poorest in the empire, and for them life became unbearable. Brought to despair, they began sporadic rebellions, which became more frequent as time went on.

The Habsburg Empire, which bordered on Bosnia, and Serbia, with its own interests in Bosnia, was eager to exploit this discontent. The Habsburgs believed they could add Bosnia to Croatia, and Serbia hoped to expand into Bosnia. A considerable part of the Serbian political elite at the end of the nineteenth century held Bosnia to be Serbian land, with a Serbian majority. In addition, they claimed, Hercegovina, the southeastern part of the country, was the home of the Serbian dialect considered by the father of modern Serbian language and grammar, the linguist Vuk Stefanovic Karadzic, to be the purest.

Vuk, as he became known, traveled, peg-legged, to the most remote Serbian-speaking areas to record dialects, compile a dictionary, and collect folk stories, poems, and proverbs. He reformed the Cyrillic alphabet to adapt it to Serbian usage and created a singularly simple and logical spelling system. "Write the way you speak," Vuk was known to say, insisting that each sound be represented by a single letter. His *Serbian Lexicon* remains a classic, unsurpassed work. Seeking to replace prior standards that were based on the ancient Church Slavonic, far from the speech of the people and an obstacle to their literacy, Vuk elevated the idiom of the Serb masses in Hercegovina to the status of a national literary language. Having found the "purest Serbian," as he called it, in Hercegovina, he unwittingly encouraged the ambitions of some Serb nationalist politicians to claim Hercegovina—the land awaiting liberation from the Ottomans—as Serbian land.

The intoxicating idea of liberation from the Ottoman yoke penetrated the discontented Bosnian peasantry, as it did in Bulgaria, Macedonia, and other Ottoman provinces. Indeed, Bosnian Muslims and Jews also rebelled against the Ottoman power. Many, and not just Serbs, spoke of the unification of Bosnia with "free, Slavic" Serbia. And so the idea of national freedom came to be linked, for certain influential politicians, with the idea of expanding Serbia into Bosnia.

Serbia had already been, to a very great extent, freed of Turkish rule. Uprisings beginning in 1804 under a remarkable figure known as "Black George" or Karadjordje, a pig trader from the Serbian heartland, forced the sultan to issue a firman, or ruling, in 1830 granting Serbia significant freedom under Russian protection, although it remained officially a Turkish possession.

The slow advance of the Serbian national cause, aided immensely by the Russian tsars, led to the concept of a Great Serbia that would unite all the Serb lands—"Serbia proper," within its late-nineteenth-century borders, along with Montenegro, long considered a Serb territory; "old Serbia," as Kosova to the south was known; Vojvodina to the north; the Serbian-inhabited Krajina in Croatia; and Bosnia. South Serbia, as Macedonia came to be labeled, was eventually added to the scheme.

The national rebirth of Serbia excited tremendous hopes. Yet the rhetoric of liberation of the "historic Serb lands" inevitably implied territorial expansion at the expense of others: the Croats, Bulgarians, and Albanians. In the nineteenth century, however, this level of political consciousness was rare, although, most notably, the Serbian political writer, a member of the Socialist International, Svetozar Markovic warned of the pitfalls of the Great Serbian dream.

Serbia found itself, along with Bulgaria and Greece, at the forefront of the Balkan movement to overthrow the Ottomans. Greece, which had attained full national independence, was its closest ally; Bulgaria, although Slavic-speaking and still struggling against the Turks as late as 1878, was Serbia's rival for support from Russia. Serbia and Greece together began planning the division of Macedonia and Albania once the Turks were expelled.

In 1876–78 Turkey was soundly defeated in a war with Russia, in which Serbia participated alongside the tsar's armies. Bosnia rebelled, with Serbian help; Bulgaria gained its freedom and seized much of Macedonia and part of Albania. Serbia believed the war would end with Bosnia united to it. But the central and western European powers—Germany, Austria-Hungary, Britain, and France—were concerned that the total collapse of the Ottoman Empire, the "Sick Man of Europe," would strengthen Russian power, enabling the tsar to dominate the Bosporus and thus control access to the Black Sea. This was seen as threatening to the European balance of power as well as to the Mediterranean and the gateway to the Middle East.

Russia, for its part, worried that British control of the Turkish Straits would allow Britain to attack the Russian Black Sea ports and to advance into the Caucasus. The anxieties of the great powers became evident when it required not one but two diplomatic congresses to end the Russo-Turkish War. The first congress ended with the Treaty of San Stefano, and the second, convened before the ink had fully dried on the first one, with the Treaty of Berlin. The 1878 Berlin Congress charged Otto von Bismarck, the German chancellor, to act as an "honest broker" and work out a compromise regarding former Ottoman lands, a compromise that would make everyone happy, particularly the great powers.

Bismarck did his best. He granted Serbia and Montenegro full independence but allowed Austria-Hungary, not Serbia, to gain control over Bosnia. Three hundred thousand Austrian soldiers marched into Bosnia, to Serbia's great displeasure.

Some Croatian politicians saw the Austrian occupation of Bosnia as a positive development. Once again, Serbia and Croatia found themselves at cross-purposes. Their growing conflict over Bosnia, added to their subterranean conflict over the Krajina, became exacerbated as the twentieth century dawned. In 1908 Bosnia was fully absorbed into Austria-Hungary, exciting hope in Croatia that at least the western part of Bosnia would be joined to Croatia. On the Serb side, needless to say, the legal annexation provoked extraordinary bitterness.

The Serb desire to absorb Bosnia implied a confrontation with Austria-Hungary; the trend toward such a conflict was heightened when, in 1903, the dynasty ruling in Serbia, the Obrenovici, long considered pawns of the Habsburgs, were brutally overthrown by Serb military officers and replaced by the Karadjordjevici. But Serbia was not prepared to contemplate outright conflict with the Dual Monarchy—not in 1908 and not in 1914, when a Serb youth from Bosnia, Gavrilo Princip, fired a shot at the Habsburg crown prince Franz Ferdinand and his princess in Sarajevo. Princip was a member of a revolutionary group, Mlada Bosna (Young Bosnia), that included Croat and Muslim members and had anarchist as well as nationalist tendencies. But Vienna accused Princip of acting as the instrument of Belgrade. The truth is that he was a patriotic idealist, not a hired hand. And Belgrade itself was not too eager to provoke the monarchy. Serbs knew they would be taking on too much.

But shots had been fired and Serbia was pushed into war. Austria-Hungary made demands; Serbia, backed by Russia, rejected them. Armies mobilized on both sides of all borders. For the first time in their history, Serbia and Croatia found themselves fighting each other, the former as one of the Allied powers, the latter—including the Croatian Serbs—as part of the Habsburg Empire. In the war, Serbia was devastated, its armies and thousands of its people driven out of the country; it saw one-quarter of its population dead. But, as A. J. P. Taylor has written, "The Great Habsburg Monarchy had shrunk to a single room where elderly bureaucrats and professors gloomily surveyed each other." The South Slavs were free to unite, and the Serbs, who have indeed borne the brunt of the war in the Balkans, gave themselves credit for it.

World War II brought Serbs and Croats again into bloody confrontation as the Croatian fascist puppet regime sought to implement a "final solution" in dealing with the Croatian Serbs. The genocide of Serbs in Croatia, however, was less an expression of existing hatreds than of an infusion into Yugoslavia of Nazi racial radicalism. Deep scars were left after the war in the collective memory of the Serbs, who saw themselves as martyrs. Slobodan Milosevic appealed to this sense of martyrdom and to the colossal price in human lives that the Serbs have paid in both world wars when he sought to sell his war plans to the Serbian people.

But before Milosevic came to exploit the Serbo-Croat grievances, he manipulated the grievances of the Serbs in Kosova. A plateau of some hundred square miles in the southwest of today's Serbia, surrounded on all sides by mountains, Kosova represents yet another historical fault line in the Balkans.

Three days before the Berlin Congress was to open in June 1878, the League of Prizren, the first Albanian national organization, which had been formed shortly before the congress, addressed Bismarck, asking the congress to grant Albanian autonomy within the Ottoman Empire.

Albanians were the largest non-Slavic ethnic group in the Balkans, and they converted to Islam during Ottoman rule in greater number than any other Balkan population, although a third of them remained Christian (Catholics in the north, Orthodox in the south). The Muslims among them were considered peers of the ethnic Turks in the Ottoman Empire, employed as governors and soldiers; an Ottoman saying was "To the Armenians, the pen; to the Arnauts [Albanians], the sword." But the Albanians are not ethnic Turks; rather, they are the descendants of the Illyrians, who predate the Slavic invasions of the Balkans.

In addition to denying that the Albanians are Illyrian, and therefore the indigenous peoples of the region, Serbian extremists claim that Kosova has never been anything but "old Serbia," the heart of its medieval kingdom and the place where a cataclysmic battle for Serb power was fought and lost in 1389. In spite of help from the Bosnian King Stjepan Tvrtko I, the Serbian King Lazar lost his kingdom at Kosovo Polje, "The Field of Blackbirds." In reality, the Serbian kingdom was not fully subdued by the Turks for another seventy years, until the battle of Smederovo in 1459. But the conflict at Kosovo Polje was sung in numerous folk songs

and poems that have survived to the present and are honored by
Serbs as their greatest literary treasure.

Another aspect of historical reality, as opposed to myth, is
the fact that Albanians fought alongside the Serbs in the Christian
armies at Kosovo Polje; epic songs of the battle exist in Albanian
and were traditionally sung by Albanian folk poets as well as by
Serbs. In addition, the Albanian clans helped protect Orthodox
monasteries in Kosova during the long centuries of Turkish rule.

Many Serb historians deny these arguments, insisting that Albanians held high administrative posts, served as soldiers for the
Ottomans, and have always been enemies of the Serbs. Serbs blame
Albanians as well as the Turks for the violence that led to the mass
migrations of Serbs northward from the sixteenth through the
eighteenth century.

Herein lies the core of the long Albanian-Serb conflict, to this
day unresolved. The Albanians are the only people in that part of
the Balkans (with the exception of Gypsies) to remain ethnically
isolated to this day. It was perhaps understandable, then, that they
would seek, in their request to Bismarck in 1878, limited autonomy under the sultan, not full independence. The members of the
League of Prizren knew that Serbia sought to regain Kosova. In
their advance during the 1878 Russo-Turkish War the Serbs
reached the town of Prizren itself, in the heart of Kosova. In the
minds of Serb soldiers the issue was liberation of the ancient Serb
heartland, something they were convinced was foretold in dreams,
in signs from God, and in wondrous events. For the Kosovar Albanians to request full independence from the Congress of Berlin
would have made Kosova immediately vulnerable to Serbian designs.

Bismarck, however, did not believe there was such a thing as
an "Albanian nation," and he therefore found no grounds for autonomy. This suited Serbia quite well; its leaders considered the
League of Prizren an anti-Serb organization. The further outcome
of Bismarck's response, however, suited the Serb leadership less.
The congress assigned Kosova to Turkey, not to Serbia, and Der-
vish Pasha, a Turkish governor, took control of it in 1881. Serbs in
Kosova paid a brutal price in blood.

The next transfer of power, however, thirty-two years later,
when finally Albanians won the desired autonomy, passed in peace.

Albanians launched no reprisals and no revenge against Serb civilians. At the end of 1912, in the First Balkan War—launched by the Balkan League of Bulgaria, Greece, Serbia, and Montenegro to complete the destruction of what was then called Turkey-in-Europe—the Serbs and Montenegrins captured Kosova and drove deep into northern Albania proper, aiming for the town of Shkodër and the Albanian Adriatic coastline. Montenegro, its Serbian character mainly religious, yet still considering itself part of the Serb nation, had borne the brunt of the anti-Turkish struggle for long years, always with the ideal of a free Serbian nation at heart. In 1912, while Greece attacked Albania from the south, the Montenegrins captured Shkodër, at the cost of ten thousand Montenegrin lives.

In the process of liberating what they considered a Christian birthright, the commanders of the Serb forces ordered looting and massacres of Albanians, including the sick and wounded, women and children, many of them Christian themselves although speaking Albanian rather than Serbian. Five thousand were executed in and around Prizren alone; a total of twelve thousand to fifteen thousand Albanians perished in the Balkan Wars. Any settlement where an Albanian weapon was fired was ordered destroyed. Thousands of Albanians, as well as Turks, fled to Turkey. Leon Trotsky, then working as a war correspondent for the Russian liberal press, sent home fiery dispatches describing and denouncing the atrocities. In one, he declared, "An individual, a group, a party or a class that is capable of 'objectively' picking its nose while it watches men drunk with blood, and incited from above, massacring defenseless people is condemned by history to rot and become worm-eaten while it is still alive." Elsewhere he wrote, some ninety years ago but in words that echo with relevance today, that the large and hostile Albanian population included within the borders of Serbia "may prove fatal to the historical existence of Serbia."

The Albanians fought back. Alarmed at the Serbo-Montenegrin advance, Austria-Hungary meddled in the conflict, inciting the Albanians. In response, during the fall of 1913, Serb troops further razed Albanian villages, an action Dimitrije Tucovic, a leading Serbian socialist of the time, described as the "Third Balkan War." The Serbian socialists bitterly opposed their government's military policies. They also offered a solution: the unification of the Balkan countries with full political and cultural autonomy for all the constituent nations. They pointed out the deep gulf between Serbian war propaganda, which rapturously proclaimed the glory of Kosova's redemption, and the low morale of the Serbian forces in Albania. Although atrocities continued, few of the ordinary soldiers, or their officers for that matter, were avid for the occupation of what, according to Tucovic, was clearly a foreign land. The Serbian troops were starving and poorly dressed, toes sticking out of their torn shoes. Their enthusiasm, as they slowly made their way to the Adriatic coast, was so lacking that the decision to order a battalion into battle would be made, it was said, by a throw of dice the night before.

In 1919, at the end of World War I, the Serbian socialists argued that the newly formed Kingdom of Serbs, Croats, and Slovenes, which included Kosova, should support the maintenance of the Albanian state—whose independence had in any case been recognized by the great powers—and work toward friendly relations with it. This was not done, but worse, in Kosova the improvement of relations was not even attempted. The Kosovar Albanians again fought back; but an uprising was quelled in blood. After that, a popular Albanian guerrilla movement, known as the *kaçaks* and exemplified by Azem Bejta and his wife Shota Galica, who in the highly patriarchal Albanian society was compelled to disguise herself as a man while fighting, continued an insurgency for five years more. *Kaçaks* attacked Serbian officials, bombed government buildings, and sabotaged trains. They urged Albanians not to pay taxes or serve in the Yugoslav army so long as the Serb authorities violated their rights. Bejta was killed by Yugoslav gendarmes in 1924 and the *kaçak* resistance was stifled.

In 1941 the monarchist Kingdom of Yugoslavia, in existence since 1929, collapsed under Axis aggression; fascist Italy, which had already conquered Albania in 1939, secured the unification of Kosova and western Macedonia with Albania proper. It was small wonder that Kosovar Albanians viewed this action as a liberation. Italy permitted schooling in Albanian along with other things that Yugoslavia had forbidden: the use of Albanian in the state administration, the display of the Albanian flag, and the carrying of arms by Kosovar Albanians. Italy also turned a blind eye to the actions of Albanians against Serb and Montenegrin civilians. During

World War II, although many within Albania proper joined the Communist partisans, few Albanians did, even after direct control of Kosova was taken over by the Germans. Needless to say, relations with the Serbs did not improve.

With mutual animosities unresolved, the restless nationalism of the Kosovar Albanians remained an abiding feature of their twentieth-century history. Slobodan Milosevic brought the tensions in Kosova to a high pitch in 1987 and has sustained them on that level for the last seven years. This has only strengthened the resolve of the Albanian community to resist Serbia. Should war break out in Kosova, Albanians in Macedonia, in addition to Albania proper, would likely be drawn in, widening the horror.

The fault line running through Macedonia is equally complex and dangerous. Bismarck disappointed Serbia and Bulgaria at the 1878 Congress of Berlin by restoring Macedonia to Turkey, as he had Kosova. Bismarck was making sure that Serbia wasn't getting too strong. His task at the congress, after all, was safeguarding the balance of great powers in the Balkans as the Ottoman Empire crumbled. In the ensuing twenty years, an exceptionally strong and radical nationalist movement emerged in Macedonia, with factions subsidized by Serbia, Bulgaria, and Greece. In 1912, Serbia, Montenegro, Bulgaria, and Greece united to correct Bismarck's decision of 1878.

The collapse of the Ottoman Empire was accelerated when, in 1908, a modernizing revolution broke out in Turkey. That movement stimulated the Macedonians, Albanians, Armenians, and other restive nationalities under Turkish rule to further action. The Serb faction in Macedonia declared Macedonia to be South Serbia; the Bulgarians described it as West Bulgaria; the Greeks harked back to the Hellenic culture of the Macedon that produced Alexander the Great. The large Sephardic Jewish and Macedonian Muslim communities in the country were caught in the cross fire, but many of them also supported the various national revolutionary efforts.

In the Middle Ages Macedonia, although linguistically closest to the Bulgars, fluctuated between their rule and domination by the Serbs, beginning in the ninth and continuing through the thirteenth and fourteenth centuries. In 1331, in the Macedonian town of Skopje, the greatest of all Serbian kings, Tsar Stefan Dusan, was crowned emperor of the Serbs, Greeks, Bulgarians, and Albanians. After the Turkish conquest, however, Skopje was reduced to a Turkish garrison town. The whole of Macedonia became a military stronghold, a base for Ottoman scouting missions and military expeditions south into Greece, west into Albania, and north into Serbia and Bosnia. Part of the Macedonian population was enslaved, another part dispersed. The rich, hilly pastures were settled by Turkish herdsmen from Asia Minor and by Albanians, although a considerable Slav population remained in place.

Nevertheless, the Orthodox archepiscopate, the most vital religious institution of the Serbs and Macedonians alike during the five hundred years of Turkish rule, was permitted to remain in the Macedonian town of Ohrid, acquire land, and thrive. This was a strong link between the Serbs and Macedonians. During the Turkish invasions at the end of the sixteenth century (1593–1606) and again in the eighteenth century, when Macedonia and large portions of Serbia were thoroughly devastated, Serbs and some Macedonians and Albanians fled together into southern Hungary, today's Vojvodina. A new war between Turkey, Austria, and Russia two hundred years later (1787–92), brought new raids, plunder, arson, and massacres. Desperate, Macedonians abandoned their villages, towns, and fields, again fleeing northward. In Macedonia "all life and trade died out," a French traveler through the wasted land wrote at the time, "and the sultan's laws were disregarded."

In 1878, after the Congress of Berlin, Macedonia was again plunged into despair. Unchecked by foreign powers, Turkey levied excessive taxes on the exhausted population. Those unable to pay were locked up, beaten, and tortured. Wanton violence descended on the land. Captured men had their eyes gouged and ears cut off. Women and girls were raped in an orgy of Turkish revenge. Never having known the good life, Macedonians accepted their brutal history, and poverty, with the fatalism of the doomed. Still, a remarkable capacity to take delight in small pleasures and to give their subdued sufferings a deeply sensual, nostalgic expression through their exceptional folk songs survived.

The Ottoman Empire continued to weaken, and the first Macedonian uprising broke out in 1881. The Turks suppressed it with extraordinary brutality. Nine years later the Internal Macedonian

Revolutionary Organization (known internationally as IMRO and in Macedonian as VMRO) was formed, led by the young schoolteacher Goce Delchev, a former Bulgarian military cadet. Goce, a wise and broad-minded insurgent leader, was committed to Macedonian autonomy. His name is still honored by street signs and the plaques of cultural societies across Macedonia as well as in Bulgaria and Serbia. Both Serbia and Bulgaria laid claim not only to Macedonian land but also to its heroes.

In May 1903 Goce Delchev was gunned down by the Turks at the age of thirty-one. Three months later, on St. Elias's Day, Ilinden (August 21), VMRO launched a desperate uprising, which lasted for two months. In retaliation, more than forty-five hundred civilians as well as a thousand anti-Ottoman guerrilla fighters were killed by Turks, and one hundred fifty villages burned. Thirty thousand Macedonians sought refuge in Bulgaria.

The liberation of Macedonia by Bulgaria, Greece, Serbia, and Montenegro in the first Balkan War of 1912 marked an incomparably larger event: the virtual dissolution of the Ottoman Empire, which was completed with the close of World War I. The victory of 1912 was celebrated in Serbia as the triumph of a long campaign to end the Turkish presence in Europe. But rather than bringing autonomy to Macedonia, the victory provoked a further bloody scramble over the Macedonian lands, between the erstwhile war allies. Their conflicting appetites in Macedonia precipitated the Second Balkan War of 1913, with the Serbs and Greeks successfully joined against Bulgaria by an ally, Romania, which had designs on other parts of Bulgaria. After Bulgaria was defeated, Macedonia was partitioned anew: Greece grabbed more than half of the region's total territory, known as Aegean Macedonia and including the coveted jewel of Salonika, a rich port city that until the late nineteenth century actually had a Sephardic Jewish majority; Serbia received Vardar Macedonia, named after a major river and its valley; Bulgaria had to settle for the smallest part, Pirin Macedonia.

It is no wonder that following the brutality of the Balkan Wars, in all respects matching Turkish brutality of the previous centuries, VMRO—which sought an independent Macedonia where all nations would enjoy equal rights—became a terrorist organization. After World War I, with the division of Macedonia reaffirmed, VMRO continued its terror. It was active against the Kingdom of Serbs, Croats, and Slovenes, in which Macedonia was included but was granted no autonomy at all. The kingdom persecuted the Macedonian nationalists, seeing in them, primarily, an anti-Serbian force.

VMRO split between a rightist wing that insisted on Macedonian independence and a leftist, Soviet-oriented faction that called for the old socialist ideal of a Balkan federation. The former group allied with the Croatian ultranationalist Ustashe and was bankrolled by fascist Italy and Hungary. In 1934, a Bulgarian member of VMRO, Vlado Chernozemski, known as "Vlado the Chauffeur," with support from the Ustashe, assassinated Yugoslav King Aleksandar in France.

VMRO ceased to function in Titoist Yugoslavia, when for the first time in its history Macedonia was granted the status of a separate republic. With the breakup of Yugoslavia, beginning in 1990, VMRO reappeared as VMRO-DPMNE, a party of Slavic Macedonians. In the meantime, the considerable Albanian community living in western Macedonia also organized politically and demanded and gained a share of power, with tensions between Albanians and Slavic Macedonians persistent although at a fairly low level.

In a destabilized Balkan region, Macedonia today faces Serb, Greek, and Bulgarian nationalism. But it must also contend with an Albania concerned for the condition of its people in the new state as well as in neighboring Kosova and, most ominously, with a Greece overwhelmed by hostility to the very concept of an independent non-Greek state bearing the name of Alexander's native territory. Macedonia is also now host to six hundred U.S. military personnel sent to monitor its security and has been promised aid by Turkey in case of a war, which many people fear is close, too close. Macedonia could again find itself up for grabs by its neighbors.

Watersheds of Balkan history, having little to do in the final analysis with indigenous hatreds, and much to do with the long and tortured experience of the region's domination by foreigners, have turned the peninsula into a complex environment of ethnic ambiguities, painful memories, and bitter grievances, as well as cautious but determined strivings for reconciliation and national unification.

All the fissures and fault lines notwithstanding, there was nothing inevitable about the most recent Balkan wars. Despite Western media myths about "ancient hatreds" hibernating under communism, these are not people's wars. Before the war, the vast majority of Yugoslavs regularly drank Turkish coffee with their neighbors, became godfathers to each other's children, and married persons of different nationalities. Almost everywhere, their caring for their neighbors and neighborhood, the *komsiluk*, overshadowed their national concerns. That virulent nationalism prevailed in the end was not the result of indigenous processes. The nationalist deluge ran against the authentic concerns and real interests of all the Yugoslav peoples. For extreme nationalism to arise, despite the intuitions of most citizens of former Yugoslavia, a long-term, planned, systematic, relentless, and tightly controlled propaganda campaign was necessary, aimed at the Serbs in Serbia, Croatia, and Bosnia. The Croats were also manipulated in this way, as were the Slovenes and even, although to a much lesser extent, those who were most innocent and naive, the Bosnian Muslims. Until bloodshed came to the door in Sarajevo, these latter victims, the saddest of all, could not believe war was a reality, or that it would last.

TWO

The Making of Yugoslavia (1830–1945)

Branka Prpa-Jovanović

"The whole world sees morning, but in the Balkans daylight never comes," begins a poem written in 1842 by Ognjeslav Utjesenovic Ostrozinski, a Serb from Croatia. It was a lament about the condition of the ignored, backward, and divided South Slavic peoples, who in the first half of the nineteenth century still lived under the rule of the Austro-Hungarian Habsburg dynasty and the Turkish Empire.

At the time Ostrozinski wrote, a movement toward the unification of South Slavs had just begun. It was not a movement led by political thinkers or reflecting popular discontent. Rather, the early movement for South Slavic unity was created by a group of Croatian scholars who called themselves "Illyrians" after the oldest tribe known to have inhabited the Balkan peninsula, dating back to classical Greek times. The name also evoked memory of the Illyrian Provinces, as the Habsburg possessions on the Adriatic, including Croat-speaking lands, were known when they were briefly annexed after 1805 to the modernizing empire of Napoleon Bonaparte. But the name further expressed the desire for a historically neutral identity that all South Slavs could accept. The scholars who joined the Illyrian movement in the 1830s and 1840s tried to establish a common language as a means of uniting the South

Slavs, who spoke and wrote in different idioms. A common language, they thought, would be the cornerstone of a unified national culture—a major step toward liberation from foreign domination.

Yet in the Balkans, dialects and languages, both vernacular and literary, were many. The choice of one that would prove acceptable to all Slavic ethnic groups turned out to be a daunting task. In an admirable act of wisdom and restraint, the Croat Ljudevit Gaj, the leading figure among the Illyrians, opted not for the *kajkavian* dialect spoken in his own place of origin, Zagreb and the northwestern part of Croatia, but the *stokavian,* spoken in much of the rest of Croatia, a dialect in which, Gaj argued, "everything that heart and mind demand can be expressed" and which was also spoken by Serbs. Gaj insisted that the Croats and other South Slavic communities should each give up something to allow the formation of a single literary language and a unified, Illyrian culture.

To achieve their goal, the Illyrians sought to open schools, publish intellectual journals, start cultural associations, and, above all, standardize their written language. This was a way not only of strengthening Slavic unity but also of emphasizing cultural differences between the Slavs and the non-Slavs who ruled over them, whether German-speaking Austrians, or Hungarians, or Turks.

The Illyrianism of the 1840s was revived in the 1860s, but under the name of Yugoslavism (*jugoslavjenstvo*), that is, unification of the South (*jug*) Slavs. The most famous representatives of the new movement were two members of the Croatian Catholic church hierarchy, Josip Juraj Strosmajer and Franjo Racki. Their program, like that of the Illyrians, pursued national spiritual unification through establishment of a single literary language and development of the characteristics deemed unique to South Slav culture. Only through building their own distinct culture and linking up with their Slavic kin, such as the Czechs, Poles, and Russians, Strosmajer and Racki argued, could the Croats resist the continuing efforts of the Austrians and Hungarians to assimilate Croatia. Strosmajer, a wealthy Catholic bishop, generously donated his large fortune to support efforts toward unification. Not only was he instrumental in the creation of the University of Zagreb and the Yugoslav Academy but he also supported numerous other, lesser cultural institutions and publications.

Strosmajer hoped to unify the South Slavs then under Habsburg domination through federalization, in which the numerous peoples of the Austro-Hungarian Empire (ranging from Italians to Romanians, from Slovenes to Serbs, from Germans to Ukrainians) would gain equality, with the German-Austrians, Hungarians, and South Slavs as the leading nations. This form of Yugoslavism was called by some "Austro-Slavism." Creating an independent state of all South Slavs would have been more desirable than uniting them under the Habsburg roof, but Strosmajer and Racki insisted that the end of the empire was not yet in sight. In addition, the Serbs, who had gained more than the Croats or other South Slavs in terms of independent nationhood, were still not strong enough to push the Turks out of the Balkans. Under more favorable circumstances, Strosmajer and Racki argued, they would urge forming an independent Yugoslav state.

Simultaneous with the emergence of Strosmajer's Yugoslavism, a new movement of Croatian national affirmation developed, stressing the constitutional achievement of a strictly Croatian state rather than the unification of all South Slavs. This movement, led by Ante Starcevic and Eugen Kvaternik, called itself the Party of Right. It called for a reborn Croatian state on the legal foundation of the ancient "Croat state right" that had been recognized by the Hungarian and other foreign rulers of Croatia since 1102 A.D., when the previously independent Croatian kingdom was joined in a "personal union" with the Hungarian throne.

The ideology of Starcevic and Kvaternik held that Croatia had maintained itself as a distinct legal entity since that time and that, although Croatia had undergone long Hungarian and then Austro-Hungarian rule, its special legal character had never been abrogated. The party's focus on the Croatian state and Croatian medieval traditions implied a clear rejection of Strosmajer's Yugoslavism. In contrast to Strosmajer, Starcevic and Kvaternik not only opposed the program of Croatian unity with other South Slavs under the Habsburgs but also also viewed some other South Slav groups as inferior to the Croats. The Slovenes were, they alleged, merely "Mountain Croats," with no legitimate identity of their own, while Serbs were held to be an "unclean, servile race" without culture.

By the end of the nineteenth century, educated Croatians,

whose prosperity and sophistication had increased in the epoch of imperial investment and the rise of industry, were politically split. Some supported Strosmajer and Racki, others rallied to Starcevic and Kvaternik. But the imagination of many young people was fired by a new movement, a political club of students at the University of Zagreb called Progressive Youth (Napredna Omladina). This group attempted to combine the South Slavic claims of "Austro-Slavism" and the particularism of the Party of Right.

Progressive Youth held that a pragmatic politics aimed at reconstitution of a Croatian state should be based on cooperation between Croats and Serbs to oppose the march of German-speaking culture eastward (*Drang nach Osten*). In this environment, three men, Franjo Supilo, Ante Trumbic, and Josip Smodlaka, gave the ideas of Croatian statehood, as defined originally by the Party of Right, a new, Yugoslav orientation. In 1905 a Croatian-Serbian electoral coalition was formed in Croatia. The concept of Croatian-Serbian integration thus gained broad currency and support in the period leading to World War I.

The Serbs, for their part, viewed the rise of Yugoslavism from an entirely different perspective. Serbia had attained a considerable degree of national independence, and for a long period Yugoslavism was of interest to most Serb political circles, if they took notice of it at all, only as a means to the reconstruction of a strong Serbian state. In 1804 Serbia was the first Balkan region to sustain a national rebellion, directed against the Ottomans. Although the progress of liberation was uneven, in 1830 the sultan granted Serbia broad autonomy under Turkish rule. Serbia was in a radically different position from any other South Slav nation, including the Croats, who remained subordinate to the Austro-Hungarian Empire. For the Serbs, who had already attached a considerable degree of independence, Yugoslavism was a not very attractive alternative. Until the end of the nineteenth century no political party in Serbia included Yugoslavism in its program. For the Croats, by contrast, unification under the Yugoslav banner was the sole probable means of their emancipation.

As early as 1844 a leading Serbian political figure, Prime Minister Ilija Garasanin, had developed what amounted to a blueprint for an expanded "Great Serbia," the Nacertanije or Memorandum. Garasanin advocated the expansion of Serbian rule into Bosnia-

Hercegovina, Montenegro, and northern Albania as essential for Serbia's national survival. Garasanin was also open to Strosmajer's Yugoslavism and suggested to Strosmajer in 1867 a loose plan for liberating Christians from Turkish rule and the "unification of all South Slavs in one federal state." Serbia was to be the axis of unification. Serbian rulers followed the philosophy of Garasanin's Memorandum by pushing their frontiers into neighboring regions where Turkish rule had been weakened and where Serbian-speaking peoples were present. These territories also included large numbers of non-Serbian peoples, who were brought into the Serbian cultural sphere on the basis of historical arguments. The Obrenovic dynasty, then ruling Serbia, believed that a strong Serbia, absorbing all territories that could be claimed historically, was a preferable goal to that of a broader South Slav unification. Serbian political leadership therefore called for unity of all Serbs, of which there were many living in Croatia, Bosnia-Hercegovina, and southern Hungary.

However, as the twentieth century began, Serbian leaders saw expansion southward as the means to attain these objectives. Their ideas reflected the pragmatic reality of a decaying Turkish empire, hardly able to resist its redivision, in contrast with a still militarily intimidating Habsburg power to the north and west. Yugoslavism, which challenged the latter, therefore remained a secondary concern even as, in 1908, Bosnia-Hercegovina, under de facto Habsburg rule since the late nineteenth century, was officially absorbed into the Austro-Hungarian Empire.

The oldest and strongest political party in Serbia, the Radical Party, simply rejected Yugoslavism as unrealistic, and its position remained unchanged from 1881 into the early twentieth century. The Radicals called for a union of Balkan states, but one that would merge Serbia, Montenegro, and Bulgaria. A new youth group called the Slav South (Slovenski Jug) was formed in Belgrade in 1904; it argued for a pan-Slavic unification, but its brand of Yugoslavism could make little progress in a Serbian political scene still dominated by nineteenth-century political thinking.

Serbia was transformed by the two Balkan Wars of 1912–13. In these conflicts, the four nations that made up the Balkan League (Serbia, Montenegro, Greece, and Bulgaria), with the support of tsarist Russia, resolved to drive the Ottomans out of Europe. In the First Balkan War (1912) the Turks were deprived of all their remaining European territories except a small strip adjacent to Constantinople. The ensuing territorial settlement predictably produced a great deal of discord among the allies. As a result, in the Second Balkan War (1913), Serbia, Montenegro, and Greece aligned against Bulgaria to divide Macedonia, which they had together seized from the Turks.

The Balkan Wars had varied results. Serbia acquired Kosova and the largest portion of Macedonia, the territory around the upper Vardar River. Montenegro and Serbia seized and divided the *sanjak* of Novi Pazar, which linked Macedonia to Bosnia, and this conquest gave Montenegro a common border with Serbia. Greece got Aegean Macedonia, and Bulgaria obtained Pirin Macedonia, the smallest part of all. In addition, Albania secured its independence.

Success against the Turks gave Serbia a great deal of self-confidence; if the Ottomans could be so easily defeated, why not the Habsburgs as well? More important, it stimulated sentiment for a South Slav union. The Radical Party began to call for pan-Slavic liberation from Austria-Hungary, with Serbia leading the way. In 1903 the Obrenovic dynasty was overthrown in Serbia and replaced by the Karadjordjevic dynasty. This move helped shift Serbian politics toward Yugoslavism and increased tension with Austria-Hungary.

However much Serbia now enjoyed seeing itself as the liberator of the South Slavs, it was not strong enough to immediately confront one of Europe's great powers. Nevertheless, Serbia, backed by imperial Russia, found itself at war with Austria-Hungary following the assassination of Archduke Franz Ferdinand in Sarajevo on June 28, 1914. Austria-Hungary seized the opportunity to settle accounts with Serbia; it accused Serbia of sponsoring the assassination plot and, supported by Germany and later joined by Bulgaria and Turkey, declared war on Serbia on July 28, 1914. Russia, with France and Great Britain, rallied to Serbia's side. At the beginning, Serbian objectives were defensive. But soon the Serbian leaders defined their war aims in terms of broader South Slav liberation. If the war with Austria-Hungary could not be avoided, it at least offered a possibility for Serbia, in case of victory, to create a powerful Slav state, uniting Serbs, Croats, and Slovenes.

Yugoslavia was thus born in the chaos and blood of World

War I. In battle, as in the past, South Slavs found themselves fighting on opposite sides: Croats, Slovenes, and Serbs from Croatia and southern Hungary, in the trenches of the Habsburg forces, fought against Serbs and Montenegrins in the armies of those two monarchies. In effect, Croats, Slovenes, and "exiled" Serbs were obliged to combat Serbia's stated goal of South Slavic liberation and unity.

War produced the collapse of Austria-Hungary: Croatia saw nationalist and social uprisings, Hungary underwent a brief Soviet revolution, and the remaining non-German peoples who had been ruled by the Habsburgs demanded their independence under the doctrine of "self-determination" enunciated by U.S. President Woodrow Wilson. Serbia was jubilant, at the height of glory and prestige, although it had lost one-fourth of its population and half its economic assets in the war. At long last, the chance to create, if not a Great Serbia, then at least a united South Slavic state was at hand.

The formation of the new state was outlined in 1917 when the South Slav Committee, consisting of such prominent Croatian figures as the sculptor Ivan Mestrovic and the politicians Trumbic and Supilo, joined the Serbian government in issuing the Corfu Declaration, calling for a democratic, constitutional monarchy of Serbs, Croats, and Slovenes. At the same time, the Slovene politician Antun Korosec had organized a Yugoslav National Council, advocating South Slav unification. The movement for unity was fed by traditional fears of German cultural domination combined with anxieties over the ambitions of Italy, a member of the Allies whose leaders had demonstrated that their appetite for annexation of the Slovene- and Croat-speaking territories along the Adriatic from Trieste to Dubrovnik was not to be discounted.

In the world destined to be defined by the Versailles Treaty, Yugoslav unity had ceased to be an abstraction and had become an urgent reality. A revolutionary State of Slovenes, Croats, and Serbs quickly gave way to a new Kingdom of Serbs, Croats, and Slovenes, announced on December 1, 1918, and ruled by the house of Karadjordjevic from Belgrade. The new state was recognized by the great powers at Versailles on July 28, 1919, although the United States, in which South Slavic immigrant political groups were active and articulate, had already recognized the kingdom in

February 1919. To the former Serbian monarchy were added Slovenia, Croatia, Bosnia-Hercegovina, Montenegro, and Vojvodina, the latter being an area, formerly part of Hungary, with a considerable Serbian population and tradition. Italy, the least influential of the victorious Allies, was the only power resolutely opposed to recognition; it saw in Yugoslavia a rival for control of the Adriatic.

This was a transcendent historical moment, the fulfillment of the dreams of generations of South Slav advocates. The South Slavs were joining together not only because of shared cultural and linguistic traditions but also in search of prosperity, modernization, autonomy, and equality in the new European order. The aggressive habits of Germans, Hungarians, and Italians further strengthened the union as a means of national survival. Yet the manner by which Serbs, Croats, and Slovenes would resolve their differences, once a united kingdom was proclaimed, remained unclear.

The new state, under the rule of regent Alexander in Belgrade, was not an equal partnership. A new constitution picturesquely described Serbs, Croats, and Slovenes as "three tribes" of the same nation. The Montenegrins, however, were not recognized as a separate "tribe" because their parliament had voted on the eve of the new state's creation to incorporate themselves into Serbia. The Macedonians were not recognized as a nation because they had been part of the Kingdom of Serbia since the Balkan Wars and were treated as Serbs. The Muslims were recognized as a religiously separate entity and were allowed to have political parties but, like the Montenegrins and Macedonians, were not recognized as a separate "tribe" or nation. The large Albanian minority in Kosova was simply ignored.

Other aspects of the political situation showed that profound tendencies toward the disintegration of the new state existed within it from the beginning. The distinct regions exhibited drastically different levels of economic development. Legal traditions were separate one from the other. Virtually all the communities in the new state disagreed over one issue: Should the regime be centralized, or should it be a decentralized federation? These differences deepened with time. Very soon the country resembled a building under construction during the day and destroyed each night.

Modernization encountered some insurmountable obstacles

in addition to the frailty of democratic traditions and the variety of legislative and executive regimes inherited from the previous rulers. Since it was mainly a traditional peasant society, the whole Balkan region had seen a retarded process of urbanization and development of the middle classes. In 1921 agriculture was still the main occupation of some seventy-nine percent of the Yugoslav population, and in 1931 of more than seventy-six percent. But Yugoslav agriculture was in permanent crisis, and reform and mechanization were elusive. Landholdings were typically very small, often too small to be productive beyond immediate subsistence. In 1931 some two-thirds of farming households had less than five hectares of land; seven hundred thousand households owned less than two hectares, and the tendency was continually toward smaller and smaller, less and less efficient landholdings. The crisis in agriculture was worsened by the low level of technical development and labor productivity and by rural overpopulation.

Industrial development was also stunted, as well as being unequally distributed. The greater part of industry had been established in the former Habsburg realm, in the northwest regions of Slovenia, Croatia, and Vojvodina. Slovenian industrial development was four times greater than Serbian and twenty-two times greater than Macedonian and Montenegrin. Compounding the problems facing the young country were the heritage of four different railroad systems, seven different bodies of law, and several different currencies. The merging of these multiple systems was slow, and the kingdom, from the beginning, lagged well behind the rest of Europe in embracing twentieth-century methods.

Yugoslav leaders wanted to fashion the key features of the country's social and political system after European models of capitalist efficiency and political liberalism. In practice, the stability of the new state depended on the willingness of the Serb, Croat, and Slovene political elites to minimize their major conflicts in the interest of modernization.

The constitution of June 28, 1921, which became known as the St. Vitus's Day Constitution (Vidovdanski Ustav), was intended as a major step in this direction. It defined the new state as a constitutional, parliamentary, and hereditary monarchy. The constitution enshrined the principles of European bourgeois life: the abolition of feudal obligations, the inviolability of private property, and guarantees of equality under the law, freedom of religion and of the press. This constitution promised modernization but in practice offered only a step in that direction. In a simpler context, the liberalism of the constitution might have prevailed; in the Balkans, it could not.

The new constitution brought about several disputes. Because of maneuvering by Serbian politicians, the text was adopted only by a simple majority of the Constitutional Assembly, not by a two-thirds majority. The Slovenian and Croatian representatives bitterly objected to the adoption process, which institutionalized the domination of the Serbian majority over representatives of the other Yugoslav nationalities. Furthermore, the constitution conceived of a highly centralized state. That worked to the advantage of the Serbs, who ruled the state from Belgrade, but greatly exacerbated the sense of grievance of the non-Serbs. In theory, the national interests of the three "tribes"—Serbs, Croats, and Slovenes—were meant to be fused in a new nation. But as it turned out, the proposed Yugoslav nation-state consisted of nothing more than a geographic framework, while politically it remained the cockpit of conflicting Serbian, Croatian, and Slovenian national interests. Neither the force of the state machinery nor the strength of South Slav unitaristic idealism could succeed in forging a genuine, single people or nation out of these three. Consequently, the kingdom never became a true nation-state. The leading principle of the European liberal world—that of "one-man, one-vote," as promised in the constitution—abstractly represented progress. In the political practice of the multiethnic kingdom, however, it enabled the most numerous nation—the Serbs—to outvote and dominate the others.

Some leading Serbian personalities who spent World War I in exile in Western Europe understood as early as 1918 that Yugoslavia could not be constructed on a centralist basis without provoking an irresolvable political crisis. They anticipated an inevitable collapse of Yugoslavia and tried to find solutions that would appease differing national interests. In 1918 Ljubomir Stojanovic, a prominent Serbian linguist and professor at Belgrade University, predicted in a letter to Jovan Cvijic, a geographer and Belgrade University colleague, that Yugoslavia would end up like Austria-Hungary unless it adopted a federal structure in which Serbia,

Montenegro, Croatia, Slovenia, and Bosnia-Hercegovina enjoyed equal status. Cvijic, for his part, theorized a Yugoslav community along federal lines which he called a "United States of Yugoslavia."

Other members of the Serbian intellectual elite also considered the generation of old Serbian politicians—and especially the long-popular Nikola Pasic—unable to guide Yugoslavia in the direction of a modern European state, simply because they belonged to the past in their political practice and outlook. Cvijic said of Pasic, whose political career had begun in the era of revolutionary pan-Slavism, influenced by anarchist extremism at the same time as it was subsidized by the Russian tsar, that "he did not understand and could not understand the mentality of Western Europe."

Yet, as the head of the Serbian government before and during World War I and as leader of the Radicals, Pasic enjoyed a decisive influence in the creation of the Yugoslav state. After unification, from January 1921 to April 1926, Pasic formed ten governments and remained the dominant figure on the Yugoslav political scene. His outmoded, centralist conceptions provoked increasing resistance by Croatian and Slovenian representatives. Croatians were especially sensitive on these matters because their whole political tradition was based on centuries of struggle against the centralism of Vienna and Budapest. The federalist Yugoslavism that Croatian intellectuals pursued during the nineteenth century was conceived as an alternative to the centralism of the Austro-Hungarian monarchy, not as a means for its substitution by another form of centralism. Croatia expected the new state to grant what it had been denied under the Habsburgs: national sovereignty and a chance for unhindered economic and cultural growth. Croatian Yugoslavism, the current that triumphed during World War I over Croatian ultranationalism, gradually lost its sense of optimism and enthusiasm in clashes with real-life Yugoslavism. The Croatian public came to view the formula of "three tribes" in the constitution as a mask for Serbian expansionism and the assimilation, if not the destruction, of the Croatian people.

The centralism established by the 1921 constitution encountered its most serious obstacle in the form of the dominant trend in Croatian politics after World War I: the Croatian Peasant Party. Its leader, the remarkable Stjepan Radic, exercised a commanding hold over the loyalties of the Croatian public, by combining peasant protest and an antimonarchical and pacifist program. The Croatian Peasant Party took up the crusade against centralism. A sense of common purpose—the preservation of the Croatian nation and its historical tradition of statehood, melded with a program of agrarian radicalism—bridged social differences.

In the same period Slovenian politics was divided between "Yugoslavs" and "nationalists." In a 1918 manifesto, some Slovenian intellectuals had criticized Slovenian "separatist political aspirations," but by 1921 another group had assembled yet another manifesto, declaring the impossibility of a mechanical unification of Yugoslavia. That tendency soon demanded Slovenian autonomy within Yugoslavia. Although the majority of Slovenian politicians and intellectuals saw Yugoslavia as a necessary vehicle for political unity, they would not grant it the power to forcibly combine the existing nations into one new Yugoslav nation. The initial good faith with which Yugoslavism had been received by Slovenes vanished, and doubts mounted. Like Croats, Slovenes could not accept a state that was controlled by Serbia. The split between centralists and autonomists in Slovenia ended in decisive victory for the latter.

The "three-tribe" nation thus stood divided from the very beginning. No awareness of distant, common Slavic ethnic origins and no unifying state policy could change this reality. Yugoslavia was viable only so long as its Serbian rulers did not openly seek to suppress the identity of any of the other constituent nations. That and the aggrieved agitation of the federalist opposition, especially as it gained momentum in Croatia, made open conflict between Croats and Serbs inevitable.

Misunderstanding, distrust, and intolerance became the main features of political life in the kingdom. The parliament was paralyzed, working less and less frequently: either it waited for the end of yet another extended ministerial crisis (some lasting more than six months) or it called new elections.

This political struggle was carried out in an unfavorable economic environment as well. Economic liberalism was mandated by the constitution; the adoption of new legal codes should have stimulated development. Yet the social and economic differences between the regions persisted in their profound influence on political life. The regions that were more developed industrially (Slovenia and Croatia), in which seventy-five percent of all industry had been located in 1918, increased that percentage between 1920 and 1930 to eighty percent. The underdeveloped southeastern regions showed much slower industrial growth. The predominantly agrarian economies of Serbia and Montenegro were especially hard hit by the worldwide recession of the early 1920s, in which commodity prices collapsed, as well as by the deeper world economic crisis that began in 1929.

The northwestern regions of the country sought to preserve their advantageous situation in the internal Yugoslav market, while the southeastern regions, especially Serbia, wanted to close the economic gap as quickly as possible. Hence, Croatians and Slovenes expected their economic position to win them political authority, while the Serbs expected their political authority to strengthen their economic position, mainly through the power of taxation. Disparities in economic and political power were dramatic: according to one calculation, Serbia accounted for a mere one-fourth of Yugoslav capital, but its representatives made up three-fourths to four-fifths of government personnel.

The crisis of the new state was also complicated by the special powers of King Aleksandar Karadjordjevic, the first Yugoslav king and the son of the Serbian King Petar I. The prerogatives the constitution granted to Karadjordjevic and the use to which he put his prerogatives weakened the parliamentary system, and the constitutional monarchy soon became an autocracy. The king was endowed with inviolability—that is, he could not be politically challenged or forced to account for his actions to parliament. The Belgrade government was responsible for all his actions, yet all state functions—the legislative, the administrative, and the judicial—were held in the king's hands. In a form very distant from that of the European parliamentary monarchies, in which the ruler discreetly influenced government and did not in practice test the limits of royal authority, King Alexsandar, as he was known, constantly interfered in the political life of the country, above all in the choice of cabinet members. By frequently using his constitutional right to convene and disband parliament, by allowing the country to be governed by governments that lacked a parliamentary majority, and by nullifying governments that had a parliamentary majority, he undermined the basic principles of parliamentarianism. For example, according to the testimony of Svetozar Pribicevic, a politician very close to the king, of twenty-three cabinet crises, the parliament had provoked only two; all the rest were provoked by the king or by officials close to him and acting on his instructions.

A critical turning point came ten years after Yugoslavia emerged out of the ashes of World War I. On June 20, 1928, three deputies of the Croatian Peasant Party, among them the famed Stjepan Radic, were shot in parliament by Punisa Racic, a Montenegrin deputy and member of the Radical Party. Two were killed immediately, and Radic suffered a lingering death. With that tragedy, parliamentarianism also died, and with it many illusions about the future of a democratic Yugoslavia. The death of the beloved Radic deeply radicalized the Croatian national movement and irreparably aggravated the Serbian-Croatian split.

King Aleksandar took advantage of the crisis created by the parliament murders to carry out a coup d'état. On January 6, 1929, he suspended the constitution, outlawed all political parties, and dismissed the National Assembly. Although the coup was publicly justified in the interest of peace and order in the country, in reality it was the last attempt in the history of the Yugoslav monarchy to maintain a centralist regime. The king set up a dictatorship, suppressing all forms of parliamentary and democratic activity in the name of Yugoslavism. The Kingdom of Serbs, Croats, and Slovenes was officially renamed the Kingdom of Yugoslavia.

For a while, it seemed as though the king had found the formula by which to stop the escalating crisis. His attempt to settle ethnic antagonisms by denying their existence—as in renaming the state—was welcomed by elements of Croatian and Slovenian public opinion who believed the Yugoslav king really wanted to establish interethnic balance and prevent chaos. The king accused Yugoslav politicians of instigating strife among the people; he insisted that their opportunistic struggle for power was the basic cause of the political crisis in the country. He therefore offered the framework for the establishment of an "ideal" form of Yugoslavism; the "unifying king," as a symbol of the unified state, promised to communicate directly with the Yugoslav people. He eliminated the liberal legal-political structure in order to establish "direct democracy." Between the monarch and the people, he claimed, there should be no intermediary. But the success of these seemingly effective maneuvers was of brief duration.

The refurbished version of Yugoslavism served the king as a political rationalization for authoritarian rule. The centralistic model created by the constitution was reaffirmed by a new administrative division of the state into nine provinces (*banovine*), named after major rivers. Dividing the Yugoslav territory geographically, the king sought to erase all trace of the state traditions of the different Yugoslav nations, as well as ethnic and religious borders. The constitution of September 3, 1931, which the king's supporters called the September Constitution and his opponents called the Imposed Constitution (Oktroirani Ustav), offered an illusion of democracy through a pseudo parliament.

Reality had exposed the false nature of monarchical Yugoslavism. Still, few expected the price to be paid in blood—and by Aleksandar Karadjordjevic himself. Macedonian and Croatian extremists assassinated him in Marseilles in 1934. With him, the illusion of monarchical Yugoslavism was also buried.

The death of the king brought about a regrouping of political forces, but the democratic, liberal foundations of the Yugoslav state had been thoroughly eroded. On the one hand, Yugoslav parliamentarianism had been compromised by the parliament murders of 1928 and further subverted by royal dictatorship. On the other hand, fascist Italy and Nazi Germany, as well as Hungary, were encouraged to exploit Yugoslav national conflicts for their own objectives. The world economic crisis exacerbated the situation. These were the circumstances in the final chapter of Yugoslavia's short and turbulent life. A race against time began.

Demands for Croatian independence from the Yugoslav state continued to threaten the government with new crises. The question was put on the agenda in 1934, but not until February 1939 did Prince Pavle Karadjordjevic open the way for settling Serbian-Croatian relations. An agreement signed on August 26, 1939, between the Serbian politician Dragisa Cvetkovic and the Croatian politician Vladimir Macek, successor to Radic as leader of the Croatian Peasant Party, initiated a reordering of the Kingdom of Yugoslavia. The state and its "imposed constitution" underwent a radical change, with Croatian autonomy recognized through the establishment of a special *banovina* (province) of Croatia.

Banovina Croatia, as it was known, was granted a specific territory and a separate government organization. Croatia now was qualitatively different from the nine previous *banovine;* it now en-

joyed a degree of recognized statehood, which although it was subordinate to the central government and king, held out the possibility of a federal Yugoslavia.

But a federal Yugoslavia might have had a better chance at
another time. It was now too late—not only because the Serbian-
Croatian agreement was reached on the eve of World War II, in
difficult international circumstances, and because the other Yugoslav nations were bitter for being left out, but also because the
solution satisfied neither the Serbs nor the Croats. Croatian politicians were angered by the limited nature of autonomy, Serbian
politicians by the loss of their dominion, the abandonment of
centralism, and the new division of administrative powers. Nevertheless, the 1939 agreement began the revision of Yugoslavia's national foundations, as historian Branko Petranovic has noted, a
process that remained incomplete in failing to encompass Slovenia,
Bosnia-Hercegovina, and even Serbia as separate units. The national demands of the Macedonians and Albanians continued to
be ignored.

Only eighteen months after the agreement was signed, Yugoslavia collapsed. There was hardly enough time for the range of
national and party differences to be overcome. On April 6, 1941,
Hitler's air force leveled Belgrade, dragging Yugoslavia into World
War II on its own territory. The first South Slavic state perished as
it had been born, in fire and smoke. The creative energy symbolized
by the unification and the accumulation of human, intellectual,
and economic potential had foundered on the phenomena of permanent political crisis and national antagonism. Yugoslavia had
gambled away its first historical chances.

In less than two weeks, Hitler and Mussolini abolished the
country of Yugoslavia. Its territory was partitioned between Germany and Italy, with parts also handed out to Hungary and Bulgaria. Once again, new borders were laid out by foreign powers,
trenches were dug, barbed wire strung, bunkers built, concentration camps opened, armies formed, and local chiefs installed.

Society was reorganized on the basis of ethnic separation and
inflamed hatreds. There began a war of all against all. Armed attacks on the occupying power began almost immediately in Italian-
controlled Montenegro, which had ancient traditions of guerrilla

warfare, as well as in Serbia, marked for "exemplary punishment" by the Nazis. With the German invasion of Soviet Russia less than three months later, the Communist Party of Yugoslavia, which had been a negligible political factor after a brief leftist upsurge in the 1920s, called for partisan warfare. The occupiers answered both non-Communist and Communist resistance with terror and mass executions, compounded by further atrocities by their local collaborators.

The pro-Axis forces that emerged to rule the ruins of the South Slav state included the Ustashe, or Rebels, the extremist wing of the Croat nationalist movement, which had gained the patronage of Italy and Hungary in the period before the outbreak of war and which, with the fall of monarchist Yugoslavia, set up a puppet "Independent State of Croatia" that absorbed Bosnia-Hercegovina. The Ustashe, although a small minority of the Croatian population, also recruited among the Slavic Muslims of Bosnia-Hercegovina, on a program of brutal repression of Communists as well as outright genocide against the Serbian population within the "independent state." In addition, the Ustashe enthusiastically fulfilled Nazi demands for the extermination of the historic Jewish communities of Croatia and Bosnia-Hercegovina (in the latter case, a Sephardic Jewry of great age and distinction) as well as many Gypsies.

In Serbia, a collaborationist regime was also set up, run by military and police officers, and an array of ultranationalist formations, known as Chetniks (Irregulars), began pursuing vengeance against Slavic Muslims, Croats, and Communists. In Vojvodina, the combined efforts of local German colonists and the Hungarian authorities resulted in the wholesale destruction of the local Jewish population and serious losses among the Serbs.

Against this range of extremely unattractive options, only one force existed that was committed to united South Slavic resistance to the invaders, that is, to something like the original ideal of Yugoslavia. That was the Communist Party under the half-Croat, half-Slovene Josip Broz Tito, which included many members of the International Brigades in the Spanish civil war.

The rest of the old political organizations and parties disappeared. The royal Yugoslav government and its king found refuge in London, representing a country that no longer existed. The Allies, committed to support for resistance efforts throughout occupied Europe, were faced with two such movements in Yugoslavia: a faction of Serbian Chetniks loyal to the king and led by General Dragoljub (Draza) Mihailovic, formally representing the national Yugoslav army in its occupied homeland, and the Partisans of the National Liberation Movement set up by Tito. Although both Mihailovic's Chetniks and Tito's Partisans were members of the Allied coalition, the two movements never succeeded in uniting for a joint, patriotic fight against the German and Italian occupation. The Chetniks fought for a return to a Great Serbian, centralist monarchy, the Partisans for a socialist federation. Ideologically opposed, advancing conflicting war aims as well as different visions of the renewal of Yugoslavia, they would fight a war within the war. For all these reasons, World War II in Yugoslavia was not simply the bloody destruction of a conquered state by the Nazi-fascist coalition. It was also a civil war within each of the Yugoslav communities.

From this pandemonium of evil that broke loose in Yugoslavia, only one faction emerged victorious—the Communists. Their historic victory would be difficult to explain had they relied on ideology alone. The Communists were a small, illegal organization, fiercely persecuted in pre–1941 Yugoslavia. Soon after the war began, they launched sporadic and isolated armed actions. However, as the war progressed, it was clear they were alone in maintaining a consistent struggle against the invader. Their appeal to the Yugoslav peoples invoked patriotic, local, and democratic, rather than ideological, principles. Thus, in Slovenia they allied with the Christian Democrats; in Croatia they recruited followers of the Peasant Party as well as Dalmatian Croats angry at the Italians who sought to colonize the area and Serbs who had suffered under or feared the Ustashe regime; in Bosnia-Hercegovina they brought together Croats, Serbs, Muslims, and Jews; in Serbia and Montenegro they harked back to national traditions of mutual aid from and for "Holy Russia," now ruled by Stalin but, to many Orthodox peasants in the Balkans, no less Russia and no less holy. In the past political life of the kingdom, the Communists had unequivocally demonstrated their commitment to a federal Yugoslavia—to the principle of full equality for all the peoples living within it. During a war with all the features of a religious and ethnic war, the Communists offered—at the time when the renewal of Yugoslavia seemed entirely impossible—a new vision of Yugoslavia, expressed in the slogan "Brotherhood and Unity." Yugoslavism was reborn in blood, but on new foundations. The Communists hoped not to repeat the errors of their predecessors.

In 1943, the second session of the Antifascist Council for the National Liberation of Yugoslavia—the political leadership of the Tito Partisans—decided to recognize Bosnia-Hercegovina, Montenegro, Croatia, Macedonia, Slovenia, and Serbia as federal units of a Democratic Federative Yugoslavia. National status was granted to the Macedonians, Montenegrins, and implicitly, through recognition of Bosnia-Hercegovina, to the Muslims as well. The status of Kosova and of Albania itself in the future Balkan socialist commonwealth was left unmentioned. The intention in forming the federation was to establish a national equilibrium and prevent any nation from dominating the others. It was on this platform and on the basis of their undeniable successes on the battlefield that the Communists won widespread support.

But the Allies recognized the Yugoslav government in exile and the Chetnik commander Draza Mihailovic, the representative of the exiled king, as the representative of the country. As the war continued, however, it became increasingly clear that the Communists were the only real military force to contend with in Yugoslavia. British policy backed away from Mihailovic's Chetniks as a political or military alternative. Churchill, in 1943, recognized the internationalist Partisans as the major partners of the Allies, shocking the royalist Yugoslavs exiled in London. The leadership of the Mihailovic Chetniks held an underground congress, offering a reborn constitutional and parliamentary monarchy of Serbs, Croats, and Slovenes. But the attempt to make this an all-Yugoslav platform did not bring Mihailovic the support of the Allies, nor did it reinforce his position in the country. The Allies concluded that the Mihailovic Chetniks were not fighting the Germans and Italians but, rather, were collaborating with them against the Communists. The Chetniks also compromised themselves before the Yugoslav people because of their violent Serbian chauvinism and the atrocities they had committed against Muslim, Croat, and other non-Serbian civilians. By 1943 the Communists faced no serious rivals in the anti-Axis camp.

From small action groups committed to desperate and poorly organized actions against the occupiers, Tito's National Liberation Army grew to become a force of eight hundred thousand fighters. Tito triumphed in the halo of military success and ascribed his glory to the power of Communist ideology. The real victory, however, was that of the resurrected Yugoslav idea. Once again, Yugoslavs looked to the future with enthusiasm and hope. The first, post–World War I Yugoslavia had been created by intellectual and political elites. The new Yugoslavia that emerged from World War II was seen as a creation of the people. Despite the legacy of the ill-fated royal state, and despite the terrible crimes committed in the name of nationality during World War II, Yugoslavism provided a context for reconciliation. Common life was not only possible, but necessary.

THREE

Tito's Yugoslavia

Mirko Tepavac

In 1941 the kingdom of Yugoslavia collapsed under the assault of Nazi Germany and its Axis allies. The disintegration, twenty-three years after the foundation of a unified South Slavic state, was dramatic and appeared final. Few in the country or abroad believed the pieces could ever be put together again in a revived single state. Yet the impossible proved possible, in the hands of Josip Broz Tito.

Soon after the German invasion in April 1941, two figures emerged as apparent resistance leaders: General Dragoljub (Draza) Mihailovic, who led the Chetniks, a faction of Serbian irregular forces loyal to the exiled king, and Tito, who directed the Partisans under Communist political control. The Mihailovic strategy was to avoid direct battle with the German and Italian occupiers so as to preserve the strength of the royalist Serbian nationalist forces, in anticipation of a return to power by the prewar Karadjordjevic dynasty. Tito's Partisans, in contrast, waged an uncompromising war against the invader and gained strength in the struggle. While Mihailovic was able to rally only Serbs and Montenegrins to his stationary units in the mountains, Tito recruited his Partisan troops among all the peoples in Yugoslavia and maintained a continuous military campaign against the occupation. Once the war ended, their sacrifices and successes in battle rewarded the Partisans with unchallenged power.

Mihailovic had promised a rebirth of the Kingdom of Yugoslavia, under Serbian rule. Tito promised a new, federal Yugoslavia, national equality, and a change in the prewar sociopolitical order, which was much disliked even by Serbs, notwithstanding their domination of the royalist state.

Tito called for an "all-out war against fascism," with the victory of communism as the ultimate goal. Mihailovic called for defense of the Serbian nation and the defeat of communism. The war ended with the Allied powers overwhelmingly supporting Tito's Partisans, despite Tito's revolutionary objectives.

On November 29, 1943, the wartime Partisan parliament convened in the Bosnian town of Jajce, liberated from the occupiers, and voted for a new Yugoslavia that would, in its final form, be a federation of six republics, with two autonomous provinces, Kosova and Vojvodina, joined to Serbia. Bosnia-Hercegovina was restored to its historic parity with Slovenia, Croatia, Serbia, and Montenegro; Macedonia was also granted full republic status. In reality, the shape of the new state was not fully clear until after the war. Only one thing was certain at Jajce: a new Yugoslavia had to guarantee national equality. The Partisan parliament meant what it said, and, with the war over, it did much of what it promised.

The victorious, strong Tito regime immediately tried and punished a range of pro-Axis war criminals, along with a sprinkling of nonfascist political opponents, and acted to suppress what it viewed as reactionary nationalistic tendencies, above all in Croatia and Kosova. The slightest manifestation of nationalism was treated as a major crime. But within two years, one could travel safely from one end of Yugoslavia to another, irrespective of nationality, religious beliefs, or language. In a country where one-tenth of the population had died fighting the occupation or had fallen victim to genocide, this amounted to a miracle. Tito's slogan "Brotherhood and Unity," which today is frequently an object of scorn, was not empty demagoguery in a country where hundreds of thousands of men, women, and children had lost their lives in the most brutal ways because of ethnic hatred. The slogan reflected new hope in a population that had undergone a catharsis.

Contrary to recent claims, Tito was a sincere Yugoslav, an internationalist and cosmopolite, unencumbered by his Croat and Slovene origins. He bore no grudge against any of the Yugoslav nations, Serbia included. As a pragmatic politician, however, he saw Serbian nationalism, because it appealed to over one-third of Yugoslavia's total population and reflected a tradition of imperial rule, as a greater danger to the federation than, for instance, Macedonian or Slovenian nationalism.

If the concept of national equality was now clearly affirmed in Yugoslavia, the sociopolitical and economic vision of the future was, at best, cloudy and burdened with considerable ideological baggage. Abstract generalizations about "socialism" and "social justice" were the rule. A romanticized picture was conjured up, invoking a Soviet-style system with unassailable values for Yugoslavia to emulate. The Communist leadership seemed to believe that the destruction of private capitalism—which had brought neither freedom nor prosperity to Yugoslavia—was sufficient to accomplish a social and political transformation.

The educated elite, which had supported Tito and gladly continued to do so after the war, did not really grasp the full scope and complexity of constructing an entirely new country from its foundations. In the early postwar years, their vision went little beyond the idealized Soviet model, of which few had any direct knowledge. Tito and several of his closest associates had experienced Soviet reality through visits to the USSR before the war. They knew that the picture was not idyllic, but they, like other Communists, sought to ascribe the difficulties to the growing pains of an otherwise positive system. The Tito regime had genuine popular support and could, they thought, avoid the mistakes of the Soviet leadership. Many Yugoslav Communists honestly believed that the Soviet Union would do everything to help Yugoslavia and other Soviet bloc countries deal with their problems.

It was not long before illusions about the Soviet Union were shattered by the Soviet leaders themselves. A brusque, contemptuous, and provocative letter from Stalin to Tito in 1948, which announced the split between Moscow and Belgrade, was a landmark example of dictatorial arrogance. Stalin resented what he viewed as the excessive self-confidence of the Yugoslavs. Foreign Communist leaders were supposed to be reverent, not proud and independent, and, of course, the last thing in the world Stalin wanted was a ruling communism he could not control. Stalin made it clear to Tito that the achievements of Yugoslavia's antifascists—a movement that was proportionately as great and combative as that among the Soviet peoples themselves and that had excited the admiration of millions around the world—must be considered very small in comparison with the wartime exploits of the great Soviet Union. The main point of Stalin's message was that Yugoslavia must not imagine that it enjoyed a privileged position in the Soviet orbit. Stalin threatened, and carried out, a purge in the world Communist movement in response to Tito's defiance.

Only three years after war's end, Yugoslavia and Tito were again faced with a mortal danger, threatened this time not by a traditional foreign enemy but by the "greatest friend" and "elder brother of the Yugoslav peoples," as the Soviets had been described throughout the war. Tito categorically rejected Stalin's attempts to call him to account. However, some Yugoslav Communists, who honestly believed that the rejection of Soviet orders was the rejection of communism itself, believed that a socialist patriotism that was more faithful to one's own country than to the USSR was bitter betrayal. They were soon to find themselves labeled "traitors to their country and party" and were sent to prisons or concentration camps.

Yet a historic, courageous, and resounding no had been delivered to Stalin, with the overwhelming support of the Yugoslav people. Tito, at the head of the Yugoslav Communist Party, emerged from this confrontation the authentic hero of all Yugoslavs, unquestionably the most admired figure in the history of Yugoslavia. His popularity made his people forget and forgive his many absurd and arbitrary policies.

In the late 1940s, for example, blind dogmatism led to the nationalization of all private businesses, to the collectivization of agriculture, and to the compulsory sale by the peasants, at state prices, of farm produce—policies intended to feed the populace as well as to undermine the political power of those "rich peasants" labelled *kulaks*. Tito had broken with Stalin, but not with his political methods. The rigid Stalinist conception of state and society remained intact in the minds of Tito and his colleagues at the heights of power, however much they hoped to avoid Soviet errors. In the end Tito was able to avoid some Soviet errors but not to surmount those errors that were strictly his own.

Titoist Yugoslavia enacted a constitution and laws for a one-party, unitary, strongly centralized state, in contradiction to its official multinational federal structure. Private enterprise and property were reduced to a minimum. Political freedom and civil rights were restricted and the media placed under total state control. The West, for its part, was willing to overlook all that because Tito had clearly demonstrated his geopolitical independence from Moscow. With Western aid, the military was strengthened, disproportionately to the country's size, at the same time as internal security was modernized. On the surface, it appeared that the chief aim of the military, police, and other repressive organs of the Titoist state was to counter the Soviet threat. In reality, while supported by his people and lauded by almost the entire world, Tito was carrying out exactly the program he would have completed as an orthodox Communist, by establishing an uncontested dictatorship regardless of his foreign policy toward Stalin.

Resisting the Soviet threat, Tito nevertheless always saw himself as a Communist first and foremost, even as he had become a patriotic symbol of Yugoslav honor and independence. Ideologically distrustful of the "capitalist world," but now an outcast from the Communist one, he had no choice but to link his own and his country's survival to the West, which, pursuing its own interests, provided willing and effective assistance.

To develop an independent foreign policy for Yugoslavia, Tito had to navigate between the Soviet model, the commands of whose leaders he rejected, and a Western model, which he found ideologically distasteful. He turned out to be a master of such a difficult and delicate course. The Soviets were unable to push him entirely over to the Western side, but neither did his dependence on the West force him to renounce Yugoslavia's socialism. Of course, he was not guided by principles alone. He defended his own power and everything he had personally accomplished. Fortunately, his personal ambitions and the interests of the country happened to coincide. He was a pragmatist, not a sage. But successful pragmatism requires wisdom.

As much as Tito had been able to say no to Stalin, seven years afterward he found himself unable to say yes to Khrushchev. The arrival of Nikita Khrushchev and Nikolai Bulganin in Belgrade in 1955, hoping to redress the wrong Stalin had done to Yugoslavia in 1948, was spectacular and historic. Tito's attitude was made visible before the eyes of the world. He turned away when Khrushchev attempted to embrace him in the Russian style. Khrushchev then made a repentant statement before live microphones, and he gestured to Tito to follow him to the podium; Tito responded by pointing coldly to an open car door. Tito offered the Russians no more than a diplomatically correct normalization of relations between two equal members of the international community. The Belgrade Declaration, a carefully worded document drawn up by the best minds in the Tito government, was published at the end of the visit and signed reluctantly by the disappointed Soviet leaders. Everyone was left with the impression that Yugoslavia's internal affairs and its socialism would never again be the object of interference by the Soviet regime or international communism. Unfortunately, things did not work out that way.

Tito reciprocated Khrushchev's trip to Yugoslavia with a series of visits to nearly all the Soviet bloc countries. Wherever he went, he was given a hero's welcome as a "great revolutionary and Communist" whose words should be respected and advice sought. In many such countries attractive offers were made for cooperation with Yugoslavia. Everything was done to soften the heart of Tito, the "comrade in arms and in ideology." Khrushchev himself needed a reconciliation with Tito, in his own struggle with Stalinist restorationists; at the same time, the ineluctable imperial Soviet logic required that he attempt to dilute Tito's heretical independence.

Tito was not an innocent, but his ideological loyalties were extraordinarily deep. In the end, they made him susceptible to Soviet overtures and incapable of recognizing that the new Soviet embrace was no less risky than the earlier threats. Tito believed that he had become the most influential leader in the Communist world, which was the only world in which he truly felt at home. Emboldened, the cautious statesman gradually, unwittingly acquiesced.

The Moscow Declaration, signed by Tito during his state visit to the Soviet Union in 1956, formalized cooperation between the Soviet and Yugoslav Communist Parties "in the common interest of the struggle for socialism." Over the next few years the USSR offered Tito, on a number of occasions, full readmission to the Warsaw Pact and other institutions of the Soviet bloc. Tito remained too shrewd to accept such membership as a favor; he was aware that in 1948 the loss of the same membership was a punishment.

But a shift in relations with the Soviet Union had taken place, with a strong impact in Yugoslavia. Ill at ease with liberal reformism and still burdened with the traditions of Soviet socialism, Tito began to obstruct attempts to loosen up the one-party political monopoly and free the economy from state supervision. Milovan Djilas, one of the four men closest to Tito during and immediately after the war and the first public advocate of a democratization of Yugoslav communism, had already been removed from the leadership in 1954. Attacks on Djilas were stepped up; he was arrested and sentenced to a long prison term.

The 1956 rebellion in Hungary, against the remnants of the harsh and violently anti-Tito Stalinist regime of Matyas Rakosi, followed by the brutal Soviet intervention that crushed it, swept away many illusions that a fundamental change would come to the post-Stalin Soviet Union. Once again, Yugoslavia found itself resisting Soviet pressure, which now was encouraged by Tito's incautious acceptance of reconciliation. Still, like Khrushchev and Leonid Brezhnev after him, Tito never broke entirely with the basic Soviet style of governance, regardless of his defiance of Soviet hegemony. In the higher echelons of the Yugoslav party and state, democratically oriented officials had been arguing for years against making ideology the basis of relations with the socialist countries, given Moscow's history of manipulating ideology to disguise naked, aggressive imperialism. But these efforts were, of course, hopeless. In truth, the ideology of the Warsaw Pact countries had never been fully abandoned in Yugoslavia; it was merely given a liberal interpretation.

The 1958 Program of the League of Communists of Yugoslavia—the new title of the ruling party—promised reform, with Yugoslavia professing a liberalism inconceivable in any other socialist country. The program envisioned a limit on one-party rule; a narrowing of state planning; evolution toward a full market economy; and economic efficiency as the test of the political system. The role of the state in general was to be circumscribed, with the introduction of "self-management," democratization of the federal structure and increased autonomy of the constituent republics, and finally, greater openness toward the West. The "leading role" of the party was redefined as a "guiding role." The party would become a participant in decision making instead of the sole decision maker:

it would argue for its positions instead of handing down orders. The party's program ended, "Nothing in our established practice may ever be considered so sacred that we dare not move on and replace it with practices that are more progressive, freer, more humane." Sadly, the dogmatic nature of Yugoslav Communist practice had already become too entrenched to be easily replaced. Yugoslavia's "soft totalitarianism" was yet incapable of fundamental change. As rapprochement with Moscow proceeded in the coming years, the spirit and the letter of the 1958 program were defended with less and less vigor; the program never fully came to life.

Fluctuations in Yugoslav domestic policies and in the country's role in the cold war world centered on the sole reliable constant: Titoist Yugoslavia was and remained an authentically independent country. Yugoslavia continued using, to maximum advantage, its cooperation and close relations with the West, while avoiding the maximum damage of its relationship with the Soviet Union. Yugoslav success in this area stemmed partly from Tito's personal commitment to the new idea of "nonalignment," that is, of a broad neutrality between the capitalist and Soviet powers on the part of nations in Asia, Africa, and Latin America. Tito was a leading figure in the Movement of Nonaligned Countries, which was formally established in September 1961, and he remained prominent in it until his death. For the better part of two decades, the 1960s and 1970s, Yugoslavia was in the forefront of "nonalignment" and contributed effectively to the movement's leadership. Although Tito's involvement with the nonaligned movement has been fiercely criticized in former Yugoslavia, nonalignment did at least as much for Yugoslavia as Yugoslavia did for nonalignment.

Tito may have exaggerated, for domestic consumption, the nonaligned movement's international importance, and he may have been overambitious in seeking to play a major part in world affairs. But nonalignment had real importance for Yugoslavia's independent international position. The Russians were not happy about Yugoslavia's nonalignment and were even less happy when nonalignment gained favor in other Soviet bloc countries or led to the weakening of Soviet influence in some nonbloc countries. Still, the Soviet Union never dared to attack Yugoslav nonalignment or demand that Tito renounce the movement. In any case, Yugoslavia could never have achieved the degree of liberalization it enjoyed—a liberalization surpassing by far that of the other Soviet bloc countries—had it not been aggressively open to the entire world. And that openness was necessarily intertwined with nonalignment.

Yugoslavia departed decisively from Soviet dogmatism in that it genuinely attempted to create a more democratic socialism, moving ahead under the impetus of postwar enthusiasm and significant foreign aid. Industrial growth reached impressive levels, above ten percent annually. During the first two postwar decades, broad modernization and industrialization were accomplished, and the standard of living showed constant improvement. Yugoslavia became the "showcase" of socialism, surpassing Hungary and Czechoslovakia, which were much better developed before the war. Yugoslavia was the only country that was well off, indeed rather comfortable, under communism, above all in its living standards. Many inside and outside the country thought Yugoslavia had successfully found an original road for socialism. But the essential prerequisite for maintaining growth and progress, a policy of fundamental democratic changes from top to bottom in the political system, was out of the question. Tito, who was actually a reluctant reformer, began putting the brakes on change. He preferred socialism to prosperity, if and when the two seemed to conflict. In 1968, he told Belgrade University student demonstrators that he agreed with demands for greater democracy, but he then turned around and blocked all change.

In 1965 a broad economic reform had been launched, with the objective of establishing a market economy by removing administrative price controls. In Slovenia and Croatia, the richest regions, this led to a dramatic rise in production and income; in Kosova, the poorest, it led by contrast to further stagnation. Prices for agricultural and industrial products soared, and the government responded by temporarily imposing new controls. From 1965 on, Yugoslavia attempted to keep its own brand of "market socialism." The attempt was, however, fainthearted and generated no more than a hybrid economy plagued by the many problems implicit in an untested experiment, whose direction was not clear to Tito or anyone else.

Titoist Yugoslavia was, therefore, permanently characterized by a zigzag progress between liberalism and authoritarianism. In

1974 the constitution was amended to redefine the complicated lines of authority between the federal government, the republics, and the autonomous provinces of Kosova and Vojvodina. The new constitution granted the latter two complete economic and political autonomy, in a de facto status as full republics. But this effort at decentralization resulted in a more fragmented economy and society, with centralism intact as a policy of governance. Centralist power was simply transferred from the federal authority to the republics. Over time the republic leaders duplicated, in their own environments, the same centralism they resented when it had originated with the federal administration: the result was eight tightly controlled, centralist regional governments. The 1974 constitution allowed them to act freely and openly in pursuit of their national interests, oblivious to those of the federation as a whole. In addition, regional leaders promoted their careers by offering their peoples a romantic vision of harmony within each single, ethnic community. Within a few years of Tito's death in 1980, each republic and autonomous province had become a state within a state. The center no longer held. Gaps between the nations began widening uncontrollably.

Tito was not blind to signs of the eventual decomposition of the new Yugoslavia that was the product of his lifework. Yet he was aware he could not stop the trend without risking his unchallenged position. He opted for self-deception and acted as though he himself believed the popular song, heard more widely than the Yugoslav anthem, "Comrade Tito, we pledge not to veer from your course." He believed that Yugoslavia was safe as long as he lived. Afterward, others would face the responsibility of having "veered from Tito's course."

One night in autumn 1971, aboard the presidential Blue Train on his return from a state visit to Romania, Tito began discussing, with the delegation that accompanied him, news of unrest at the University of Zagreb. Tito's associates condemned the rebirth of nationalist sentiment in Croatia. Tito had already made up his mind, although he did not disclose it, to purge the Croatian Communist leadership, which he blamed for the growing discontent. In the middle of the conversation, Tito suddenly looked up at his comrades and said, "If you saw what I see for the future in Yugoslavia, it would scare you." There were many valid reasons for fear, and his words were obviously prophetic. In the meantime, he was determined to come down hard on the Croatian Communist leadership. He was incapable of opening up the party and government to a democratic debate that would explore the social and national problems that underlay Croatian nationalist concerns.

In the early 1970s, an article was added to the Yugoslav constitution stating, "Josip Broz Tito is President-for-life of Yugoslavia." Among others, a certain Belgrade University professor criticized this article during public discussion of the draft constitution. Tito undoubtedly lost no sleep when the professor was arrested, tried, and imprisoned. Tito could no longer face the new or abandon the old. He had ceased to be simply the head of state; he now was the state.

In 1971 and 1972, with the help of the conservative wing of the League of Communists of Yugoslavia, Tito purged the Communist leadership and the intellectuals in Croatia, crushing demands for federal reform. The movement, although nationalist in its consciousness, embodied a broader democratic outlook. One year later, Tito repeated this performance in the repression of reformist democrats in Serbia led by Marko Nikezic and known for their explicitly antinationalist and liberal attitudes. The Serb reformers also desired democratization not only of their own republic but of the entire federal structure. But genuine democratization remained a far greater potential danger to Tito's rule than nationalism.

The confrontations with Croatia and Serbia were each followed by purges, including several thousand dismissals, at all levels. Prominent figures in academic and cultural life, and even in trade and industry, were targeted. The vacancies in the bureaucracy were quickly filled by Tito's loyalists. A new peace descended on the country, though the real problems remained untouched and the illusion of solidity and unity was emptier than ever. Tito's solutions were obsolete. He continued accumulating power even as it grew more and more problematic. Beneath the calm surface, the ground was turbulent. The foundations of Yugoslavia, weakened by the fragmentation into virtual mini-states by the 1974 constitution, were increasingly shaky.

Another negative side emerged from Tito's long-lasting ability to maintain Yugoslav independence. Still perceived as a country that had rebuffed the Soviet Union, Yugoslavia in the 1970s obtained cheap loans from many foreign sources. The federal government borrowed and spent ever more recklessly. Meanwhile, the 1974 constitution encouraged the republics to believe that mutual responsibilities would disappear in the near future. Concerning themselves only with their own affairs in the late 1970s and 1980s, the republics dragged the federation into an enormous foreign debt. Regional spending was not determined by economic criteria but orchestrated by local bureaucracies increasingly overtaken by nationalist selfishness. The facade of prosperity was maintained, but the economic foundations of Yugoslavia were crumbling. The overriding concern was to keep up the appearance of progress, measured by the fictitious standards of "self-management." In reality, Yugoslavs were wasting away their future.

Titoist Yugoslavia, now in decline, had become nothing more than Tito's Yugoslavia. Tito was not only the supreme and unchallengeable first citizen of the country; he was, at the end, the only effectively functioning institution. All the levers of power operated through his hands. Government rubber-stamped his will. The League of Communists was not a political party, if for no other reason than that it was the only party; the parliament was a debating club and not much more; the army and internal security were Tito's private domains. The members of the federal government came to view any initiative on their own part in foreign policy, defense, or security as "meddling" in Tito's jurisdiction and carefully avoided these areas. The government had never been much more than a council for economic affairs, economy being the one area in which Tito preferred to avoid involving himself. While the ministers of defense and foreign and internal affairs were in constant personal contact with Tito, with access to him whenever they liked, the speaker of parliament and the prime minister could not see him even after repeated requests. He discussed the details of their work with the first three, but with the other two, instructions were sent through underlings.

As their autonomy increased, however, the more important was Tito's direct contact with the republic governments and League of Communists leaders. With them he met regularly, if not frequently. As a result, relations among the republics, and their conflicts, were more and more removed from the purview of federation officials. Republic delegations officially reported to Tito and increasingly turned to him for approval of many measures they believed could not be adopted through constitutional channels. Furthermore, Tito was inclined to agree with everybody. When a problem arose between two or more republics, republic leaders learned to approach Tito separately instead of meeting together. Tito often would satisfy the parties individually, sometimes at each other's expense, and without resolving the underlying issues.

Tito liked to travel around the country meeting local leaders. He journeyed in high style and was welcomed and seen off by huge crowds; every word he had to say at a meeting or in a speech was carried in full by all media. He was generous with praise, and his public criticism was judicious. Whatever he said was received with gratitude, as "helping our work," and was enshrined by the government and party bodies. There is almost no record of anyone voicing criticism of Tito himself at such meetings or disputing his observations or evaluations. He believed that public acceptance of his word was proof of unity and unanimity and a demonstration of democracy, when it only masked the self-serving careerism of the republic leaders.

Tito would exclaim, "They say there is no democracy in our country, but aren't these talks with the people the highest form of democracy?" or "They say there is no criticism in our country, and I myself am the greatest critic of anything bad." He was hard on "weaknesses" and criticized his associates for not doing a better job. "I will single them out by name when the time comes," he would say and then leave everybody guessing whom he had in mind. He spoke out against lawbreaking, willfulness, ambition for power and extravagance, never imagining that for the growing number of skeptics in his audiences his reproaches should very obviously apply to himself. He had long since stopped seeing himself through the eyes of the "ordinary citizens" and "working people" to whom he most often addressed his words. Once, in a small circle, when the growing abuse of privileges in the construction of private vacation homes was mentioned, he grumbled, "I wouldn't mind building a place I would actually own, but one has to think about what the people would say." It was clear that it never occurred to him that those present might consider private ownership of a vacation home to be a much humbler form of ownership than his own possession (if not ownership in the strict sense) of dozens of luxury vacation homes around the country, replete with servants.

The conservative nature of the system affected the selection of individuals for public service, including the political leadership. In early postwar Yugoslavia, the criteria for public responsibility had been meritorious war service, belief in the party's goals, and readiness to work hard. The party's choice and a person's public reputation were affirmed through a process of thoughtful appointment from above rather than democratic selection. Gradually, however, personal loyalty became the decisive element. In the 1970s an unconditional pledge to one's republic and ethnic leaders was required for advancement. "Negative selection," as the filling of offices with loyal cadres was called, gained momentum. Finally, in the 1980s, all restraint was lost, and totally arbitrary promotion became the rule. Like mushrooms after rain, a multitude of power-hungry bureaucrats emerged from the pseudo-populist jungle of post-Tito Yugoslavia. To the leaders of the republics, the worst extremists became indispensable.

Still, only a few years before fighting broke out in 1991, Yugoslavism, or, more precisely, the principle of a Yugoslav federation, would have won a majority in any honest referendum in all the republics and autonomous provinces, without exception. Why then did Tito's Yugoslavia, after only fifty years, perish in a bloody ruin?

Was communism to blame? The Communists were certainly not free of all blame. Yet Balkan evils have a deeper history than Balkan communism. Being antinationalist and even, in theory, internationalist, communism did not foster ethnic antagonisms. Many decades of Yugoslav communism passed in genuine national and religious equality and tolerance. Laws against inciting national hatreds were unambiguous and harshly enforced. In any case, nationalistic offenses were rare until the 1980s. The constituent Yugoslav nations enjoyed a considerable equality of rights, unknown in any other socialist country. Missing in Yugoslavia were the democratic political rights that affect all, regardless of their national affiliation or the rights of their communities.

In its seventy years of existence, Yugoslavia tried monarchy and communism, centralized and decentralized government, "self-management"—everything except genuine democracy. And only as a genuine democracy could Yugoslavia have held together or, if proven a failure, have dissolved honorably.

Tito died in 1980, two days before his eighty-eighth birthday. But even had he lived much longer, he would have been unable to preserve the Yugoslavia he left. Tito was the courageous leader of Partisan antifascism, the uncompromising opponent of Stalin, the skillful guardian of his country's independence, the architect of post–World War II Yugoslavia, and the driving force behind the policy of national equality—long the best and most consistent aspect of Yugoslavia's governance. He was, however, also the watchdog of a political system that wavered between dogma and democracy. The collapse of Yugoslavia was a consequence of this unsustainable political system, not its policies, whatever their failings. Tito will not be forgiven for valuing the preservation of his own power above progress and greater democracy, thereby condemning his country to survive him by no more than a decade. But it was not Tito who murdered Yugoslavia. The murderers are among us.

FOUR

The March to War (1980–1990)

Slavko Čuruvija and Ivan Torov

Tito died on May 4, 1980, but the slogan "After Tito, Tito" continued to describe Yugoslavia's reality. Like a drug, the promise of Tito's "immortality" created the illusion of safety; nothing bad or dramatic would happen even after Tito's death. The majority of Yugoslavs sincerely mourned him. He had given them nearly five decades of peace in the restless and explosive Balkans, and their life had been incomparably better in living standards and political freedom than anything known elsewhere in Eastern Europe.

Tito, however, left a leadership vacuum. It was most obvious in the absence of goals and ideas about the inevitable changes that would follow his death. Tito was succeeded by an eight-member collective presidency made up of one representative for each of the six republics and the two autonomous provinces. It proved a weak institution, incapable of arriving at consensus regarding the country's intensifying economic difficulties. By the beginning of 1980s, the policy of heedless borrowing thanks to cheap credit from the West had begun to haunt the Yugoslav economy. Misguided past investments in heavy industry were now a painful burden, and the foreign debt had increased four hundred percent by 1980: from $6 billion in 1975, it climbed to $17 billion in 1979 and $23 billion by 1980. Interest on the foreign debt alone brought about three-digit inflation. Prices for electricity, food, clothing, and other daily necessities rose sixty percent every six months. Public disenchantment with Tito's economic and political legacy grew apace.

Although a shopping trip was enough to leave many Yugoslavs confused and upset, daily life did not change that much, particularly for the burgeoning middle class. Instead of monetary controls to slow inflation, the federal government continued issuing newly printed bills. A relatively high standard of living was maintained artificially, but people knew that something was very wrong. There was a growing gap between the way people tried to continue living and the increasing economic chaos reported in detail in the media. Stores still offered a tempting variety of products, most of which remained within reach of the middle-class budget. While less money might be left over for vacations abroad, many could still eat in good restaurants and buy Italian leather goods and French cheeses as well as imported baby strollers. However, wage workers had begun striking for higher pay and demanding lower prices for the basics: meat, bread, milk, and local farm produce.

The destructive consequences of this fictitious prosperity reached a climax in summer 1990 when Yugoslav banks ceased to cover their customers' foreign currency deposits, with the excuse that such was made impossible by the national shortage of hard currency. Thus, if a Yugoslav had $50,000 in U.S. funds on deposit in a local bank, it could not be withdrawn. Officially, the funds remained on the books; it was yours; it had not been seized or removed. In reality, it no longer existed.

With no serious plan for alleviating the economic crisis spinning out of control, with doubt and uncertainty reaching degrees unimaginable under Tito, and, last but not least, with the collapse of Soviet communism, there was little that local leaders could use to maintain their positions and inspire popular confidence. They opted for radical nationalism.

National contradictions were nothing new in Yugoslavia. During World War II ethnic conflicts had turned into open civil war with a brutality that sometimes seemed to exceed that of the Nazi occupiers. After the war, Tito ordained that the public expression or promotion of nationalism was a crime. Tito understood—as Stojan Cerovic, the columnist of the independent Belgrade weekly *Vreme* has written—the qualitative difference between expressions of personal hostility and the expression of collective, nationalist, racial, or gender hatred. Nations are not individuals, and nationalistic outbursts do not offer the therapeutic benefits of a personal catharsis. Thus, under Tito open nationalism would not be tolerated. Yugoslavia began to fall apart when Serbia, Croatia, and Slovenia violated this, Yugoslavia's fundamental taboo.

Nationalist tendencies existed even in Tito's time. Pressure from Slovenia and Croatia for greater autonomy had culminated in the adoption of the 1974 federal constitution giving the republics and autonomous provinces much greater powers than they formerly enjoyed. The six republics and two provinces were given veto power in the federal assembly, tacitly transforming federative Yugoslavia into a confederation. The federal government was crippled, encountering obstacles whenever any one of the republics or provinces felt that a proposal threatened its interests. Decision making became virtually impossible at the federal level. After 1974, each of the eight federal units acted primarily against competition from the other federal units and felt free to take account only of its own needs. Each considered itself the master and manager of its own local economy, investment policy, and foreign trade. None worried about the common household.

This led before long to what Harold Lydall, the author of *Yugoslavia in Crisis*, called "feudal socialism." Capital investment was duplicated, economic and transport infrastructure became fragmented, and communication between the eight federal units broke down. The situation was politically absurd and economically disastrous. Federal paralysis worsened to a point where it was irreversible. The final breakup of Yugoslavia and the ensuing wars had roots in the 1974 constitution, which left the federation economically impoverished and politically defenseless.

The 1974 constitution granted considerable autonomy to the two autonomous provinces of Serbia—Vojvodina in the north, bordering Hungary and including a Hungarian population of half a million, and Kosova to the south, bordering on Albania and with an Albanian-speaking majority. The powers vested in these two provinces were close to those enjoyed by Serbia as a federal republic. The provinces had their own police forces, judiciaries, media, schools, and universities. The education of Hungarian children in Vojvodina was conducted in Hungarian, that of Kosovar Albanian children in Albanian. In the latter case, textbooks for use in the elementary and high schools, as well as the University of Prishtina, were imported from Albania.

Until Tito's death, the high degree of autonomy of Vojvodina and Kosova was considered one of the outstanding features of Yugoslavia's policy toward nationalities. Yet despite that achievement, Kosova remained the least economically developed federal unit of Yugoslavia. Its underdevelopment was a source of tension between the Kosova ethnic populations: Albanians on the one side, Serbs and Montenegrins on the other. The situation was quite different in Vojvodina—but Vojvodina was not underdeveloped, like Kosova. On the contrary, it was always the most developed part of Serbia. Further, in the decade before Tito's death, the Albanian population in Kosova increased from forty percent to more than eighty percent. While Kosovar Albanians claimed that they had been systematically undercounted in the past, it was unarguable that Albanians had a higher birthrate and that Serbs had emigrated from the province.

With Kosova's autonomy strengthened under the 1974 constitution, a movement for Albanian "separatism," part of the media and political landscape of Serbia since the late 1960s, began to demand full status as a Yugoslav republic for Kosova, in name as well as in constitutional prerogatives. But opponents of such a measure argued that full republic status would give Kosova the constitutional right of self-determination, placing the region only one step away, at some future time, from secession from Yugoslavia and union with Albania. For Serbia, this would have meant the loss of a significant portion of its territory as well as the loss of symbolically important land considered to have been the heart of medieval Serbia, with major historical and religious landmarks.

Lazar Kolisevski, Yugoslav presidency member for Macedonia at Tito's death and for some time thereafter, was the first to argue, in the 1980s, that excessive autonomy had been given to Kosova and Vojvodina in the 1974 constitution. He declared that constitutional contradictions existed between the three federal units that made up Serbia; that Serbia had lost governing authority over a large part of its territory; and that Serbia had suffered a de facto partition into three mini-states: Serbia proper, Vojvodina, and Kosova. The two provinces had representatives in all governing bodies in Serbia, while Serbia had none in the provinces. Such a contradiction, warned Kolisevski, would help nobody, least of all Yugoslavia as a whole. Kolisevski was unaware of the eventual outcome of his comments on the situation.

In spring 1981 Kosovar Albanians had provided the first major challenge to Tito's heirs. Several thousand took to the streets acclaiming a "Kosova republic," that is, separation from Serbia.

Tito was widely believed to have arrived at a bargain with the Kosovar Albanians, as well as with the Communists in Albania, during World War II. The documentary record of the Antifascist Council for the National Liberation of Yugoslavia shows, however, that no promises were made to the Kosovar Albanians, although some Serb historians have viewed this very absence as evidence that Albania itself and Kosova as a part of it were intended for entry into Yugoslavia through a Balkan socialist federation. Moves toward the realization of such a merger did take place after the war, alarming anti-Serb elements in the Communist leadership in Albania and leading Enver Hoxha, the Communist ruler in Tirana, after some dithering, to appeal to Stalin for help against Tito. Stalin supported Hoxha, less out of love of the Albanians than out of resentment of Tito's style. In any event, any presumed bargain fell through.

Kosova, however, was the scene of a major anti-Serb uprising in 1945, and other disorders, large and small, by the Kosovar Albanians were suppressed in the first ten years of Titoist Yugoslavia by the chief of the federal police, a Serb named Aleksandar Rankovic. For the Serbs, these were good times, for the Albanians, bad. After Rankovic was purged in 1966, the Albanians set out very concrete demands to Serbia: they wanted autonomy in which they, as the ethnic majority, would rule Kosova.

These demands were fulfilled by a constitutional restructuring from 1968 to 1974. The Albanians obtained much of what they sought: their own representatives in all federal organs; a turn at the head of the Yugoslav state and the League of Communists of Yugoslavia; autonomous courts, police, health, and educational systems; and an academy of sciences. From the perspective of the Serbian establishment, it may seem strange that Serbia agreed to such a high degree of autonomy for an ethnic group they considered to be proven in their antagonistic attitudes. Two explanations suggest themselves. First, the Serbian leadership in that period was reformist, more prepared to compromise than in the past. Second, the leadership considered the underdevelopment of rebellious Kosova to be a burden on Serbia. Serbia would be much better off with Kosova as a federal constituent unit and, hence, a problem for the federation as a whole.

By its concessions and pragmatism, the Serbian leadership enabled the Albanians to assume full power in Kosova by 1971. The degree of autonomy for the Albanians in Serbia during that period could serve as a model for minority rights anywhere in the world. In addition, as the least developed of the federal units, Kosova received substantial financial aid without repayment obligations. All the Yugoslav republics, including the other Serbian autonomous province, Vojvodina, were donors to this fund.

However, because of many bad investments in the period that followed, Kosova's economic transformation never took place. Neither did political concessions lessen tensions between its Albanian and Serbian populations. On the contrary, old historical patterns reemerged. Serbs claimed that some of the young Kosovar Albanian bureaucracy used its newly acquired ascendancy not as an opportunity for national reconciliation, but as a chance to organize Kosova as an exclusively Albanian region. Serbs and Montenegrins complained that they felt pressured to leave Kosova from 1971 to 1986. The 1981 rebellion demanding recognition of Kosova as a separate republic was viewed as an expression of an Albanian determination to see Kosova become a separate state.

The 1981 demonstrations stirred deep anxieties and resentments in Serbia. Many Serbs suspected that the Albanians, given the void opened by Tito's death, would attempt to secede from Yugoslavia altogether, not because the Albanians saw themselves as oppressed, but because they had been granted too much autonomy already, which encouraged "separatism."

The Serbian and the federal leaderships were confused by Albanian discontent. Neither had expected serious problems from that direction. The Albanian protest movement was declared to be "counterrevolutionary." The League of Communists took things in hand, accused the Albanian leadership of separatism, and put an ethnically Albanian "good party man," Azem Vllasi, in charge, ordering him to strike at the roots of the "counterrevolution."

Calm was, however, elusive. The Kosovar Albanians were determined in their struggle for greater local power, much of which they had achieved. The situation was made even more complicated and dangerous by the rising anger of the ordinary Serbs in Kosova. Repeated assertion of their grievances, including the allegation that Albanians were forcing them to leave the region, were ignored by both the federal and the Serbian authorities. In Tito's Yugoslavia, calling nationalism by its real name was normally discouraged; ethnic disagreements were labeled as "counterrevolution" and subversion of "brotherhood and unity." Legitimate issues were swept under the rug and authentic solutions became impossible. This happened in Kosova.

The Serbs complained of differing kinds of harassment from Albanians. The milder problems were merely psychological. Albanians would, it was said, offer repeatedly to buy Serb houses despite refusals by the owners to sell. In a less hostile climate such frictions would be nothing more than a nuisance; but in the tense atmosphere growing in Kosova, Serbs interpreted these offers as threats. In addition, numerous local incidents—the purportedly deliberate burning of a Serb crop, a cow blinded, a goat killed, gardens and orchards destroyed here and there—were magnified by fear and rumor. Bullying, assaults, and murders were viewed as part of a conspiracy; in an environment less emotionally charged they would have been seen as criminal activity. In Kosova, however, they were interpreted as ethnic aggression. Serbs verbalized their anxieties as a personal and collective frustration. The Albanian authorities in Kosova, for their part, paid little attention to growing Serb irritation.

The problem was exacerbated by the apparent indifference of the authorities in Serbia proper, along with the authorities in the other republics, to anything having to do with nationalism. They were unwilling, it was believed, to assist the Kosova Serbs in any way. Helping the Kosova Serbs would have required acknowledgment that a conflict existed and would have destroyed the illusion of peace, equality, and a balanced order—the "brotherhood and unity" that the political leadership considered indispensable. The pleas of Kosova's Serbs were relegated to the distant margin of politics and media.

In early 1986, in an effort to attract public support, two thousand Serbs signed a petition asserting that Serbs in Kosova were

threatened and sent it to the highest Serbian and federal government institutions. This protest, like that of the Kosovar Albanians
before it, was also immediately characterized negatively by the federal authorities, as a "provocation." The Kosovar Albanian leadership, believing that a "Serb rebel headquarters" already existed in
Kosova, threatened a repression of their own. The person whose
name appeared first on the petition was arrested, but several hundred Serbs gathered in front of his house, determined to stay there
until he was freed, and he was released. The Serbs attempted to
organize a massive march, a "protest emigration" from Kosova,
but it was forcibly prevented by the local authorities.

One year later, in April 1987, a broader movement broke out
among the Kosova Serbs. This incident deeply influenced the
course of events in Serbia and in Yugoslavia. The Serb protest was
unexpected. Significantly, it occurred during a highly publicized
visit to the battlefield at Kosovo Polje, considered the greatest
shrine of Serbian nationalism, by the head of the Serbian Communists, a hitherto obscure figure named Slobodan Milosevic. Until
then, nobody suspected any interest in the Kosova Serbs on the
part of this man.

Little is known, even today, about the background and personal life of Slobodan Milosevic. He was born in 1941 in Pozare-
vac, a small town in eastern Serbia, the son of a Serbian Orthodox
priest. Both his parents committed suicide, but that did not prevent
him from gaining an economics degree and launching himself on a
technocratic career combining economics and politics. Between
1966 and 1968 he was an economic adviser of the mayor of Belgrade before becoming general director of the Belgrade firm Tehno-
gas, a post in which he remained from 1970 to 1978. He moved up
to the presidency of Beobanka, one of Yugoslavia's most important
financial institutions, both domestically and internationally, where
he served from 1978 to 1982. In 1982 he became a member of the
presidency of the Central Committee of the League of Communists
of Serbia. In 1984 he was the head of the Belgrade League of Communists. During this period he was a protégé of Ivan Stambolic, his
longtime college friend, then head of the League of Communists of
Serbia. Milosevic was considered by many who knew him to be a
good apprentice, intelligent and ambitious, although far overshadowed then by Stambolic. Stambolic saw Milosevic, who became

known as "Little Sloba," as his man, a young and diligent cadre, different from the old hard-liners who still filled much of the state bureaucracy.

Milosevic typically delivered closing speeches at party meetings, in a mass-rally style, as if he had forgotten that he was usually speaking to executive sessions of people he had known personally for years. But TV cameras were there, too, which must have given him the sense of a bigger and more impressive audience. With his chin pushed out, he was clearly addressing himself to more than a party auditorium.

In June 1986 Slobodan Milosevic became president of the League of Communists of Serbia, and it was in that capacity that he went in April 1987 to Kosovo Polje. The incident at Kosovo Polje, which one of the authors of this chapter (Ćuruvija) witnessed, was a remarkable occurrence, to say the very least. It was a hot, dusty day. A column of official cars appeared around five in the afternoon. Only minutes before, the street and square in front of the town's Cultural Center had been more or less empty, with a few groups of people standing around in Balkan somnolence even though a meeting had been announced, in which the head of the Serbian Communists would meet with representatives of the Kosova Serbs. Suddenly, as if on order, fifteen thousand Serbs poured into the square. The column of cars was surrounded. When Milosevic got out of the car, the air was broken by booming chants: "We want free-dom! We want free-dom!"

Milosevic, whose first name means "freedom-loving," was astonished. So were the Kosova Communist leaders, most of them Albanians, who accompanied him. Nobody expected such an outpouring; journalists were also stunned. The whole previous day as we had moved in and out, around the small town, talking to people, we had noticed that the coffeehouses were full and that conspiratorial conversations seemed to be taking place everywhere, but we had not expected to witness a major demonstration by the Kosova Serbs. Some people had told us that "every Serb in Kosova will come," but we did not believe them, particularly since until then all public manifestations by Serbs in Kosova had been carried out under strict police control and had never amounted to much. At most, a few hundred people would gather, seldom exceeding a thousand.

The police had to virtually carry Milosevic into the run-down

Cultural Center, and Azem Vllasi, political boss of Kosova province, pushed in alongside him. The rest of us had to fight our way in, with the multitude determined to fill an auditorium whose maximum capacity was three hundred. Then chaos broke out.

The regional police formed a cordon around the building, but the people broke through the police line, still trying to get in. The police officers, Serb and Albanian, unsheathed their batons and, as always on such occasions, began dealing out blows. The people picked up stones and stormed the building. In retrospect I believe they would have leveled the place if the local Serb leaders had not brought Milosevic outside to calm the situation. Then something happened that I believe defined the future of this man and of the country.

By accident, I found myself right next to him. He was pale, bewildered. The people carried him, yelling and pulling at him. We were pressed together when an old Serb, his hair completely gray and his mustache yellow from tobacco, yelled directly in his face: "They are beating us, President! Don't let them beat us." The old man was crying and Milosevic began trembling. "You must go upstairs, address them from the window," my colleague Milos Antic yelled at Milosevic. "How? How can I get myself up there?" he asked.

The next thing we knew he was up there, addressing the crowd. From the window of the Kosovo Polje Cultural Center Slobodan Milosevic gave a short speech, later infamous, which marked the beginning of the end of Yugoslavia. The main point was to call for people to calm down and select representatives to participate in a closed meeting inside the building. But Milosevic, nervous and improvising, uttered one of those dramatic phrases that changes history: looking down into the eyes of the old Serb who had appealed to him for help, he cried out to the frenzied crowd, "Nobody must ever again dare to beat this people!"

His words had their effect: the protesters settled down and chose representatives, who went into the hall for what became known as the "Night of Hard Words." Until six in the morning, people took turns at the podium outlining their personal and collective grievances. Women in black, mourning husbands or sons whom they said had been killed by Albanians; men who claimed their daughters had been raped; people who had lost jobs; young men attacked or beaten; peasants whose crops had been destroyed. In front of the Cultural Center the mass of people who had not succeeded in entering the building stood waiting all night.

The next day, our newspaper, *Borba,* carried an article with the headline "A New Phase." We argued that at Kosovo Polje the Serbs and Montenegrins of Kosova had held a convention, articulating their national goals. In the "socialist" Serbia and Yugoslavia of the time, where the slightest expression of nationalism was taboo, this bordered on the impermissible. The Serbian leadership was baffled; it was impossible to cover up a protest of such proportions.

Official Serbia was, nevertheless, aware of the situation in Kosova. Ivan Stambolic had himself gone there several times to talk to the Serbs but had left them unsatisfied. He had tried too hard to quiet them down, which was not what they wanted. Stambolic was frightened by the rapid growth of Serb dissatisfaction and especially wary of its public expression. He tried to solve the problem institutionally, by changing the constitution and gaining control over the funds sent to Kosova. Stambolic respected Kosova's autonomy, although he favored stronger ties with Serbia and greater authority for the Serbian government over local authorities in Kosova. He pressured the Kosovar Albanian leadership to work on solutions. His approach, however, was acceptable neither to the Serbs nor to the Albanians. The Serbs sought a leader who would understand and protect them, while the Albanians considered themselves masters in their own house. The latter formally accepted some demands of the Serbian leadership, but few were put into practice. The Albanians had an absolute majority in all Kosova institutions and rejected anything they considered contrary to their interests.

The "Kosova question" became the burning issue in Yugoslavia. It offered a chance for all democratically oriented intellectuals to honor legitimate complaints by the Serb population in Kosova, while still supporting the autonomy of the Albanians and hastening the political liberalization of Serbia as well as Yugoslavia in general. The Kosova problem, after all, reflected the clogged nature of the overall political regime, as much as it did intrinsic Serbian or Albanian attitudes. But a group of prominent Serbian intellectuals who intervened in the debate just then, all of them members of the Serbian Academy of Sciences and Arts (SANU), avoided such an opportunity and brought about a worsening of the conflict. The anger and real grievances of Serbs in Kosova were not used to promote democracy in Kosova and elsewhere. Instead, their plight served as a pretext to launch a wide campaign alleging that Serbs were threatened not only in Kosova but throughout Yugoslavia. A new vocabulary emerged, bearing the mark of the SANU and centered on exaggerated and confrontational slogans: "genocide against the Serbs," "the Serbian Holocaust," "Serb martyrdom," "the Kosova Serb tragedy;" "the sacred ground where Serb graves lie," "the Serb exodus," "Serbian honor," "enemies of Serbia," "the anti-Serb coalition," and many more.

This aggressive self-pity had already been given a fraudulent legitimacy when a draft "Memorandum of the Serbian Academy of Sciences and Arts" was leaked to the press in September 1986, quickly becoming a scandal. Central to the memorandum was the claim that the equilibrium of Tito's Yugoslavia had been maintained at the expense of Serbia. The memorandum insisted that Tito had believed that a weak Serbia was the condition for a strong Yugoslavia. Thus Tito allegedly permitted Serbia neither true economic nor cultural development. And the Serbs were not, according to the SANU memorandum, exposed to "genocide" in Kosova only. In Croatia too, it declared, they were kept subordinate, and it was no accident that the regions where they were the majority remained the least developed. The memorandum warned that Serbs living outside Serbia would face a mortal danger should Yugoslavia fall apart; they would be at the mercy of the proven enemies of the Serbian people.

Tensions were exacerbated by the reaction of the Serbian political elite to the publication of the SANU memorandum. Instead of dealing directly with this ultranationalist challenge, the establishment merely condemned the memorandum and banned its distribution. The whole affair was temporarily covered up, but the memorandum opened up a Pandora's box, leading eventually to war.

The political establishment outside Serbia was shocked. The head of the Croatian police warned the Croatian parliament against the dangers of the SANU memorandum. One younger Vojvodina politician told the Serbian academy: "You, the authors of the memorandum, are unwelcome in Vojvodina, and you should know that here your security cannot be guaranteed." Serbia waited for a reaction from the top Serbian politicians. But the Tito method called for "nationalism and other hostile manifestations first to be dealt with by the Communists of the nation in which such manifestations occur." Slobodan Milosevic kept silence, although as president of the Serbian Communists, he should have been the first to express his position in such a crisis. Milosevic never said a public word about the memorandum. When, a year later, he became the unchallenged leader of Serbia, his first official act was to praise the Serbian Academy of Sciences and Arts.

Following his infallible instincts, Slobodan Milosevic saw in the wake of publication of the memorandum that the Kosova issue offered him the best chance to win the support of the Serbian people quickly and triumphantly. He also understood that, if he were to make good on the opportunity, it was necessary for the relationship of Serbia to Kosova to be changed from top to bottom. This implied a far-reaching operation, above all breaking the power of the Albanian majority in Kosova. To achieve this, Milosevic first had to squeeze out his mentor and former friend, the moderate and relatively liberal Ivan Stambolic, now president of Serbia.

Stambolic, as previously noted, respected the autonomy of Kosova; he sought an administrative reintegration of the Serbian republic and the province, but not the stirring up of Serbs against the Albanian population, and he thought Milosevic had gone too far that day in Kosovo Polje. Sure of his own position, however, Stambolic refrained from criticizing Milosevic publicly. But for the first time there was a conflict between them, even if only a latent one. Milosevic saw the conflict as useful in ways of which Stambolic was entirely unaware. Milosevic perceived, quite farsightedly, that the conflict offered him a chance to shake off the tutelage of his mentor and become his own political personality. He had in fact began to prepare the terrain for this as early as 1984, by placing his supporters in the various subcommittees of the Central Committee of the League of Communists of Serbia. Those people would fulfill their responsibilities to him at the Eighth Congress of the Serbian League of Communists in September 1987.

At the time, Ivan Stambolic was engaged on two fronts: trv

to overcome the conservative federal hard-liners and trying to quiet the Serb nationalist authors of the inflammatory memorandum. He did not need a conflict with Milosevic on top of his other burdens. In addition, Stambolic still saw Milosevic as just a "Little Sloba."

To strengthen his position against Stambolic, Milosevic began with an approach to Stambolic's archenemies, the federal hard-liners. He declared that at the Eighth Congress of the Serbian League of Communists he was going to defend the legacy of Tito. That was exactly what both the army and federal leadership circles wanted to hear. In the second half of the 1980s Tito's memory was increasingly attacked in public, and such attacks threatened to undermine the positions of his heirs. Milosevic's maneuver won him sympathy from the army and the federal bigwigs.

Regarding Kosova, also to be discussed at the Eighth Congress, the leaders of other republics wanted to avoid involvement. Ivica Racan, head of the Croatian Communists, and even Azem Vllasi, the chief of the Albanian-dominated government in Kosova, both insisted that any conflict between Milosevic and Stambolic regarding Kosova was an internal Serbian affair.

Many politicians in the other republics believed that in the long run it would be easier to handle Little Sloba than the experienced and principled Ivan Stambolic. So at the Eighth Congress of the Serbian League of Communists, when Milosevic and his supporters in the party subcommittees made public a Stalinist-style defamation campaign against Stambolic and his policy of gradualism in Kosova, they encountered little resistance. The congress lasted three days and left the TV audience across Yugoslavia amazed. The disbelieving Stambolic was voted out office and forced to resign.

Nobody in Yugoslavia at the time seemed to understand this as an ominous, far-reaching event. "Sloba exaggerates just a wee bit too much," said the Croat Ivica Racan in an interview. "How can he say that Serbia will be one, or that there'll be no Serbia?" How slowly the elites of the other republics gained awareness of the real situation was illustrated when, almost two years later, in the summer of 1989, the entire federal leadership attended the celebration of the six hundredth anniversary of the Battle of Kosovo Polje—the event that marked the crowning of Milosevic as the strongman of Serbia.

The common people were also taken in by Milosevic, although they were, perhaps, confused about the implications of his new pledges, beginning at the Eighth Congress, to right the wrongs done to the Serbs. Milosevic also promised them that in ten years Serbia would reach the level of Switzerland. The masses were overwhelmed by his short, upbeat, and quotable populist speeches. In Serbia Milosevic was seen as a man who would put an end to Serbian concessions, to Serbia's "guilt complex as the biggest nation," and to "the sacrifice of Serbia's interests" in the name of "higher common goals." And nothing dangerous could happen, since the enormous television audience had witnessed Milosevic proclaiming himself "totally committed to Tito's policies"; a "defender of Tito's work and memory"; "a Communist from head to toe"; a proven fighter for "brotherhood and unity"; and a "fierce opponent of every nationalism," meaning Serbian nationalism as well. Milosevic had no solutions for the worsening economic crisis, and he lacked the political charisma of Tito, but he bet on the right horse—the nostalgia for the good old days of past Serbian heroes and glories—and he won.

His photographs, like Tito's in his time, were soon pasted on the windshields of trucks and buses all across Serbia; they appeared on mantels and bookshelves in many private homes. Meanwhile, a thorough political purge took place. Politicians, journalists, editors, professors, company executives—everybody was removed who had or was suspected of having the slightest diffidence toward Milosevic's platform for resolving the status of the Serbian autonomous provinces.

Milosevic understood the power of mass rallies in the volatile situation of 1987–88. He even believed that the legitimate grievances of the Kosova Serbs could be harnessed to spread anti-Albanian sentiments across Yugoslavia and to win public opinion in Slovenia and Croatia to his position. All he had to do was send demonstrators to Slovenia and Croatia. Public support in other republics for the plight of the Kosova Serbs would, in turn, allow him to act resolutely to safeguard their rights. And for Milosevic this meant abolishing the autonomy not only of Kosova to the south, but also of Vojvodina, Serbia's autonomous province to the north.

But for politicians outside Serbia, the problems of Kosova and Vojvodina were one thing; spreading anti-Albanian mass rallies to other republics was quite another. Slovenian and Croatian politicians and intellectuals were dumbfounded and outraged at such a prospect. But in 1987 and 1988 most of them remained silent, hoping Milosevic would soon play himself out and leave them alone.

Vojvodina had been quiet and free of Serb protests before the end of 1987. There were no tensions between its Hungarian and Croatian populations and Serbs living in the region. Vojvodina was doing quite well; both its countryside and its cities were prosperous, and its people were content. Yet its degree of autonomy, Milosevic insisted, was equal to Kosova's, and that was unacceptable. Like Kosova, Vojvodina was functioning as a federal unit and not as a territory belonging to the republic of Serbia. To bring Vojvodina back into the Serbian fold, Milosevic used an exceptionally effective tactic. The protests of the Kosova Serbs, condemned as "counterrevolutionary" only a year earlier, were now not only allowed but officially organized; and not only in Kosova but throughout Serbia, including, of course, Vojvodina. Needless to say, at that point the protests no longer bore the slightest element of a spontaneous expression of anyone's legitimate grievances. They had became mere instruments of Milosevic's policy.

In summer 1988, the first staged demonstrations of Serbs were held in Novi Sad, the Vojvodina capital. Vojvodina politicians immediately accused the Serbian leadership of having organized the incidents, that is, of nationalism and aggression against their autonomous province. In disregard of the protests by the Vojvodina government, meetings in "solidarity with the Kosova Serbian victims" continued week after week. They became larger, more provocative and militant, and further removed from the authentic problems of the Serbs. "We want weapons," the demonstrators began to yell, already carried away.

The Vojvodina leadership strongly opposed the aggression from Serbia but lacked the support if its majority population, the Serbs. In fall 1988, some one hundred thousand Serbs gathered in Novi Sad and demonstrated around the clock until the entire Vojvodina leadership resigned. People who supported Milosevic's political line were put in charge. A few months later, in January 1989, the same thing happened to the Montenegrin leadership. There Momir Bulatovic, a Milosevic supporter, came to power, in the guise of an "antibureaucratic revolution" reported with naive enthusiasm by anti-Communists in Western media.

In Kosova itself, however, the process required a great deal more trouble, even bloodshed. The federal leaders now hoped to pacify Milosevic by making concessions, that is, by using their authority to force the Albanian leadership to resign. And the Albanian leaders indeed resigned in November 1988, or were driven out of power.

Following this, Kosovar Albanians began demonstrating again, for the first time since 1981. These peaceful demonstrations lasted continuously for five days and nights in the larger towns of Kosova, without a window or even a bottle broken. The Yugoslav presidency declared a state of emergency, and troops were sent into Kosova. Serbia sent its special police force. In March 1989 the first serious clashes occurred, and sixty Albanians were killed. In response, Kosovar Albanian workers, led by miners, began mass strikes. The Serbian regime reacted in June 1990 by disbanding Kosova's parliament as well as all other organs of the Kosova provincial government. A widespread purge of Albanians from government and state positions ensued. Nearly all Albanian media were suppressed. Direct rule by Serbia was established, maintained to this day by the police and the army. Thus Milosevic established what he called "historic Serb rights" to sovereignty in Kosova. Serbia prevailed in the competition between Serbs and Albanians over Kosova.

Beginning in 1990, the Albanians acted with great wisdom in dealing with martial law in Kosova. They defined the issue as one of aggression by an anachronistic Communist regime against the democratic forces in Kosova. (Croatia and Slovenia would formulate their secession from Yugoslavia in much the same way.) The Albanian leadership placed the problem in the context of human rights for Albanians, which successfully brought it to international attention and helped obscure the original issue of the human rights of Kosova Serbs. The Albanian leadership received international support for autonomy and maximized the chances of Kosova's eventual departure from Serbia. The Kosovar Albanians are aware that Serbia's future in world affairs depends as much on a solution of the Kosova issue as on ending the war in Bosnia-Hercegovina. It could be said that although today they are the colonial subjects of the Serbian regime, in the long run the Kosovar Albanians hold Serbia hostage.

Slobodan Milosevic had declared martial law in Kosova on the pretext of "correcting injustices done to the Serbian people." This was the first of a series of acts by him that would lead Serbia to ruin. And it served him well that until summer 1990, Croatia and Slovenia mainly observed silence, doing nothing to stop him.

By the end of the 1980s, it was obvious to Yugoslavia's political establishment that Milosevic was a nationalist and a political bully. But the larger part of that establishment in the other republics, fearing for their own power, closed their eyes to Milosevic's campaign of Serbian mobilization, viewing it as a kind of controlled catharsis for Serb dissatisfaction. The Croatian leadership of the time kept quiet because it was afraid that any firm opposition to Milosevic would stir up the Serbs in Croatia. While it was still possible to do something, at least until mid–1989, both the federal and republic leaderships played for time in the hope that small sacrifices could satisfy Milosevic. By reintegrating Kosova and Vojvodina into Serbia, and therefore with Serbia, Kosova, Vojvodina, and Montenegro under his thumb, Milosevic had taken over four of the eight Yugoslav federal units. From that moment, he held half the votes in the federal institutions. That meant that, whether or not he might form coalitions with hard-line Communists in Croatia, Slovenia, Bosnia, or Macedonia, he still controlled a determining share of the Yugoslav presidency. The balance of forces in the federal structure was now such that virtually nothing could be done against Milosevic.

However, playing for time with Milosevic did nothing to save the false peace covering the ever more fragile ethnic equilibrium in Croatia. That illusion of peace disappeared when new mass meetings of Serbs were called in Croatia. For the first time, the Yugoslav federal leadership expressed opposition, and Croatia and Slovenia made it clear they would prevent such meetings by force.

They could not, however, prevent the celebration of Serb patriotic anniversaries, least of all the celebration of the six hundredth anniversary of the Battle of Kosovo Polje. On June 28, 1989, the Serbian Orthodox church organized a gathering of Croatian Serbs in a small village not far from Knin in the Lika region between Zagreb and the Dalmatian coast. For days, it was repeated in the media that "every Serb in Croatia will attend." Croatian authorities recognized the danger; they could not prevent the event, so they joined it. They invested a considerable amount of money in the event and tried to give it the character of a country fair. They almost succeeded. Forty thousand people, mostly Serbs but also Croats, came, indeed as to the country fair, and gathered around the village Orthodox church. It all looked like an oversized village wedding, with everyone in Sunday best, eating roasted and grilled food, sharing drinks and souvenirs. But it lost its benign character when a special train from Serbia arrived at the Knin railroad station.

The train was decorated with Serbian national and church flags, and the locomotive had started to blow its whistle several miles before reaching the station. When it stopped, hundreds of men streamed off, carrying flags, banners, large photographs of Slobodan Milosevic, and other national symbols. "We have come to help our brother Serbs in Croatia to fight for their rights," they yelled. "This is Serbia," they shouted. The word "guns" was in the air. They called on Milosevic to rally the people and lead them into battle.

The gathered locals viewed these interlopers as strange apparitions. They were astounded. They got out of the way. The extreme heat of the day and alcohol subdued the new arrivals relatively fast, but boisterousness erupted again as soon as twilight fell. The official program was interrupted, and stones were thrown at the Orthodox priest who tried to calm the crowd. A local Serb leader, Jovan Opacic, was pushed onto the stage to speak.

A few hours earlier I (Čuruvija) had interviewed Jovan Opacic, an administrative employee at a local firm. We stood during the interview in the yard of the old Serbian Krka monastery, situated in a pristine valley on the banks of the beautiful Krka River not far from Knin. A few yards away, a Croat member of the secret police listened in. The police watched Opacic constantly. As soon as we began talking, a secret agent simply walked up, without hiding his identity, and listened. This did not bother Opacic in the least. He spoke breathlessly, as though transported. This was the first interview in his life for a "big paper" and he dredged up everything he knew. He had studied economics but seemed mired in quasi-philosophical concepts and half-baked locutions picked up who knows where. When everything he said was sifted through, what remained was the refrain of "the threat of assimilation of Serbs" and "protection of Serbian cultural and national identity" along with a demand for renewal of Serbian institutions in Croatia. He looked through me, his stare focused somewhere far off, and spoke as though to a crowd of thousands, not just to one reporter and one Croat agent of the state security service.

The next day he was arrested, tried, and sentenced to several months in jail for disturbing the peace. The celebration of the six hundredth anniversary of the Battle of Kosovo marked the beginning of a campaign by Croatian leaders against "Serbian aggression in Croatia." The Serbian media responded with a call to protect the "Serbian people in Croatia." Neither campaign was reined in; on the contrary, both continued until in 1991 both peoples plunged into mutual slaughter.

It was in this atmosphere that the first multiparty elections took place in Yugoslavia. In 1990, the elections were won by parties that in Slovenia, Croatia, and Bosnia-Hercegovina had existed openly, on the average, for only a few months. In Slovenia, ethnically homogeneous and bordering on two solid capitalist democracies, these parties reflected the differing ideological trends of Western society—classical liberalism, conservatism, and social democracy, such as existed in Austria, and reform communism, as in Italy. In Croatia and Bosnia-Hercegovina, however, these tendencies, although they sometimes existed (more in Croatia than in Bosnia-Hercegovina), were deformed or overshadowed by the rise of purely ethnic parties. Aside from the reform factions of the former Communist bureaucracies, the new parties had been formed semilegally or illegally, sometimes in the hinterland. Parties were headed by, and elected, individuals who only five or six months before the elections would have been considered fanatics or exhibitionists rather than serious politicians. At the beginning of the elections the fiery nationalism these new politicians expressed often provoked sneers, and the lists of their candidates were a joke to the public.

It may sound paradoxical, but at that time most Yugoslavs still believed that Yugoslavia was headed toward integration with Europe. The disintegration in winter 1989 of the League of Communists of Yugoslavia offered hope for the economic reform developed by the Yugoslav prime minister at the time, the Croat Ante Markovic, which called for a degree of privatization and a wider play of the market. Rising nationalist euphoria was accompanied by rising wages. People had money, and the stores were full of imported goods. The average Yugoslav was able to exchange his or her wages, equivalent to about one thousand deutsche marks ($650) per month, at any local bank for any hard currency. Prime Minister Markovic happily cited figures on the growth of hard currency reserves and increasing Yugoslav exports. We were all suddenly awash in a new freedom and intoxicating enthusiasm. It seemed as though dawn had finally come.

At the same time, the nationalists were holding public meetings, making promises within their own republics, of even more money and even greater freedoms to be brought by their parties. Franjo Tudjman, "the man with the shark tooth grin" as he was known, then a joke candidate, today president of a battered Croatia, promised Croatians the advent of more than one hundred billion dollars in foreign capital, provided of course that they elected him. This promised prosperity was directly tied to a loosening of Croatia's ties with the federation, its independence and eventual departure from Yugoslavia. In Slovenia as well as in Croatia, independence was represented as the precondition for prosperity. A process aiming at independence was deliriously offered by the nationalists in spring 1990. Prime Minister Markovic, who formed his own party prior to the elections in Croatia, offered no more than gradual, evolutionary reform and declared that nationalism would be the certain ruin of Yugoslavia. The people chose delirium.

Tudjman's campaign speeches and the nationalist fanaticism and excesses of his party associates were applauded by tens of thousands of Croatians in the squares of Croatia's largest towns and cities during the last weeks of the election campaign. Tudjman offered a state that would be Croatian in name and sovereign in power, "democratic and rich." As Milosevic did with the Serbs, he offered them enemies to blame for their frustrations: in Tudjman's case, the Serbs and Yugoslavia.

Tudjman made very skillful use of clashes between Serbian and Croatian Communists and of growing, systematic attacks by Serbian nationalists on the Croatian authorities. In February 1990, in the most impressive Zagreb meeting hall, Tudjman called the first convention of the Croatian Democratic Union (HDZ). Numerous domestic Croat extremists, along with representatives of the Croat ultranationalist émigrés, many of them Hercegovinian in origin and with origins or associations in the World War II Ustashe regime, were represented in the HDZ organization.

Yugoslavs, particularly Serbs, but a significant part of the Croatian public as well, were shocked by this event. The tide of Croatian nationalist symbolism and rhetoric at the HDZ convention had been unheard of since the fall of the Ustashe-ruled Independent State of Croatia. Many were stunned when Tudjman declared without blinking an eye that during World War II, although the Ustashe state in Croatia had been a regime of Nazi collaboration and fascist crimes, it also expressed the historical aspirations of the Croatian people for their own state. The HDZ audience broke into a standing ovation.

Tudjman and the HDZ had defined Croatia as, first and foremost, the state of the Croatian nation and only secondarily as that of the citizens of Croatia, including its Serb population. But to elevate a fascist past to the level of historical national aspirations was too much. Everything else Tudjman said after that was heard against the background of that February declaration. Tudjman never missed the opportunity during the election campaign to point to "the privileges enjoyed by Serbs in Croatia" and to announce that one of his first moves would be to reduce their influence "to reflect their ten percent in the population of Croatia."

Tudjman was elected as head of an HDZ majority in the Croatian Sabor (parliament). In his first year, Tudjman gained inviolable power for himself. In the early weeks of his government, he used his influence within the ruling party to reduce his colleagues in the presidency to a purely ornamental status. Cabinets, which he changed like shirts, were appointed by him alone. After only six months he had already changed the Croatian constitution twice. The changes were fundamental, totally altering the structure of power in the republic. He immediately imposed strict HDZ control over the television and print media, and from its first days his government began a fierce nationalist propaganda campaign.

All of this was done at great expense, with primitive posturing intended to add luster to the new regime. Franjo Tudjman spent his first year in power delivering toasts at banquets and outdoor feasts, waving his party flags, designing coats of arms, and posing in ceremonial regalia. Celebration of his election victory "deepened the division between winners and losers," wrote a Croatian colleague, while it was still possible to write freely. "War measures" were later instituted under which any public statement against Tudjman's regime was a criminal act. Opposition barely existed in the "democratic" state of Croatia. Once serious clashes between Serbs and Croats broke out, even mild opposition to Tudjman effectively disappeared.

Conflict with the Serbs had already begun, in a relatively mild form, during Tudjman's electoral campaign. A Serbian Democratic Party had been organized, posing as the sole party of Serbs in Croatia. Jovan Raskovic, a psychiatrist who was the founder and president of the Serbian Democratic Party, broke all contact with Tudjman as early as May 1990. Although Tudjman offered Raskovic a vice presidential position in the new government, Raskovic refused to send his party's elected deputies to the first session of the Croatian parliament and informed the parliament by telegram that his party would boycott it and any other public offices offered to it.

In an atmosphere of fear, overheated emotions, and conceptual confusion, carried away by his triumph and under pressure from his Hercegovinian hawks, Tudjman made a series of moves that only inflamed the Serbian minority. He spoke repeatedly of "the thousand-year dream of the Croatian nation for an independent state" as the foundation of his program. In a very short time Tudjman changed the republic's flag, emblem, and constitution in ways that Serbs considered provocative. His constitution reduced the Serbs to national minority status, where previously they had been considered a partner nation in Croatia, on equal footing with Croats; for the Serbs the symbolic significance of this was tremendous. He placed the checkerboard (*sahovnica*), the historic Croat coat of arms, on the national flag. Aggrieved Serbs declaimed that the *sahovnica* was used by the Ustashe regime during World War II and was therefore frightening and unacceptable to them, although it was also employed by the Socialist Republic of Croatia under Tito on official government emblems, although not on the flag. "The flag under which we were slaughtered shall never again fly over us," insisted the Serbs.

This pledge marked the beginning of the Serb uprising in Croatia. Officially, the uprising began when Serbian members of the Croatian police, of whom there were many, and particularly the local police in the Serb regions of Croatia, refused to put these emblems on their uniforms and join the new, centralized police force loyal to Tudjman's government. The first to express this refusal were the Knin police, headed by Milan Martic, later minister of defense of the rebellious Serbian Krajina in Croatia. The separation of Serb territories from Croatia began simultaneously with Tudjman's first moves toward independence for Croatia from Yugoslavia.

"Croatia and Croats may, if they like, leave Yugoslavia. As for ourselves, we are staying in Yugoslavia," declared the leaders of the Serbian Democratic Party. The Croatian Serbs did not hesitate to move from words to action. A number of Serb townships came together to form the Knin Regional Union and made the inaugural announcement of Serb political and territorial autonomy within Croatia. In June 1990 the Serb leaders in Knin called their "first Serb convention" and adopted a declaration on the "sovereignty and autonomy of the Serbian people in Croatia."

Meanwhile, the media in Serbia and the Serb intellectuals in Belgrade increased the uproar. Old conflicts were resurrected to prove that no trust was possible between Serbs and Croats. In World War I, the argument went, the Croats fought for the Austro-Hungarian Empire against the Serbs; in that war the Serbs lost one-fourth of their population. In World War II the Croat Ustashe, it was said again and again, had sought to exterminate one-third of the Serbs in Croatia, to expel one-third, and to convert one-third to Catholicism. In 1990, the Belgrade media shouted, the secessionists in both Croatia and Slovenia demanded that Serbia compromise by accepting a confederation, which would lead to a probable secession of Croatia. In reality, Slovenia was much more set on complete separation from Yugoslavia than Croatia, whose leaders, Tudjman included, wavered between confederalism and secession. But, the Belgrade media trumpeted, Tudjman's regime has already demoted Croatian Serbs to second-class citizenship. What could Serbs expect in an independent state of Croatia, if not a repeat of the horrors of World War II? The Serbian press began to take on a virtually pornographic character as it revived, in gruesome detail, the worst tortures, executions, massacres, and other atrocities of the fascist era. The implication was that the Ustashe had returned.

Meanwhile, Milosevic insisted that the "confederalists" were pushing an agenda on which Serbia could not, and would not, ever compromise.

Prodded by their supporters in Belgrade, a newly formed Serb National Council in Croatia rejected all the constitutional changes made by Tudjman in the first months of his rule and voted to hold a referendum on Serb autonomy in Croatia. The reaction in Zagreb was fierce. All the measures taken by the Serbs in Croatia were declared unconstitutional, the referendum was forbidden, and the Serbs were informed it would be suppressed. In addition, the Croatian minister of police announced an inventory of weapons owned by Serb citizens. The Serbs in Knin answered: "We advise you not to send heavy police units to Knin; we are not sure such a move wouldn't provoke ethnic clashes."

In August 1990, fighting began. Croatian police tried to disarm the Serb reserve police in the town of Benkovac. Serbs in the surrounding villages rose up, broke into the police station, and seized the weapons kept there. The Croatian authorities dispatched special forces with armored personnel carriers and three helicopters to Knin. Neither the armored vehicles nor the helicopters arrived. The federal army stopped the first somewhere on the road, and MiGs intercepted the helicopters and forced them back to their base. The chief of operations of the Yugoslav army warned, "If a single head rolls, we will intervene."

The Croatian administration demanded that the Yugoslav presidency take a stand on the incident. Borisav Jovic, then Yugoslav president, a Serb and Milosevic supporter, answered that "the right of citizens or people to express their political will or to political activity may not be questioned," thus siding with the Serb rebels. Milosevic demanded that the Yugoslav presidency "make any violation of the rights of Serbs in Croatia impossible." Milosevic's Socialist Party of Serbia—the renamed League of Communists of Serbia—announced that it had set up a fund to aid Serbs in Croatia.

The polarization was complete and the temperature was extremely high. The Croatian authorities, for their part, abstained from any further actions backed by force. The Serbian Democratic Party in Croatia had, however, taken wings. It blocked all the roads toward Knin with logs and other barricades and put armed civilians at the barricades, stopping cars and checking the identity documents of passengers. Transportation was completely disrupted at the height of the tourist season, and Croatia was literally cut in half and separated from its coastline. Despite these conditions, the Serb referendum for autonomy was held. Whoever wanted to vote could do so, as many times and wherever he or she wished. All the identification needed was to say that one was a Croatian Serb. And so, the Serb Autonomous Region of Krajina was proclaimed on October 1, 1990.

After the first clashes in Knin, some Croatian intellectuals warned that the mentality of Croatian Serbs, their traditional sense of courage and dignity, and their memories of the Ustashe crimes during World War II had to be taken into account. Croatian intellectuals also warned that the "young Croatian democracy," as Tudjman called his regime, was "a mother to some and a stepmother to others." In their view, the Croatian administration had reacted in an undemocratic and counterproductive manner. Threats of the use of force, sporadic attempts to remove road and town signs in the Cyrillic script favored by many Serbs, the disappearance of Cyrillic subtitles from Croatian television, physical attacks on Serb deputies in the Croatian parliament, arrests, persecutions, firing or demotions of Serbs, imposition of a loyalty oath as a requisite for Serbs to keep their jobs, nocturnal threats by telephone and gunfire in mixed communities—all this exacerbated the feeling among Serbs that they were under serious threat. In this situation, the Serbian Democratic Party, relatively small before Tudjman's election, easily established its influence over the entire Serb population in Croatia, even that section that voted for Croatian parties in the elections. This was Tudjman's greatest defeat; it was hard to find a Serb in Croatia who recognized the authority of his regime.

Croatia was confused. Increasingly, Serbs were officially described as "terrorists," and the police continued threatening that the Croatian authorities would "use all means allowed by the law to restore order to the Krajina." The newly formed HDZ branch in Dalj, a small town on the Danube in eastern Croatia, bordering on Serbia and with a very large and until then relatively peaceful Serb population, allegedly declared that "Serbs have no place in Croatia." The Croatian government rejected an offer by the federal government to send a special unit, made up of police from all the Yugoslav republics, to secure peace and communications in the Krajina, a rejection that upset many Croats as well. The Croatian authorities did not send special police to the Krajina, but searches and arrests of Serbs in Western Slavonia and throughout those regions of Croatia where Serbs had not previously shown rebellious tendencies began. Incidents became increasingly numerous, as relations between Serbs and Croats worsened. Several thousand Serbs from Petrinja in Slavonia fled to the woods, and several thousand more took refuge in the federal army compound in Petrinja. Serbian extremists from Serbia and Montenegro began to offer "help" by their volunteer units for the Serbs in Croatia. War was approaching.

In early 1989 the Slovene leadership, observing the political developments in Serbia and Croatia, described what they saw as a "Chinese cultural revolution." From the Eighth Party Congress to the collapse of the federal-level League of Communists in January 1990, Serbia and Slovenia were in constant confrontation. The confrontation ended with Slovenia's unilateral secession from Yugoslavia in June 1991 and the Slovene ten-day Independence War that immediately followed.

The Slovenes regarded Milosevic's removal of Stambolic in September 1987, and the purges that followed, as a blatant return to Stalinist governance, believed to have been long since superseded in Yugoslavia. Ljubljana, the Slovene capital, had already produced a very different political environment. Few spoke openly of secession yet, or of abandoning socialism. Slovenia wanted "socialism in the interest of the individual"; in any event it felt more and more distance from Serbia. Belgrade, for its part, accused Slovene president Milan Kucan of encouraging separatist tendencies. At first, in 1987, Ljubljana had said nothing about events in Serbia. In 1988 and 1989, however, a number of events prompted Slovenia to movement. In Kosova the two most prominent Albanian Communist leaders, Azem Vllasi and Kacusa Jasari, were dismissed, and demonstrations spread throughout Kosova; the miners at the Trepca silver mine in Kosova began a hunger strike. All this provided the final proof to Slovenia of the repressive nature of the

Milosevic regime. Slovenia had tried to treat it as an internal affair of Serbia. But it began to look as though what was happening in Serbia was Slovenia's business after all.

Slovenia wanted a multiparty system and felt that its goals were jeopardized by Serbian centralism. Dimitrije Rupel, later the Slovene foreign minister, stated that "the dispute is not simply between Kucan and Milosevic, but rather between two concepts, one closer to the West, the other closer to the East." The Slovene writer Ciril Zlobec said, "Milosevic is the only power figure in Yugoslavia who can change things to his liking with complete disregard for the constitution and the law. The essence of the erotic relationship between Milosevic and the Serbs is the creation of a belief that the provinces were stolen from them and that now Milosevic is reuniting Serbia."

Mladina, a government-subsidized Slovene student and youth magazine, with a tradition of bowing to nobody's dictates, contributed significantly to the heightening of tensions between Ljubljana and Belgrade. It carried a number of articles attacking the Yugoslav army, claiming it had the character of an occupation force. Later, *Mladina* condemned the arrest and indictment of four Slovenes who, having revealed an alleged plan for invasion and repression of Slovenia by the army, were charged with espionage. The overall impression among Slovenes was that the federal leadership, at Serbia's insistence, was preparing martial law in Slovenia, or even a military coup against the Slovene leadership, after the espionage trial. Rumors of a coup were quickly denied, but doubts remained about the military, egged on by Milosevic.

In 1989 the Slovenes decided to head off Milosevic, and in February they organized their own "truth and solidarity" rally in Ljubljana's largest concert hall. The rally was announced as an act of "solidarity with the striking Albanian miners." Kucan addressed the meeting and described the miners and their hunger strike as a valiant defense of "Tito's Yugoslavia." Yet many in Serbia saw this as a cynical move. Slovenia was the first republic to refuse to contribute to the Kosova development fund. And there have been many press reports about the almost racist treatment of both Kosovar Albanian and Bosnian migrant workers in Slovenia. Everything about the solidarity event, especially as reported by Serbian television and the other Milosevic-controlled media, enraged the Serbian public. In Slovenia, however, Kucan gained the aura of a hero, becoming the most popular public personality in the republic. He twice won the Slovenian presidential elections—once before Slovenia's declaration of independence and once after.

Milosevic answered the Slovene anti-Serb rally with a propaganda barrage against Kucan and his supporters, in an effort to split Slovene public opinion. When that failed, he called on his Kosovar Serb striking force to carry the "truth" to Slovenia and to organize, in November 1989, their own rally in Ljubljana. Slovenia then, for the first time, addressed Serbia and Yugoslavia as an "independent sovereign state." It forbade the meeting and warned it would prevent, by force if necessary, the Kosovar Serbs from crossing the Slovene border. Milosevic lashed back at Slovenia with a no less unprecedented move: he declared a trade war. Serbs were to boycott everything Slovene. This effectively ruptured economic relations between Slovenia and Serbia, at a great cost to the Slovene economy but an even greater cost to Serbia since a large part of its industry was technologically dependent on Slovenia. Appeals by Serbia's leading economists and industrial managers to reconsider this thoroughly self-destructive move were, of course, ignored. The new Serbian patriotism prevailed. Everything made in Slovenia disappeared from the stores throughout Serbia. This damaged political relations between Serbia and Slovenia beyond repair.

It was in this atmosphere of great tensions between the loosely defined east and the west of Yugoslavia—that is, between Serbia, Montenegro, Kosova, and Vojvodina on one side and Slovenia, Croatia, Bosnia-Hercegovina, and Macedonia on the other—that the 14th (Extraordinary) Congress of the League of Communists of Yugoslavia convened in January 1990.

The Serbian delegation and Milosevic brought a very clear message to the party congress: the League of Communists of Yugoslavia was to be a unified organization, regardless of what any republic might think or do, or it would cease to exist. With the sides defined, the congress turned into little more than a battlefield in the war of words between Milosevic and Kucan.

Kucan argued that boycotts of Slovene products and threats of importing mass meetings could not be tolerated. He rejected the Serbian concept of the League of Communists and the Yugoslav army as the two basic pillars of Yugoslav unity. He was categorical in saying, "Slovenia, in case it is not clear, is the sovereign state of the Slovene nation. It does not want a unitary or centralized federal Yugoslavia. It wants a new agreement for the Yugoslav community." This was Kucan's answer to Milosevic's assertion "In this auditorium, an end is being sought for the party, plans are being made to set Yugoslav Communists against each other and, I would say, the Yugoslav nations as well. Serbia is for a unified League of Communists of Yugoslavia."

A group of liberal delegates—Branko Horvat from the University of Zagreb and Zdravko Grebo and Nenad Kecmanovic from the University of Sarajevo—tried to present a third proposal to circumvent the confrontation between implacable positions. They proposed the formation of two parties, one Communist and the other Socialist. Serbia and its bloc of delegates from Montenegro, Vojvodina, and Kosova rejected the proposal as ludicrous and inconceivable. When the Slovene delegation saw that, because of the Serbian bloc, they could never put together the required majority vote for acceptance of their proposals, they did what they knew they had to do: they walked out of the congress, to frantic applause and tears. The federal League of Communists of Yugoslavia had ceased to exist.

The disappearance of the main pillar of multinational, socialist Yugoslavia left the federal structure hanging in midair. Many believe that Milosevic knew, after the congress, that he would never be able to beat Kucan and gave Kucan permission for Slovenia's relatively painless departure. Slovenia declared its sovereignty on July 2, 1991, on the basis of the Slovene nation's right to self-determination. Kosova proclaimed its independence the same day, and Croatia on June 25, 1991. The state of Yugoslavia had fallen apart. On October 1, 1990, the Croatian Serbs had proclaimed their independence. The Bosnian Serbs and Macedonia each followed with their proclamation of independence on December 21, 1991.

The collapse of the League of Communists of Yugoslavia coincided with the beginning of a turbulent but somewhat successful year for Yugoslav Prime Minister Ante Markovic. He had taken office in January 1989, and his decisive economic policy had earned him immense popularity throughout the country. As hyperinflation ate away at the economy, in December 1989 he launched his anti-inflation program, which brought the inflation of 2800 percent down to 4 percent. In May 1990, the *Wall Street Journal* recommended Yugoslavia for investment by the leading world economies because it had already accomplished "what the Eastern European countries have only set out to do."

Although a product of the managerial section of the Yugoslav school of socialist economics, Markovic did not hide his intention to reform Yugoslav socialism from the bottom up. He worked in various party committees before becoming prime minister for the economy to be opened to market forces. On taking office, he made one of his top priorities to sweep away the Yugoslav concept of "socially owned" capital and property, an imaginary category of undefined ownership and responsibility. Yugoslavia's industries, for instance, belonged "to society," that is, to everybody and nobody. Ownership was not vested in either the state or identifiable individuals or groups of individuals. Ultimate responsibility for economic performance was, therefore, everybody's and nobody's. Yugoslav industry had to be privatized, and Markovic proposed doing so by first selling shares in each enterprise to its employees. To achieve this transformation, essential for Yugoslavia's economy to become a real market economy, some five billion dinars in fresh money was necessary. The West promised Markovic the money in loans, but it was never paid out.

Markovic's program encountered intransigent resistance on the part of Croatia, Slovenia, and Serbia alike. The political bureaucracies, including the first so-called post-Communist governments in Slovenia and Croatia, saw Markovic's reform as a blow to their own positions in banking and industry. They would be left with no real say in planning, capital distribution, or managerial appointments. On the other hand, the leaders of the growing nationalist constituencies, above all in Slovenia and Croatia, saw Markovic's commitment to Yugoslavia as a threat to their confederalist agendas. In addition, for the nationalist presidential campaigns mounted in Slovenia and Croatia, the crisis in the Yugoslav economy was a major rallying point. Nationalists in the Croat and the Slovene governments were able to effectively block Markovic's efforts to save Yugoslavia and its federal economy.

Like Markovic, Milosevic too wanted to save Yugoslavia, but like the Slovene and the Croat leaderships, he also saw Markovic as a personal obstacle to his own ambitions. Every success of Markovic heightened the prime minister's popularity. The more successful he was, the more of a rival he appeared to Milosevic, Kucan, and Tudjman. Their reasons differed, but the determination to make Markovic fail was fully shared by Ljubljana, Zagreb, and Belgrade. The propaganda machines went into high gear. Milosevic trumpeted that Markovic was a con man, capitalist, Ustasha, CIA agent, Serbophobe, liar, and so on. Every economic problem of Serbia's own making was laid at his door. Threats and ultimatums were thrown one after another at Markovic and his team. Their programs were openly or subtly sabotaged. Milosevic outdid the others only in the stridency of his propaganda and the blatant character of his sabotage. Slovenia regularly made promises to abide by the fewer and fewer measures Markovic was able to get approved or to support compromises arrived at with great difficulty, and just as regularly went back on their promises.

When Markovic recognized the nationalist obstacles he faced despite his popularity in the cities, he formed his own Yugoslav Reform Party. Markovic was convinced, and he was right, that a party that stood for an undivided Yugoslavia, promising a market economy and democratic rights, with freedom for all, was the only option between the discredited Communists and the deranged nationalists. But he was blocked at every turn, until it was too late for his party to even field candidates in the Slovene and Croatian elections. And the financial help promised him by the West also never arrived. Everybody expected a big victory for Markovic in Bosnia-Hercegovina where he personally had a strong and vocal following. But by the time the first multiparty elections were held, Bosnia-Hercegovina was already being polarized by nationalism. Each of its three ethnic communities was deeply suspicious of the others. Under the circumstances, the vote for Markovic's candidates was negligible. Markovic resigned in December 1991, having realized he could do nothing to prevent the appropriation of eighty-six percent of the federal budget for war purposes, which had just been approved. The war machine rolled first into Slovenia, in early summer 1991, then into Croatia in midsummer, and then into Bosnia-Hercegovina, in spring 1992.

FIVE

The Media Wars

Milan Milošević

For seventy years, generations of Yugoslavs, regardless of ethnic background, lived daily in a multicultural environment. The music at weddings, private parties, pubs, and restaurants was always a mixture of the tunes and rhythms from across the country: Macedonian laments, Dalmatian sea harmonies, Bosnian love odes, Serbian rounds, Zagreb chansons, Slovene polkas. Television was no exception. Its programming was strongly multinational.

Until 1974, the television studios in different parts of the country coordinated their programming to include one another's productions. Entertainment and cultural as well as news programs of one TV center often had regular slots in the programming of another. News programs at peak viewing hours, 5 P.M. and 7:30 P.M., were broadcast for the entire Yugoslav TV network and originated from a different federal capital every day: Zagreb (Croatia), Belgrade (Serbia), Ljubljana (Slovenia), Pristina (Kosova), Sarajevo (Bosnia-Hercegovina), Titograd (Montenegro), Skopje (Macedonia), Novi Sad (Vojvodina). Each studio aired a program in its own language, prepared by its own reporters and camera crew, presented by local anchors and commentators. Although it cannot be said that Yugoslav TV production was ever entirely free of political control, the regular participation of the TV studios throughout the country in the common TV network made possible constant circulation of news and information.

After 1974, when the new constitution was adopted ushering in the process of strong political decentralization, things began to change radically. Each center started developing its own network and affiliated studios and beefing up its own local programming. And as the political climate in the country evolved toward increasing the autonomy of regions, TV centers gradually abandoned the traditional multiethnic style of programming. The daily and weekly press was caught up in a similar process. Media subsidies were transferred from the federal budget to the budgets of the republics, enabling regional politicians to take full control of the media. With tensions between the republics mounting after Tito's death, the regional media gradually turned into citadels defending local politicians, indifferent to the concerns of other republics. By the end of the 1980s media editors and directors and their party secretaries in Belgrade, Zagreb, and Ljubljana alike eliminated almost completely the programming of other republics from local channels. In the spring of 1991, Anton Vrdoljak, the director of Croatian TV, gave a straight-faced public statement: "It is the duty of the Croatian media," he said, "to serve in the interest of the Croatian people." A TV Novi Sad director admitted at about the same time: "By God, I'd even lie if I had to, to serve the interests of the Serbian people." As it became clear in the late 1980s, the media fragmentation was at least as fatal for Yugoslavia as was its economic and political fragmentation.

Slobodan Milosevic and Franjo Tudjman, the presidents of Serbia and Croatia, both gave top priority to completing the total isolation of the media in their republics and making them impermeable to other views. The prevailing opinion among the members of the Belgrade opposition is that since the Nazi use of radio in the 1930s, no propaganda has been as effective as the TV Belgrade and TV Zagreb propaganda was between 1987 and 1991, and after.

A mental conversion was necessary before the majority of Yugoslavs could tolerate nationalist slogans. Despite the claims of foreign journalists and politicians, there was an ample supply of mutual trust in former Yugoslavia. The trust had steadily grown among the Yugoslav nations since World War II, greater or lesser tensions between them notwithstanding. That trust had to be rooted out first, and confusion, doubt, and fear implanted in its stead. That is what television did over three and a half years preceding the war in 1991. Television proved to be a colossal medium of war engineering.

Still, it must be said, television was not effective in the main purpose of war propaganda: in mobilizing the will to fight. The drafting of reservists ordered in the summer of 1991 turned out to be excessively difficult. Young men went into hiding or left their families and fled the country to avoid having to put on the uniform. According to General Veljko Kadijevic, head of the chiefs of staff of the Yugoslav army, the army was left eighteen divisions short because of draft resistance. Several reservist uprisings occurred as well, one after another, in units in the heart of Serbia. None of this, of course, was ever reported on television.

In the buildup to the war and during the war, Serbian television served as a springboard for Milosevic's dream to replace Tito, and Croatian television for Tudjman's to champion the thousand-year Croatian quest for independence. For both ambitions, nationalism would be the means and television the instrument.

Milosevic's politics in Serbia since his rise to power in 1987 have been aptly called in Belgrade "Caesarism by plebiscite." The tool was his political use of visual kitsch. His first television mega-spectacular took place on June 28, 1989, St. Vitus's Day, an important date on the Serb religious and historical calendar. The day commemorates the Battle of Kosova of 1389 between the armies of the doomed Serbian Empire and the Ottoman Empire in expansion. The 1989 event took place in the Kosova province, at Gazimestan, the site of the historic battle. The commemoration had all the trappings of a coronation staged as a Hollywood extravaganza. Milosevic descended by helicopter from the heavens into the cheering crowd; the masses were the extras. The cameras focused on his arrival. In some vague way, the commentator placed Slobodan Milosevic at the center of the Serbian ancestral myth of Prince Lazar, the hero of the Kosova battle. Exactly six hundred years before, the voice-over told the viewers, on this very soil, Prince Lazar had chosen the kingdom of heaven over his earthly kingdom, the glory of death over survival in defeat. The relics of Prince Lazar, killed in the battle, were carried a month previously, in a procession accompanied by unprecedented media pomp, through virtually all Serb-populated regions where war would later break out.

At Gazimestan, for the first time, Milosevic explicitly mentioned the possibility of war. He did not have in mind the later wars in Croatia and Bosnia-Hercegovina; he was speaking of some

"new battles" in Kosova itself where "the Serb minority felt threatened by the ninety percent ethnic Albanian majority." To defend
the threatened Serbs, Serbia had to reestablish its authority in Kosova, said Milosevic. The TV spectacular at Gazimestan was designed to promote the myth of Kosova as the cradle of Serbian
medieval culture and, hence, the cornerstone of every Serb's national identity. The territory had been taken unjustly from Serbia
by the 1974 constitution, TV commentators never tired of re-
peating; its majority Albanian population would try, sooner or
later, to wrench it from Serbia altogether and to unite it with Albania.

That time, as so many times later, Milosevic did not talk
about ethnic conflict but addressed an allegedly justified, self-
evident, and painful grievance of the Serbs. They, his people, were
now victims in the heart of their own ancestral land. He was ready
and willing to stand up for them. When shortly afterward he virtually colonized Kosova with the Serb army and the police force,
terminating Kosova's political and cultural autonomy and banning
Albanian-language media, many of his TV viewers believed he was
doing what had to be done to restore justice in the region where
Albanians were denying the Serbs their historic right to live on their
own land—only because they were Serbs. Milosevic's appeals were
appeals to justice. Looking straight into the TV cameras, he struck
many as a real hero.

Staged mass meetings like the one at Gazimestan proved a
powerful tool for political mobilization over the next two years.
Each such meeting was a painstakingly thought-out, promoted,
and coordinated media event, carrying insistent repetition of messages drawn from the old national myths. Gradually, a socialist
ideology was being replaced by a fervently nationalistic one. At
mass rallies, television shots were framed to give the impression
of overwhelming popular attendance and magnificence. In smaller
towns the people from the crowd were delighted when they later
saw themselves on television. This was official proof that something important had occurred and that they were at the center of
events.

The amalgam of mass meetings, folk rhetoric, and electronic
media achieved a smooth switch of ideological packages from the
familiar socialist, egalitarian slogans to the nationalistic slogans

decrying the centuries-old suffering of the Serb people, their continual victimization, and their historic stamina. The Serbs have survived the wrath inflicted on them in the past, and they would vindicate their honor again and see to it that the historical pattern of injustice against them was broken once and for all. Television featured countless programs to that effect, with famous actors reading the old Serbian epic poetry of suffering, battles, and honor. A vague but stubborn link was suggested, time and again, between the five hundred years of suffering Serbs endured under the Turks and their current suffering, caused not only by the Kosovar Albanians but also by the revamped Croatian fascists and by foreign media, especially those of Germany and the Vatican.

In its effort to augment the sense of grievance in the population at large, television especially exploited World War II history. The goal was to plant the idea that the official history of World War II did not tell the complete story: there had been a cover-up of the full extent of Croatian atrocities, official television now suggested. The number of Serbs who perished during the war in the Croatian death camp Jasenovac and from the Croatian persecution, the TV claimed, was much greater than had been calculated. The "demystification of history" was launched, with television as the main medium. The campaign was in part a response to Franjo Tudjman's book *Bespuca* (Wilderness), published in 1989, a year before his election as president of Croatia, in which he alleged that official "Communist" history had greatly exaggerated the wartime crimes of the Croatian side.

To prove Tudjman wrong, the Serbian side, in the glare of Serbian television, began systematically unearthing mass graves of Serbs killed by the Ustashe. Bone-counting was supposed to revise the number of victims upwards of the seven hundred thousand claimed by Serbs. Concrete-sealed mass graves in limestone terrain were opened and the skeletons displayed. After funeral services at the site, the remains were reburied and the graves resealed, with TV cameras eagerly recording. Slowly, the sense was being awakened in the populace that the past was indeed far worse than anyone had imagined.

Simultaneously, in their effort to shake off the Nazi legacy, Croats began desecrating Partisan graves and war monuments in Croatia. In particular, the monuments marking the sites of Ustashe death camps were defaced or destroyed. The Croatian media insisted that the time had finally come to make peace with Croatia's past, which had plagued the Croatian national consciousness since 1945. Zagreb TV repeatedly accused the Yugoslav "Communist regime" of rubbing Croatia's war guilt in the face of its people. Just as Serbian TV presented Serbs as victims, Croatian TV presented Croats as victims—victims of the Communist conspiracy to attach to them forever the shameful stigma of their past.

In this context a new tactic of characterizing the leaders of other republics as monsters served to discredit other nations as a whole. In the Serbian media Franjo Tudjman was "genocidal," "fascisoid," the "heir of Ustashe leader Ante Pavelic," a "neo-Ustashe Croatian viceroy." In the Croatian media, the same man was "wise," "dignified," "steady," "a mature statesman." In the Croatian media, Slobodan Milosevic was a "Stalinist and Bolshevik," "Stalin's bastard," a "bank robber," an "authoritarian populist." In the Serbian media he was "wise," "decisive," "unwavering," "the man restoring their national dignity to the Serbian people."

Demonizing Chetniks and "Serbo-Chetnik terrorists" was another major assignment of the Croatian media. When the first uprising occurred among Croatian Serbs in 1990, the Croatian media began referring to Serbs in general as "bearded Chetnik hordes," "terrorists and conspirators," "a people ill-inclined to democracy." Meanwhile, in the official media of Belgrade, rebellious Serbs in Croatia were hailed as people spending sleepless nights defending their families, "boys with heads held high," "defenders of their centuries-old hearths from Ustashe evil."

Once the war began in Croatia in 1991, Croatian propaganda played more and more on the moral advantage of the victims. Television returned time and again to Vukovar in ruins, Dubrovnik in flames, Zagreb under air-raid warnings, but it never showed any of the Serb villages in ashes in Croatia. Long after the fighting had stopped, in the spring, summer, and fall of 1993, Croatian television greeted its viewers with "Defenders of the homeland, good morning."

Viewers of TV Belgrade were of course made amply aware of the desecrations of the Partisan graves in Croatia and of the efforts of the Croatian media to minimize the World War II genocide against the Serbs. The world did not know the truth about the plight of the Serbs—that was the refrain of virtually all official Belgrade TV commentators. But the truth will surface, and soon, they promised. The world shall find out, at long last, that our cause is just: the defense of our own homes, nothing else. This rhetoric flooded television during the 1991 Croatian war and continued unabated into the 1992–93 Bosnian war, fully eclipsing coverage of the genocide perpetrated by the Serb forces against Bosnian Moslems and Croats. The TV viewers saw Serb corpses, Serb homes in flames, Serb children orphaned—or at least that is what they thought they saw. TV Belgrade showed Serbs demonstrating in Western European cities against the false image the West had constructed of Serbia as aggressor. The world had conspired, together with the mujahideen and the Ustashe, to wipe out the Serb nation. No one ever explained why the world had come to hate the Serbs so much, but the hatred itself seemed to many common people to be self-evident. Television had succeeded in portraying the Croatian and, particularly, the Bosnian wars as indigenous ethnic conflicts, civil wars whose only tragic target was the Serbs.

Written-to-order telegrams of support for Milosevic added a sense of popular backing for his policies and provided a chorus of support to his government. Some telegrams were written in the TV studio itself. A former Serbian TV editor claims that one of the network's directors wrote a "telegram" in verse that ended on a defiant note: "There's nothing they can do; we are stronger than destiny." The strength of the Serbian nation was a constant media theme: in their history the Serbs had survived horrors much beyond anything the new world order could think up; the Serbs are not only a "just people" but, indeed, a "chosen people" by their endurance and their spirit of defiance; if life under the sanctions becomes daily more unbearable, at least Serbs will have the moral satisfaction of showing the biased, unscrupulous, evil world that their cause was just and that nothing can bring them to their knees.

A new language—a compound of formulas from folk history, the old Communist rhetoric, and the new nationalist ideology— was created. Professor Bogdan Bogdanovic, one of the most prominent Belgrade antiwar dissidents, wrote a book analyzing the new language as it was taking shape and suggesting that "the dizzying repetition of pseudo-patriotic terminology has a shamanistic effect." When Bogdanovic's book appeared, the Belgrade official daily *Politika* declared, "Serbia is sick and tired of people like Bogdan Bogdanovic." Repeated attacks on prominent intellectuals such as Bogdanovic were a way of discrediting the opposition. Every voice in discord with the official chorus was labeled as traitorous or at least as indifferent to the plight of the Serb nation facing its worst hour.

As spiraling inflation put the daily press in Serbia out of reach of the family budget, television became the only source of news and information for most people. The independent media lost ground, financially almost crushed by the international sanctions imposed on Milosevic. Independent TV Studio B, the alternative Belgrade channel, had tremendous problems trying to finance basic essentials. The independent papers press *Borba* and *Vreme* were never sure they would have enough newsprint for the next issue. In 1992 newspaper circulation hit its lowest level in thirty years. Circulation dropped to somewhat less than 300,000 for the four largest dailies in Serbia combined, the circulation of just one of them only a year and a half earlier. In a country where the population was so impoverished that only eight percent could afford a daily paper, the official TV channel, the only one with total territorial coverage, became the single information source. In this respect, the sanctions, rather than weakening the regime, brought a handsome political reward to both official TV and Milosevic. It was the alternative, independent media that bore the brunt of the sanctions.

Before the war started, early in 1991, an independent Yugoslav TV studio, Yutel, was established in Belgrade. It was objective in its news coverage and committed to the preservation of Yugoslavia, tolerance, and liberalism. At first Yutel was carried by all the regional TV channels throughout Yugoslavia, but only after midnight. A sizable audience, especially in the larger towns and cities, waited late into the night to watch Yutel news and commentary because it was the only way to find out what was really going on in the already overheated situation. Quite soon, however, Yutel was labeled "treasonous" in both Serbia and Croatia. In this regard, the two leaderships were in total agreement. Any activity supporting a multinational concept of Yugoslavia had to be silenced right away. When in late 1991 the Serbian government confiscated a transmitter that Yutel planned to install on Mt. Avala, just outside Belgrade, Yutel sought refuge in the then quiet and pacifist Sarajevo. Yutel's editorial staff knew that all programming in Sarajevo was still being made, as before, by multiethnic teams of Moslems, Serbs, and Croats. But only a few months after Yutel moved, the first attacks on Sarajevo occurred in the spring of 1992. The Yutel transmitter in Bosnia was blown up and Yutel was cut off from its Belgrade audience. From the exclusively Serb television studio in Pale, the Serb stronghold on Sarajevo's outskirts, the barrage was often fiercer against Yutel than against the television centers of the war enemies.

Using biased voice-over and poisonous commentary, glorifying its own type of death porn, official Serbian television, one might say, used the war to consolidate the powers that be as the only guarantee of national survival. The sophisticated cosmopolitan tone that formerly was cultivated on Belgrade TV and that Yutel also nurtured gave way to a closed, parochial, conservative approach. One cultural program on Serbian TV, aired late on Friday nights and occasionally featuring people from abroad like the British actor Kenneth Branagh and French philosopher Jacques Derrida, managed somehow to survive for a long time despite its determinedly antinationalist orientation. But overall, the editors of official TV sought to eliminate European names and European topics and to create an isolated and self-sufficient cultural model. The late Friday night cultural program faded from the air as its editorial staff gradually was dispatched on "extended vacation." The public, deprived first of Yutel and then of one of its favorite cultural programs, could sense that dark days lay ahead for Serbia. If foreign guests were featured on the TV shows any longer, they were not of the type of Branagh and Derrida. They were supporters of Italian fascists in late 1991 and of the Russian ultraright in 1993. TV cameras filmed the Russian playwright Edvard Limonov, who was given a celebrity welcome at his arrival in Pale, firing a machine gun in the direction of Sarajevo from an emplacement above the city. The newspapers published photographs of him and Karadzic looking at Sarajevo from their heights.

Those who saw themselves as "soldiers of the media army" filled the jobs of those dispatched or fired. Rebellious colleagues were labeled "obstacles to the government's effort to restore order."

News anchors, commentators, and staff members of drama programs were fired for such reasons as including a Slovene writer on a list of best TV dramas. Musical program editors were fired for broadcasting over Radio Belgrade "four times more Croatian and Slovene music than Serbian." The general manager of Radio Belgrade divided his staff into "reliable" and "bad" Serbs, the latter in the same category as non-Serbs. Once he had drawn up his list for the firing squad, it was broadcast by radio several times in April 1992 and read on the peak-hour TV news. Before long, a large number of nationally undesirable journalists and other media professionals had left Belgrade TV.

Serbs in the parliamentary and, especially, nonparliamentary opposition who had openly voiced their protest against Serbian politics under Milosevic were the next targets of TV propaganda. The language used against opponents of the regime, even occasional critics of a specific policy, was crude beyond limits. In the summer of 1992, Belgrade composers organized a demonstration for several days in front of the Serbian presidential offices. The following letter was delivered to the demonstrators from the general manager of Radio Belgrade: "Ladies and Gentlemen, Composers: After a discussion in which you gave your full support to a woman who slipped a Ustashe song into a Radio Belgrade program, I believe nothing you say, and nothing you do can surprise me." The composers believe that the same hand also wrote the next sentence: "Anti-Serb riffraff! Just keep on barking, you won't last long. You will all be eliminated and your places taken by real composers, real people, real Serbs. Meanwhile, off with you, animals, to the Usce [a location outside the downtown center of Belgrade, the only place where demonstrations were officially permitted] and kneel as long as you like."

The TV news program routinely called all the opposition and all free-thinking intellectuals traitors. Thugs in the olive-green uniforms of military irregulars often ambushed such people at night in front of their own homes, with shouts of "Traitor!" or "Beat him up!" Several opposition figures, like the philosopher Obrad Savic, ended up beaten one night. The offices of the Belgrade Citizens League, the most prominent antiwar group in Belgrade, were demolished, office telephones and computers taken away.

Milan Panic, Yugoslav prime minister, turned out to be another "bad Serb" when he decided to run against Milosevic in the December 1992 presidential elections. The media pounded him: he was a traitor because he insisted on negotiations with the "Albanian separatists in Kosova"; he was a secret agent of George Bush, sent to Yugoslavia to undermine the plans of Serbia's true patriots; allegedly, his real intention was to make sure the new Yugoslavia remained under sanctions indefinitely. TV attacks on Panic were accompanied by documentary inserts of civilian casualties during the U.S. intervention in Panama. The impression left behind was of Panic's personal involvement in the intervention and of his readiness, if elected Serbia's president, to pull off something similar in the new Yugoslavia. Belgrade TV showed filmed statements by individuals interviewed in the United States alleging, in the crudest terms, Panic's involvement in criminal activities in the United States and claiming he had close friends among the Ustashe immigrants in America. Panic was particularly attacked for having admitted in foreign interviews the existence of war criminals in the new Yugoslavia and for even having named them. According to the Belgrade media, he was preparing another Nuremberg for Serbia. Incredibly, despite the propaganda barrage against him, Panic won 34.2 percent of the vote to Milosevic's rigged 56 percent.

The favorite target of the Serbian official media in its mudslinging campaigns was the writer Vuk Draskovic, leader of the Serbian Renewal Movement. From his initial strident nationalism he had evolved into a moderate in open opposition to Milosevic. On the Belgrade political scene, Draskovic had been the most active and vociferous political leader in efforts to liberate the "TV Bastille," as official TV was called by the opposition. Consequently, he was a favorite target for a long time. During the 1990 Serbian presidential campaign, for example, a report was released that the CIA had bought a house for him in Geneva. As an organizer of the week-long demonstrations in Belgrade in March 1991, Draskovic was arrested on charges of "inciting the destruction of Belgrade." Under the pressure of the continuing demonstrations, he was released. During the demonstrations in Belgrade in June 1993, both Draskovic and his wife, Danica, were arrested in the street and clubbed by the police until they were semiconscious. Their lawyer and family members were not allowed to see them for several days. Neither received medical treatment for almost two weeks for serious skull and spine injuries inflicted during the beatings. This treatment was a warning to all by the "war lobby." Only days before the event, Danica Draskovic had spoken out on independent TV Studio B against the murder of Moslems in the Bosnian town of Gacko, Vuk's birthplace.

Parallel with its campaign of slander against the opposition, Serbian TV has contributed widely to the promotion of the worst extremists. The Chetnik leader Vojislav Seselj had no equal in the time and coverage he received while on good terms with Milosevic. The nightly TV news featured him calling for physical attacks on journalists, declaring prominent individuals traitors, and naming "spies" and "bad Serbs." In turn, TV commentators called Seselj "the only voice of reason in a dark tunnel." And Slobodan Milosevic, during the 1992 campaign, rated him the opposition deputy he most respected. As the TV hero of 1992, Seselj won thirty percent of the vote for parliamentary candidates.

Zeljko Raznjatovic-Arkan, a man under an Interpol arrest warrant for armed robbery and terrorist activity, was another TV favorite. He is widely suspected of having been a hit man for UDBA, the state security service of the Tito years. First, his help was enlisted for the wars in Croatia, and subsequently in Bosnia. Then his image was romanticized. He was referred to as a "restless youth," with some of the aura of a Rambo. Finally, as a war hero and patriot, he won a seat in the 1992 parliamentary elections. A TV film on his irregulars was shown on the eve of war in Bosnia-Hercegovina. The accompanying script treated the accusations against him as part of the hostile Western effort to set up a war crimes tribunal aimed only against the Serbs.

TV Novi Sad, a local Vojvodina studio of Serbian TV, had in 1992 a favorite extremist of its own, a certain Ostoja Sibincic, arrested and charged with organizing the expulsions of Croats and Hungarians from the Serbian northern village of Hrtkovci in the Vojvodina province. The indictment accused him of using psychological and physical pressures to drive non-Serbs from their homes in Hrtkovci. In this small village, Croat and Hungarian families have lived intermixed and in harmony with Serbs for more than two hundred years. Before Sibincic was given a suspended sentence in the spring of 1993, TV Novi Sad manifested its support of him by airing a documentary about Hrtkovci. No non-Serb villager and no Serb supporting the Hungarians and Croats was asked to speak, and Sibincic and his co-defendant Cakmak were described as "legendary commanders" from the war in Croatia. The statement to TV Novi Sad by Milan Panic, at the time still prime minister of rump Yugoslavia, that expulsions of non-Serbs were a disgrace to Serbia was censored.

Support of the war has led many public personalities in Belgrade to refuse participation on TV panels. In the spring of 1993, signatures were collected against the network's policy of spreading hate and intolerance. TV programming was in shambles, degraded beyond recognition. More and more frequently, the official TV studios seized upon the eccentric, the supernatural even, and on explicit sexual pornography. In the second year of the war, mysticism was rampant on Belgrade TV. Milja Vujanovic, an actress-turned-astrologist, was a regular guest on an occult show. She would cut an apple in half to point out to her audience "the diabolical pentagram" at the heart of this symbol of New York City. She would then declare, facing the cameras, that New York, the "diabolical fortress of conspiracy against Serbia," was doomed to ruin. The evil Western world that refused to hear Serb grievances would get its due in a natural-supernatural course of events.

Still, the most frequently used instrument of the official media was simple fabrication of news. The first spark of armed conflict in Croatia was ignited on February 16, 1991, by fabrication. Special correspondents of Montenegro TV announced that at least forty people had been killed in the small town of Pakrac in Croatia. Radio Belgrade picked up the report but gave the death toll at six. TV Novi Sad reported eight dead, and TV Belgrade found an Orthodox priest among the dead. The dead priest appeared live on television a few days later with a statement of his own. The Yugoslav presidency finally came out with a communiqué officially stating that nobody had been killed in Pakrac.

In the fall of 1991, when Dubrovnik was under siege, General Milan Gvero stated categorically for television that not even a grain of sand had fallen on the Old City. Meanwhile, TV channels around the world were showing pictures of the town in flames. One of the front-line officers in the devastation of Vukovar, Major Sljivancanin, explained, "Leveled but free!" In full view of television cameras, this same officer physically prevented journalists and European Community observers from entering the Vukovar hospital, shouting, "This is my country!" It took propaganda strategists in Belgrade some time to realize that the picture on the television screen usually contradicted the spoken text accompanying it. Vukovar in ruins described as "liberated" and "now free" was shown for weeks after the town's total destruction.

In Serbia and Croatia, war crime stories were fabricated and shamelessly circulated over television networks. TV Belgrade showed Serb soldiers telling of Croat prisoners wearing necklaces made of children's fingers. At the same time, Croatian TV was reporting news of Serb soldiers who "gouged out the eyes before cutting the throat of their Croat victims."

The TV death porn during the fighting, first in Croatia and then in Bosnia-Hercegovina, was without limit. For the average viewer, the television image certifies the "authenticity" of a news report, and by the end of these programs the television audiences felt fully if mercilessly "informed." Throughout the second half of 1991, parents—and their children—watched on television the dead victims of the most terrible crimes committed "against the Serbs," with long close-ups of the massacred and burned. The war was carried directly into their homes by audacious reporters sent to the scene to document "genocide against us." Most reports explained nothing: neither why nor in whose name all this killing was taking place. The official studios in both Belgrade and Zagreb abandoned any form of news analysis in favor of a sensationalized "human interest" approach that made the war scenes frighteningly direct while playing on the confusion of the audience about what was actually happening. As the constant exposure to inexplicable horror continued, less and less room was left for common sense. Irrational and intense fear grew in the viewers in proportion to the incomprehensibility of the total picture.

It was not unusual for Croatian and Serbian television to borrow each other's victims. The same person would be identified on Zagreb screens as a Croat victim, on Belgrade screens as a Serb. A dossier on TV Novi Sad published by the opposition Belgrade monthly *Republika* in May 1992 recorded that during the Vukovar offensive, a notice on the TV studio bulletin board instructed that all corpses be identified as "Serb victims." A stunning variety of instruments of death and torture were shown. A large butcher knife was presented as a "Serb-chopper," and many other implements as eye-gougers. Interviews with "war criminals," usually some distraught prisoners unsure whether they were being interrogated or interviewed, were shown as "documents of war" on Belgrade and Zagreb TV alike.

When the fighting began in Bosnia, propaganda strategists in Belgrade were thrown into a quandary. For the first time, Serbian TV found it wiser to hide the pictures of war than to promote them. The war began in April 1992 with shots fired by Serb irregulars from the roof of the Sarajevo Holiday Inn into a huge peace demonstration. Despite the presence of a TV Belgrade team on the site, the TV report in Belgrade consisted of a blank screen and a voice-over. "I can't say for sure what happened in Sarajevo today," the report went, "except that some men broke into the Holiday Inn Hotel." TV Novi Sad was better informed and said that "so-called pro-peace forces" had gathered in Sarajevo to overthrow the government and form a new, pro-Moslem and anti-Serb government. Only independent Studio B, with its limited transmission range, covered the start of the war in Sarajevo and the subsequent peace demonstration in Belgrade.

The general manager of TV Sarajevo stated at one point that the Bosnian government too accused TV Sarajevo, which covered the demonstrations live from start to tragic finish, of wanting to help a coup. The accusation was made despite the written message accompanying it on the TV screen: "Nations of Bosnia-Hercegovina unite, don't shoot!" Nenad Pejic, a Bosnian journalist, wrote in the April 13, 1992, issue of the Belgrade independent weekly *Vreme:* "TV Belgrade and Zagreb journalists are lying shamelessly. They write what they are told to write. They are building the atmosphere to bring into Bosnia more and more volunteers from Serbia and Croatia. The war in Bosnia is being fought by people who do not live here!"

For two months, TV Belgrade gave no film coverage to go with its reports of the shelling of Sarajevo. There were written orders displayed at TV Novi Sad that reports could not be accompanied by film from TV Sarajevo or from foreign TV. Archive film and static maps were used as backdrop to the shelling, and the side doing the shelling was never identified. Only on May 31, 1992, at

6:00 P.M.—two hours before the UN Security Council was to meet and vote on the first sanctions resolution—in a last-minute effort to avoid international sanctions, a Serbian government resolution was read condemning the shelling of Sarajevo by Serb forces. A large part of Serbia's television audience for the first time discovered what was happening. The Vase Miskina Street massacre a few days earlier—when a breadline was hit and many people killed— had been immediately reported by TV Sarajevo with pictures of the victims lying in blood. TV Pale, controlled by the Bosnian Serbs, reported the massacre as part of Moslem strategy to force international intervention: Moslems had done the killing, Pale reported, but it was staged to look as though the Serbs were responsible. A month later a woman "confirmed" for Serbian television that the Moslems had staged the massacre. Her proof was the speed with which the TV Sarajevo team had reached the scene. Viewers in Serbia were told, once again and to settle the issue, about the anonymous United Nations official who had "confirmed" that staged incidents were not impossible. Similarly, in summer 1992 the news about the concentration camps in Bosnia were either ignored or represented as a part of a Western conspiracy against Serbia.

The opposition's first organized action in 1991 was aimed at freeing television. The struggle endured through the following years at the cost of deaths, injuries, loss of jobs, personal propaganda, physical attacks, threats, court indictments, and self-exile. Eighty thousand Belgraders demanded freedom of the press in the March 1991 demonstrations. The government from the outset showed its determination to beat back every threat. When demonstrators demanding the fall of the "TV Bastille" were joined by university students, tanks rolled into the streets of Belgrade. The demonstrations lasted five days. Two died and hundreds were injured. No changes were made at Serbian TV.

The new peak reached by the warmongering in the fall of 1991 led to a walkout of many journalists at Belgrade radio and television. The protest was joined by a large number of other Belgraders and spread to other Serbian towns and cities. Every evening, at a given hour, news reporters, writers, and opposition figures improvised on the street a spoken "TV News," with real news and serious analysis. The evening protests gained momentum as a movement against the draft was being organized. The failure of the draft drive in Serbia and the low war morale in reservist units began to make the regime nervous. In closed sessions of the Serbian parliament, demands were made for deserters and draft dodgers, as well as those who publicly encouraged them, to be brought before a military court. The proposals for extreme repression were not accepted, but the regime did not loosen its control over the broadcast media. In September, groups of extremist nationalists were sent to break up the antiwar protests. Repeated provocations brought an end to the street TV news.

The fight for professional independence and a free press continued. A student protest against media control, among other things, began in the spring of 1992 and lasted into the summer. One of its slogans was "Turn Off Your TV and Open Your Eyes!" Among the empty promises made by the government was representation from the opposition in Serbian TV centers. That same spring, during one of many protest strikes at Radio Belgrade, lists were made of employees to be allowed access to the second floor, where the studios were located. Anyone seeking inclusion on the list was required to sign a "loyalty oath." Striking journalists reported seeing two burly men stationed in chairs in the director's office. Staff members allowed to reach their workplace said the halls were patrolled by police officers carrying machine guns.

The Serbian government proclaimed journalist strikes blatant violations of the law and demanded that measures "required by law" be taken against the strikers. Threats of dismissal or suspension followed, especially against TV employees who were also members of the Journalists Independent Trade Union, founded in 1991 to oppose government control. The trade union had a large membership, but lack of funds severely restricted its activities. In the final days of 1992, fifteen hundred journalists and technical staff of Belgrade TV—the total membership of the union—received notice of "extended holiday," a form of dismissal with pay. The complaints against them ran from absenteeism to "insufficient facial optimism" while commenting on the election victory, only days before, of Milosevic's Serbian Socialist Party. Top staff positions were filled by people who had never achieved any standing as professional journalists; people from positions somewhere between journalism and politics; and, finally, correspondents and reporters from the regions encompassed by war.

A mid–1991 survey of the Institute for Political Studies in Belgrade concluded that only 8.4 percent of the Serbian TV audience was well informed on events of vital importance for the whole country. Surveys conducted a year later indicated that over 60 percent of television audiences had no doubt about the truth of the information transmitted by the filmed images. Only 7 percent said they did not believe the images.

The loss of perspective in the public at large crowns the success of the TV propaganda and explains how the government diffused the dissatisfaction of the population trapped in radically deteriorating economic, cultural, and social conditions. The repetition of propaganda formulas from program to program, day after day, for years, helped create a virtual reflex in the minds of the viewers against everything out of line with the TV-constructed reality. The culprits of the crisis were being found everywhere but in one's own midst. The growing gap between the simulated TV reality and the one experienced daily by the viewers themselves caused profound confusion. Caught among rising contradictions in a hopeless situation, many found it easier, and safer, to accept the fiction.

SIX

The Collapse of Tito's Army

Stipe Sikavica

Decemeber 22, the official birthday of the Yugoslav People's Army, went unmarked by a celebration in 1992, for the first time in the army's fifty-year history. On that day in 1941, Josip Broz Tito had presented the newly formed first regular army unit of the wartime partisan forces with its battle colors. The army was to rescue Yugoslavia in a David and Goliath struggle against fascism and ethnic strife.

When Germany attacked the kingdom on April 6, 1941, with no prior declaration of war, it encountered the armed forces entirely unprepared for battle. Yugoslavia had no aviation, no mechanized units, no heavy artillery, no military industry to speak of. It took the Nazi war machine only twelve days to crush the royal army. The young King Peter II and his government fled from Belgrade to London, and Yugoslavia's neighbors who had joined the Axis coalition were rewarded with parts of the defeated Yugoslav state. Italy, Bulgaria, Hungary, and Romania each received a sizable piece.

At the time of the German attack, the Yugoslav Communist Party, headed by Tito, had only eight thousand members. It was, however, a tightly organized group, including a high proportion of university students, professionals, and intellectuals. With the king in exile, the Communists turned out to be the only force able and willing to rally the Yugoslav multinational community against dismemberment and occupation. Within two and a half months of the German assault on Yugoslavia, Hitler attacked the Soviet Union, and the party initiated the Partisan war. It set up a nation-wide clandestine press and underground network. Party cells in towns and cities formed immediately and began harassing the enemy with various forms of sabotage. The party leadership also turned to some willing officers and soldiers of the royal army, enlisting them to fight with the emerging units of the new military force. Directives were sent out for the collection and hiding of weapons and ammunition. Despite a German military proclamation warning that after April 17, 1941, anybody caught with a firearm would be shot on the spot, by the end of June the party was ready to order Partisan action against the occupation in all parts of Yugoslavia.

Initially, Partisan units were kept small and local, numbering from twenty to thirty members, to give the liberation struggle the broadest possible base, especially among young peasants and workers. By early September, the party had organized seventy-five hundred armed men and women in twelve higher-level Partisan detachments. By the end of the same month, Partisan forces had grown to between fourteen thousand and fifteen thousand men and women in twenty-three detachments. Heading the forces were older prewar Communists, party and nonparty members who had fought for the Republic in the Spanish Civil War, and a smaller number of officers and rank and file of the royal army.

The party had formed a Military Committee in Zagreb on April 10, 1941, just four days after Germany's initial attack. In time, the Military Committee became the high command of the National Liberation detachments. The basic idea was to wage a Partisan war by forming a united front for all patriots, regardless of national and religious identity or political allegiance, to join together to save their country. The new army would be controlled by the Communists but would lead a popular, united resistance against the enemy throughout Yugoslavia. From the start, the cornerstone of the Partisan policy was "Brotherhood and Unity," the only basis on which a popular war against fascism could be waged and Yugoslavia restored.

Like the Communists, the Croatian fascist Ustashe Party, which founded the Independent State of Croatia (NDH), organized its forces immediately following the outbreak of war, with one of the primary objectives to exterminate one-third of Croatian Serbs. The first massacre of Serbs came only weeks after the German invasion. In the town of Bjelovar, 184 Serb civilians were killed by Croatian firing squads in late April. Mass killings quickly spread to the predominantly Serb-populated areas of Croatia (the Krajinas), and to Hercegovina.

Aware of the growing threat of civil war, the high command of the Partisan forces turned its efforts to calming nationalist passions. Croat and Muslim Communists, antinationalists committed to a unified Yugoslavia, were sent into areas where Serbs were being massacred by the Ustashe terror. There was no better way to counter the rising tide of nationalism and continue the development of a broad-based unified liberation movement. For many Croats opposed to the Ustashe state, the Partisan movement offered the only alternative. But soon Yugoslav antifascists found themselves confronting a second nationalist threat from the Serbian Chetniks under the leadership of Draza Mihailovic.

Mihailovic, a colonel in the Yugoslav royal army, had remained in Yugoslavia after the collapse to rally the remnants of the former army to resistance in the name of the monarchy. The government-in-exile promoted him to the rank of general and considered him its representative in occupied Yugoslavia. Mihailovic, like the Yugoslav royal family itself, was a Serb, and he identified the monarchy's interests with Serbian hegemonic ambitions. As a monarchist, Mihailovic saw in the Communists his real archenemy; he viewed the people's liberation movement as nothing but a Communist ploy for power. He blamed the Croats and Muslims for the war and advocated a "Greater Serbia"—a Serbia that is homogeneous, ethnically pure. Chetnik massacres of the Muslim population in eastern Bosnia and in the Sandzak in Serbia during 1942 and 1943 were demonstrations of Mihailovic's policy of vengeful nationalism. Nevertheless, until September 1943 Mihailovic and his forces were publicized abroad as the leading antifascist resistance movement in occupied Yugoslavia.

Two other Serbian ultranationalist groups, led by Milan Nedic and Dimitrije Ljotic, collaborated openly with the Germans and were responsible for the deaths of many Croats and Muslims as well as large numbers of antifascist Serbs. Nedic headed the quisling government installed by the occupation forces. Tito's

national liberation movement thus found itself waging its fight
on two fronts—against the Nazi occupation and against ethnic
strife.

By the end of 1941, Partisan forces had grown tenfold, to
about seventy thousand in forty-three detachments made up of numerous smaller units. The time had come to reorganize the Partisan
forces into a regular army. On December 22, 1941, the first regular
unit of a new Yugoslav army, the National Liberation Army, was
officially formed and presented with its colors by Tito, its commander in chief.

In their earliest days, the summer and fall of 1941, the rapidly
growing Partisan forces had been able to proclaim the first liberated territory in occupied Europe: the town of Uzice and its surrounding area of seventy-six hundred square miles in the heart of
occupied Serbia. The Uzice Republic was not of long duration, but
in addition to a great deal of arms and ammunition captured during its liberation, the existence of a freed territory gave a tremendous boost to the morale of the army in formation. The Partisan
forces would wage their war entirely on their own until mid-1943,
when, after several decisive but bloody battles, they received recognition and assistance from Allied forces. The first military supplies
from the Allies were air-dropped to the National Liberation Army
in September 1943, only eighteen months before the end of World
War II in Europe. It was only at that point that the public abroad
heard of the existence of the Partisan movement in Yugoslavia and
of its army, which would emerge from the war as the third strongest Allied army in Europe.

While the Communist Party insisted from the outset that the
Partisan forces and subsequently the National Liberation Army
were free of all ties to any political group or party, the fact is that
the party was the organizational and conceptual force behind the
only effective all-Yugoslav antifascist movement. The red five-
pointed star soon became the insignia of the Partisan soldier, and
the hammer and sickle quickly appeared on the flags of the National Liberation Army. As the war progressed, the identity of the
liberation war with the Communist revolution increased, until the
two concepts became virtually inseparable. In the immediate aftermath of the war, the leadership of the new Yugoslav state, headed
by Tito, viewed the army as its surest support and guarantee of

survival in the emerging constellation of international forces and shifting allegiances within Yugoslavia.

Today nationalists of all stripes in former Yugoslavia mock brotherhood and unity, the underlying principle of the liberation war. They say that both "brotherhood" and "unity" were empty concepts used by Tito to manipulate the people. But irrespective of this revisionism, brotherhood and unity—the all-Yugoslav, grassroots character of the Partisan war—were the pillars of Tito's strategy without which he would not have won the war against fascism. On December 22, 1952, the tenth anniversary of its official birth, the armed force received its definitive name: the Yugoslav People's Army.

In the immediate postwar years, not surprisingly, Tito decided to maintain a strong army. In 1946, the force in the three traditional services—land forces, air force, and navy—was four hundred thousand strong. In the first four postwar years, the economically most difficult for the country, twenty percent of Yugoslavia's gross national product was earmarked for the military. By 1955, the military budget dropped to ten percent of GNP. By the 1960s Yugoslavia's military-industrial complex was supplying more than fifty percent of domestic military needs. During the 1970s, that percentage rose to above eighty percent, and in the 1980s to a full ninety percent.

Tito, as president-for-life of Yugoslavia, remained commander in chief of its armed forces for life. He was also the general secretary of the Communist Party, the second unchallenged authority next to the military. The party kept a close check on the political pulse at all levels and a constant guard against ideological deviation. Party membership was required for an officer's commission and "recommended" for noncommissioned officers. Indeed, ninety-eight percent of all command personnel were party members. While Tito and the party may have kept the army in its proper political place, blind submissiveness became an important factor in the army's failure to respond adequately to the tragic course of events in the late 1980s.

Another important factor was the mediocre level of education achieved by military commanders who would by the 1990s control the army's arsenal of highly sophisticated weaponry. During World

War II the National Liberation Army had consisted overwhelmingly of peasants and workers. A bare one-half of its command personnel had an elementary education, and only one in five commissioned officers had finished high school. After the war, the army relatively quickly organized a wide range of schools and academies of its own, from secondary school through university graduate level. But officer corps, soon well schooled, never became broadminded. And Tito's later choices for key military personnel would further undermine the caliber of military leadership.

In 1953, Tito had chosen as his minister of defense General Ivan Gosnjak, a Croat by origin but a Yugoslav by commitment, a distinguished veteran of the Spanish Civil War and the Yugoslav liberation war. In 1967 Gosnjak was suddenly dismissed, without explanation, and replaced by a man of little accomplishment and an undistinguished war record: General Nikola Ljubicic. Ljubicic would prove to be a shrewd political manipulator, blindly loyal to Tito, and that was what Tito deemed important. With this key appointment, "negative selection" became a rule in the army. Ability and sincerity lost out to careerism and conformity. The officer corps began its slide toward mediocrity, and the trend was never reversed.

Military spending would also contribute to the various conflicts tearing Yugoslavia apart in the 1990s. The military budget was part of the Yugoslav federal budget, to which all the federal republics and autonomous provinces contributed equally. In absolute terms, Slovenia and Croatia, the two most developed republics, always paid more than the others because they were the richest. This became an irritant to the two republics. They complained not only about what they considered to be their disproportionately large contributions, but especially about the absence of any outside control on how the army spent its funds. In 1987, for the first time in its history, questions began to be addressed publicly to the army. First in Slovenia shrill voices were heard: Why did Yugoslavia need such a large army? How was the military budget being spent? Could military spending be reduced? Why shouldn't recruits as a rule serve in their respective republics? Why was there no alternative for military service for the men who did not want to bear arms? Some media in Croatia joined the chorus. The questions were unpleasant, and, for the first time, publicly voiced. Instead of realizing that times were changing and that the army had to change with them, the military high command reacted as though every question was a direct attack on each of its officers personally.

The army was a world unto itself financially. It provided the housing for all its personnel, including civilians it employed. It had its own medical, educational, and recreational facilities, and even its own farms. Although it fostered a public image of close identity with "the people" and claimed that every military unit was a "Yugoslavia in miniature," the gap slowly widened between the standard of living of army personnel of all ranks and of civilians. By the mid–1980s an economic crisis had been building in the country for some years and Yugoslavia's economic difficulties were becoming more acute by the day. But only then, as the result of strong pressure, was it possible to reduce the military budget by one percent from the 1981 budget. The resulting 5.20 percent of GNP was still generally considered an excessive burden for the tottering economy.

The army was shutting itself off in an ivory tower more than just economically. Even after his death in May 1980, Tito continued to be venerated in virtually mystical terms as commander in chief. The slogan at every military post, on banners, on walls, and at muster was "After Tito, Tito."

Tito had never been publicly scrutinized in his lifetime. A healthy investigative and sometimes critical appraisal began in the late 1980s, but it suddenly took an ugly turn, especially in Serbia. Sensational articles and books appeared about Tito's private life, some digging into his earliest youth. Never having made the necessary adjustments to the death of their commander in chief and with this venerable giant now under attack, the army's leaders found their sense of security seriously shaken. Finally, the Communist Party's impotence in the face of economic, political, social, and ethnic crises began to strip the party of its earlier, unchallenged authority. The army was soon to find itself at sea alone, with no experience navigating on its own, much less in a storm.

Before Slobodan Milosevic undertook to consolidate his power in Serbia beginning in 1986, he had never shown any interest in the army, nor was the army ever known to have registered his existence. Once he began his power play, however, he realized that success would depend on having the army on his side. To this end, he opted for the subtle tactics of a discreet courtship. He avoided any criticism of the army himself and discouraged it among his staff, associates, and the Serbian media, on which he quickly clamped his control. Throughout 1987 and 1988, Milosevic virtually never missed a chance to make public and favorable mention of the minister of defense, Admiral Branko Mamula, and he carefully echoed the army position on all issues afflicting the seriously ill Yugoslav community. Little by little, in this way, he brought the army around to supporting him on issues critical to his ambitions.

The first test of his ability to manipulate the army was the disturbances in Kosova beginning in 1988. When the Albanian majority in Kosova organized demonstrations throughout the province in defense of its autonomy, Milosevic and the army arrived at the same diagnosis: "Counterrevolution in Kosova!" And there was no disagreement between the army and Milosevic as to the cure: "Chop off at the grass roots!" They sent tanks to Kosova in the spring of 1989. When twenty-two young Albanians and two young Serb policemen were killed in the armed confrontation that followed, a senior army officer was heard saying, "What of it—if two of ours died, we got rid of twenty-two of theirs." None of the other high-ranking officers present disagreed.

Some Yugoslav and foreign analysts predicted that war would break out first in Kosova and that the fighting would start with an armed uprising by the Albanians. This might well have happened had Kosova's Albanian community not wisely sidelined its extremist nationalists and opted for a policy of civil disobedience in response to Milosevic's policy of force. Slowly but surely, and with great dignity, the community has maintained a life of its own below the surface of Serbian occupation and in contravention of that occupation.

Slovenes and Croatians were the first to ask why the army leaders did not speak out against the dangerous approach Milosevic had chosen for Kosova and all of Serbia. The army leaders, for their part, insisted repeatedly on the inherent danger of "every nationalism" but found the Slovenian and Croatian nationalism particularly irritating. Toward Milosevic, by contrast, the army, with Serbs vastly overrepresented in its officer corps, had a blind spot.

In 1988, Veljko Kadijevic, son of a Serb father and a Croat mother, was named minister of defense. He was considered one of the army's most highly educated generals and was respected for his modest lifestyle. Kadijevic also openly supported the antinationalist program of Yugoslav Prime Minister Ante Markovic. That, however, did not help him to understand and resist Milosevic's nationalism. Kadijevic let Milosevic have his say with the army, without showing any sign of disagreement. Astonished, the media throughout Yugoslavia, with the exception, of course, of Serbia's official media, were soon raising the question "Whose army, for God's sake, is this?" Kadijevic never answered, directly or indirectly.

By 1991, feelings were running high in Belgrade against Milosevic's nationalist policies and totalitarian methods. On March 9, the opposition took to the streets in mass demonstrations that lasted for a week. The call was for Milosevic to resign. Kadijevic finally stepped in and, without consulting the Yugoslav presidency but with the full approval of the general staff, ordered army tanks into the streets of Belgrade. After that, few could doubt where the army stood.

Meanwhile, tensions were accelerating in Croatia and the situation was becoming more and more complicated. With the victory in 1990 of Franjo Tudjman and his strongly nationalist party, HDZ, Croatia was caught up in a nationalist euphoria. This was seen as a direct provocation by the many active and retired army generals living in Belgrade. Their statements warning of a Ustashe revival in Croatia and of the danger threatening Serbs in Croatia added fuel to Serbian nationalism. Every nationalist excess of the HDZ in Croatia was exploited to encourage Serbian nationalism.

When it became clear in 1991 that Franjo Tudjman was organizing an armed force of his own and recklessly buying weapons abroad, Yugoslav military leaders decided to place all the weapons of Croatian territorial defense units under direct army control. "Territorial defense" was the units organized in all parts of former Yugoslavia, for "self-defense" in case of attack. The units were made up of reservists and were under the command of local officers. In spring 1991, Belgrade television aired a military intelligence documentary on the methods and routes by which weapons were being smuggled into Croatia and its territorial defense units armed. The Yugoslav government promptly ordered the disbanding of all armed formations the army did not directly control.

After the collapse of the League of Communists of Yugoslavia on January 22, 1990, the Yugoslav crisis entered its final, tragic stage. The idea of a military solution then became a virtual obsession of the hard-liners in the general staff, who had advocated since the mid-1980s that the army should take in hand the deteriorating situation. In August 1991, when news was received of the military coup in Moscow against Mikhail Gorbachev, the Yugoslav army general staff celebrated the seizure of power by the Soviet hard-liners as favorable for the Yugoslav hard-liners. A more moderate group, headed by Defense Minister Kadijevic, sat paralyzed by indecision. Military coup or not? Kadijevic never made up his mind.

The general staff did agree on confiscating the weapons that were held by Croatia. At the same time, however, the army began almost openly to arm Croatian Serbs. When the army began to disarm the territorial defense into units in Croatia, violent demonstrations broke out in Split, a commercial port on the Croatian Adriatic coast and the home port for the Yugoslav navy. On May 6, 1991, demonstrators surrounded naval headquarters in Split. In the confusion and violence, with the Croatian police and the army shooting at each other, a young Macedonian army recruit was killed. Official Croatia manifested no regrets. Belgrade's propaganda machine rehashed the young Macedonian's death, presented as a final proof of the Ustashe revival, for a full six weeks.

With the naval headquarters under siege by a violent civilian crowd, General Kadijevic announced that the country now faced a "state of civil war," and he informed the presidency of Yugoslavia that the army would respond with force to every attack on its members, units, or facilities. He was not seeking the authorization of his commander in chief, the collective presidency of Yugoslavia; he was informing it of the army's decision.

The sparks of open conflict spread fast into Slovenia. In Maribor, an industrial center and the second largest city in Slovenia, a clash occurred between units of the Slovene Territorial Defense and the People's Army. When the army rolled its tanks into the streets of the city in June 1991, the people of Maribor poured into the streets in protest. In the general uproar of "singing and shooting," as the situation was described, one civilian died under the wheels of an armored car. All of Slovenia united against the attack.

The events accelerated the tempo of developments in Slovenia and Croatia. On June 16, 1991, the Slovene parliament in Ljubljana and, a little later in the day, the Croatian parliament in Zagreb adopted the declarations of independence of their states. The Slovenes immediately put words into action and established customs and security control over what they now proclaimed as their state border with Austria and Italy, forcing federal officials to abandon their border posts.

With independence celebrations in Slovenia at their peak, armored army units moved out toward international border crossings and Slovenia's largest international airport, Brnik. Who ordered the movement has never been made clear. At the time, the presidency of Yugoslavia was paralyzed over disagreement as to which of its members should fill the office of president, the term of the former president having expired in mid-May. In short, the army was without a commander in chief. General Blagoje Adzic, speaking for the general staff, made a public statement claiming that the decision to move into Slovenia had been made by the federal government. Whatever that decision was, Adzic transmitted it in clearly military language: "Orders were to occupy 137 points along the Yugoslav frontier on the territory of the secessionist republic of Slovenia and ensure that the federal customs services could resume their obligations at the border crossings."

The generals certainly wanted to reestablish federal customs control as quickly as possible at the international border crossings, if only because customs collection was one of the most important sources of revenue for the federal budget; the army's budget was fed exclusively from an already lean federal budget. But the generals quite likely had an even more ambitious goal in mind: to return Slovenia by force to the Yugoslav fold. They must have been sure that a show of force would be sufficient to accomplish the task and would, in addition, serve to stop the process leading to secession that had already begun in Croatia. However, the generals did not put into action the entire military power at their immediate disposal, but only a few armored units with neither infantry nor air support. They must have believed it would take no more than a military parade to bring the Slovenes to heel.

If this is what the general staff thought, it was proved dead wrong. In fact, as it turned out, people supporting a military solution to the Yugoslav crisis could not forgive the military. The general feeling was that, having undertaken to do the job in Slovenia, the army fell far short of performing a professional job. Had it used its force, critics said, the international community would have yelled a bit, because of the inevitable civilian victims and minor destruction. But the real show of force would have put a stop to any more talk of secession, and the task would have been accomplished. Kadijevic later stated that he could have reduced Slovenia to ruin but that the toll in human life would have been too high.

The fact is that the humiliating defeat of the Yugoslav People's Army in Slovenia was dealt by the best organized and most disciplined territorial defense units in former Yugoslavia, whose combat readiness proved to be above that of the army. Territorial defense units moved with lightning speed to surround and blockade army garrisons throughout Slovenia. This tactic effectively paralyzed army ground forces. The army lost forty men, mostly nineteen-year-olds who had begun their compulsory military service only four months earlier. The Slovene side listed nine deaths.

Slovenia had 15,000 territorial defense forces, including officers; it had 85,000 reservists, and, from territorial defense arsenals, about 120 tanks and 20 armored vehicles. The army had, stationed in Slovenia, the first line of former Yugoslavia's westernmost defenses, some 25,000 enlisted men and officers, who were joined during the military action by a few thousand more from Croatia. It had 250 tanks (100 more were sent in from Croatia), about 300 other armored vehicles, 90 fighter planes, and 50 combat helicopters. The total military standing force at the time totalled 200,000 enlisted men and officers, with 150,000 in the land forces, 35,000 in the air force, and the rest in the navy. The army had 1,850 tanks, 240 reconnaissance planes, 990 armored personnel carriers, 1,950 heavy artillery weapons, 490 fighter planes, 165 helicopters, 10 submarines, and 4 frigates. Yet this great military force lost out to the incomparably smaller Slovenian territorial defense.

On July 18, 1991, the high command ordered the withdrawal of all army effectives from the Slovenian territory. Most were transferred to Bosnia-Hercegovina and Serbia. The military cost of keeping Slovenia within Yugoslavia by force would be too high,

Kadijevic admitted. But political considerations probably carried more weight in the decision to withdraw. First, Slovenia had no common border with Serbia—Slovenia was beyond the scope of even Milosevic's ambitions to expand Serbia. Slovenia's secession, however, clearly opened wide the door to secession for other Yugoslav republics. Had their real purpose been preserving the Yugoslav state, Kadijevic and Milosevic would not have allowed Slovenia's departure so easily. In retrospect, it seems reasonable to assume that Milosevic was willing to permit Slovenia's quick departure precisely because he knew that Slovenia's secession would embolden Croatia's secessionist ambitions, making war inevitable. He wanted war, and this was one way to provoke it. Overnight, his propaganda machine dropped concern for the "preservation" of Yugoslavia and gave top priority to the "protection of Serbs in Croatia from genocide" and the "liberation of Serbian regions in Croatia."

The order for the army's withdrawal from Slovenia was the death sentence for Yugoslavia. Perhaps the generals believed Milosevic's assurances that the "remaining Yugoslavia," the "state of those peoples who want to live in it," would look after the army and their families and safeguard their army status. The attitude within the officer corps had for some time been that as long as there was a Yugoslavia, their elite place within it was secure. The officers allowed Milosevic to cajole them into the belief that their best hope rested with him.

Croatia's hawks were, meanwhile, becoming more and more vociferous and provocative in their public statements. The Croatian minister of defense, Sime Djodan, had announced that "for the Croatian cause" there would be no hesitation in sacrificing "as many Croatians as necessary" or killing "as many Chetniks as Serbia sent in." And, he loudly proclaimed, Croatia would extend "to Zemun and Budva," meaning that it would take over large pieces of Serbia and Montenegro. The army general staff, frustrated and humiliated in Slovenia, began to see in Croatia its chance at military rehabilitation.

Franjo Tudjman was meanwhile working to consolidate his armed forces. He began by expanding special police units, and by summer 1990 the formation of an official Croatian army was publicly ratified with great pomp by a military parade in Zagreb. The core of the growing military force was the ZNG (United Popular Guard). Training was kept behind the scenes, and the initial influx of weapons was through secret channels. Once the fighting began, Croatia's military might rapidly increased in personnel and weaponry. The largest arms purchases were from weapons merchants in Germany. According to *Defense and Foreign Affairs Strategic Policy Report* in December 1992, Germany had sold Croatia various types of weapons in the past year: MiG jet fighters, surface-to-air missiles, blowpipe and FROG missiles, and six late-model tanks. The second principal source became confiscation or capture of arms and ammunition from none other than the Yugoslav People's Army barracks in Croatia. By mid–1993, the Croatian army had 105,000 enlisted men and officers and about 150,000 reservists, 350 tanks, 4,000 artillery pieces, and 140 fighter planes.

During the summer of 1991, Croatian armed forces followed the Slovenian example of obstructing the Yugoslav army by blockading army garrisons. The regions with a significant Serb population had already been infiltrated by Serb provocateurs. Every incident involving the Croat police and the Serb inhabitants was the signal for the army to step in with its military firepower "to protect the Serb population from Croatian terror." And the army always acted with the local Serb militia or Serb "volunteers" by its side. Soon Croatia's growing armed forces were shooting back. It did not take long for this scenario to escalate into chaotic but real war.

Volunteers were a distinctive feature of the fighting in Croatia as well as in Bosnia-Hercegovina. They can be roughly divided into three groups. The first may be described as true and honorable volunteers. Many Serb volunteers joined the armed forces in the sincere belief that the lives of Serbs in Croatia were seriously in danger; Croat volunteers believed that Croats in the disputed regions of Croatia had to be protected and the regions themselves defended until independence was won. A number of these volunteers joined their armed forces when their homes and families came under direct attack by extremist bands or military forces of the other side.

The second group was made up of "forced" volunteers, men trapped in the midst of the fighting with nowhere to flee and given no choice by their own side—usually army irregulars or an extremist band—except to join the fighting, often under threat of death to themselves or their entire families. It is not unusual for men of this group to be forced to prove their loyalty by murdering a neighbor of different national origin.

The third group of volunteers came from the underclass of society—men out to make a quick buck and outright criminals. Most of these men started out in small bands and were allowed to train quite openly on their national territories. They developed a rhetoric of strident patriotism, accusing reservists who avoided mobilization or refused to volunteer of being cowards and traitors. Most of this third group of volunteers had no qualms about robbing, murdering, massacring, and raping. A large number became rich from the war, filling their trucks with the entire furnishings of homes and apartments and selling their booty on a soon flourishing black market. Many of these volunteers returned home to invest their profits in legal and illegal businesses.

There was also a fourth group, the many "weekend volunteers," men who went uniformed into war areas only on weekends and only to pillage. As the war continued, the number of these bands multiplied, and they could be thirty to a thousand strong. Some remained local, and former bar owners, self-employed truck drivers, and warehouse clerks popped up as their commanders, bringing with them new uniform and insignia designs for the local armies. Drunken orgies were the rest and recreation of these bands. Very early in the Croatian conflict, such bands, Croatian or Serb, were being referred to as paramilitary formations or irregular units. Both regimes made sure to lend them a veneer of legitimacy.

Official armies, short on personnel, turned a blind eye to the proliferation and growth of these "weekend" bands. The Yugoslav People's Army was having very serious problems maintaining its numbers when the war began in Croatia. Mothers had already demonstrated to have their nineteen-year-old sons sent home when the shooting began in Slovenia. Mothers would demonstrate again in Belgrade and in Skopje as the war progressed and passed from Croatia into Bosnia. And the level of desertion grew rapidly as Yugoslavia and its army disintegrated in tandem. Despite the three years of intensive warmongering by the Serbian propaganda machine, a huge number of Serbs throughout former Yugoslavia were horrified by the 1991 war and the way it was being fought. Mobilization calls by the Yugoslav People's Army in Serbia were met, on the one hand, by a wave of mass emigration (some 150,000 men left the country to avoid mobilization) and, on the other, by a wave of internal migrations as reservists went into hiding with relatives or friends to escape the military police arriving at their homes, often in the dead of night, to enforce mobilization orders. Under the circumstances, the army's general staff decided to accept volunteers. Recruitment was unselective, and those enlisting were predominantly from the third group of volunteers, fanatics and criminals. Both the Serbs and the Croatians allowed paramilitary formations to fight side by side with regular units, and they helped arm them. Once accepted and well armed, these formations moved quickly beyond the control of their erstwhile superiors. Their leaders asked nobody's permission before going into action and were never called to account before a military or civilian court for their mass crimes. And where regular army units might shrink from certain actions, these newly formed units were always ready for anything. On all sides, paramilitary formations became the elite units for genocide.

Some members of the paramilitary formations were celebrated in their communities as national heroes despite the terrible war crimes they committed. In Serbia, critics of these crimes were called "Serbo-Ustashe" by the "patriots."

Serbs, Croats, and later Muslims all developed a multitude of irregular forces, although the Serbs commanded by far the greatest number. One such Serbian group is the Arkanites, led by Zeljko Raznatovic, whose nom de guerre is Arkan, a murderer wanted by Interpol. Arkan and his followers fought alongside the Yugoslav People's Army at Vukovar and sowed death and destruction in many other places of Croatia and Bosnia-Hercegovina. Arkan's men are still in the field but he nevertheless served as a deputy in the Serbian parliament at the same time as he took control of Belgrade's underground. Croatia, in turn, has its HOS (Croatian Liberation Force), an openly fascist paramilitary unit that adopted the Nazi salute complete with "Sieg Heil." Fifteen thousand strong, the unit contains a large number of criminals and foreign mercenaries who are beyond official control. HOS is guilty of war crimes in both Croatia and Bosnia-Hercegovina. On the Muslim side, the best-known paramilitary formation is the Green Berets, formed and led by Jusuf-Juka Prazina, a prewar Sarajevo criminal of somewhat romantic reputation. The brutality of the men under his command led to his being expelled from Bosnia and eventually killed after he escaped abroad.

Early in September 1991, Lord Peter Carrington, as chairman, convened the International Conference on Yugoslavia at the Hague in an effort to bring some reason to the chaos in Yugoslavia. The conference achieved nothing since Milosevic proclaimed he wasn't going to give in to Carrington's "blackmail." The army applauded his attitude and announced that the international community had been taught an "excellent lesson." Ante Markovic, a committed Yugoslav of Croatian origin, was still prime minister of the crumbling country. His last effort as the head of the Yugoslav government came later that same month when he asked for Kadijevic's resignation as minister of defense. Kadijevic refused to resign. The Serbian voice on the Yugoslav presidency accused Markovic of "openly threatening war." The general staff called a general mobilization in the "remaining Yugoslavia." The order went out: "To Vukovar!"

Veljko Kadijevic claimed that the Croatian town of Vukovar, situated at the border with Serbia, on the Danube, was part of the "backbone of the Croatian army" and that therefore Vukovar had to be "liberated." The army periodical *Narodna Armija* (People's Army), in its November 20, 1991, issue, wrote that "Vukovar had for decades been prepared to support German military penetration down the Danube." Before the war, Vukovar had a population of 84,000, almost 44 percent Croat, 37 percent Serb, and 20 percent "others." Yet official propaganda insisted that Vukovar was a Serb town.

If Vukovar had any importance for Croatia, it was the town's location on the Danube. Tudjman, in all his rhetoric, never related Vukovar to the "backbone of the Croatian army." Vukovar was probably doomed to become the symbol of Croatia's defense against Milosevic's expansionist ambitions simply because it was the first large town in the path of the Yugoslav People's Army, incomparably stronger than any armed force Croatia could field, when it openly marched on Croatia.

On August 20, 1991, Croatian territorial defense units had

blockaded the two small army garrisons in Vukovar. Croatian forces were reinforced by paramilitary HOS units led by Dobrosav Paraga, the avowed neo-Nazi responsible for many massacres of Serbs. In reaction to the Croatian blockade, the army began concentrating forces outside the town. On the night of September 24–25, the army moved in, with 390 trucks carrying reservists, 400 tanks, and 280 other vehicles rolling across the fertile plain surrounding Vukovar. Operation Vukovar began on September 30, under the command of General Milan Panic.

The civilian population of Vukovar, Serb and Croat, was not evacuated from the city. And even though no battle of significance to military strategists took place, the town was pounded indiscriminately for two months by several hundred various-caliber weapons, warplanes, and ships anchored in the Danube, while its population huddled in cellars and catacombs, dying of disease and starvation. Only when the town had been destroyed did tanks with infantry support, including "volunteers" and elite units, move on it. The ratio of attackers to defenders was between thirty and fifty to one, depending on the direction of the assaults.

No official figures of the casualties at Vukovar are available. But a huge number of civilians, both Croat and Serb, died along with young, untrained soldiers on both sides. Although the devastation of Vukovar might appear a wanton act of madness, an underlying logic did exist. Vukovar, with a mixed population living in harmony, was attacked to eradicate every possibility that Serbs and Croats would continue to live as neighbors. That was the point of the war in general. Its first lesson was Vukovar, whose destruction both Serbs and Croats elsewhere watched with horror on their TV screens.

The Yugoslav People's Army units returned to Belgrade, passing through an "arch of triumph." Officers were promoted and decorated; they were congratulated for destroying Vukovar, "the toughest and fiercest Ustashe fortress."

Dubrovnik could never fit the notion of a Ustashe fortress. The Croatian police and ZNG units in the city and its environs numbered only a few hundred. There were no irregulars on the scene, no army garrison had been blockaded. There could be no talk of an endangered Serb population either. Despite efforts during the summer of 1991 by the Serbian propaganda machine to circulate rumors of the victimization of 10,000 Serbs in and around Dubrovnik, only 4,735 Serbs lived in the area, 6.5 percent of the local population. When the 12,000 refugees began leaving the area, they headed almost entirely toward Croatia or, in virtually equal number, into the Old Town to seek safety behind its thick stone walls. When the army artillery began firing on Dubrovnik on October 2, 1991, nobody in Serbia or Croatia could understand why.

The siege of Dubrovnik actually goes back to a fall 1991 Serbian parliament session, when a deputy mentioned in one of the standard warmongering speeches of the time that Dubrovnik, of all places, would be the capital of the Serb Hercegovina. The claim was outlandish. Yet in the summer of 1991, almost a year before the war began in Bosnia-Hercegovina, two army reservist corps moved into the heights above Dubrovnik in eastern Hercegovina, allegedly to prevent clashes in that region. By fall, they had dug into position directly above the Dubrovnik Riviera. The siege of Dubrovnik would eventually also include poundings by the navy from the Adriatic and by the air force.

In line with the fantasy that Dubrovnik would be the capital of Serb Hercegovina, Serbian appetite soon encompassed the entire Croatian coastal belt from the mouth of the Neretva River, northwest of Dubrovnik, to the Croatian-Montenegrin border southeast of Dubrovnik. Bosnia's Serbs under Radovan Karadjic have still not stopped talking about their "right" to an outlet to the sea. Army reservists and irregulars carried death and destruction northwest of Dubrovnik. In the southeast, Montenegrin army reservists and irregulars took the field. On the excuse of blockading an important army garrison overlooking the Montenegrin Bay of Kotor, they crossed into Croatia and moved up the coastal belt to the outskirts of Dubrovnik. They devastated everything in their path, stopping only to load their trucks with livestock, washing machines, freezers, television sets, and other booty. For days, trucks returning full of loot and drunken soldiers passed through the Montenegrin resort town of Hercegnovi, only a few miles from the Croatian-Montenegrin border. Official Serbia and the army consistently referred only to the "liberation" of the Dubrovnik Riviera.

On December 6, 1991, the Old Town of Dubrovnik was directly shelled. Among the casualties within its thick stone walls were twelve dead. The Old Town suffered widespread damage.

Late in December 1991, when Milosevic signed the Vance Plan to end the fighting in Croatia, he was putting his signature to a peace plan for a war he had always insisted Serbia had nothing to do with. Early in January 1992, Kadijevic resigned as Yugoslav minister of defense, alleging ill health. Soon the army would start withdrawing from Croatia, primarily into Bosnia-Hercegovina. Already 10,000 tons of war material had been withdrawn from Slovenia, half of it into Bosnia-Hercegovina. By the start of 1992, the army had a standing force of at least 150,000 troops and immense firepower concentrated there.

The masters of shrinking Yugoslavia calculated that Bosnia-Hercegovina would remain theirs. If not, the Serb autonomous regions being proclaimed in Croatia and Bosnia would be incorporated into an expanding Serbia. Tito's military strategists had placed Bosnia at the core of Yugoslavia's defense system. Concentrated there were huge military effectives, more than sixty percent of Yugoslavia's military industry, large air force and other bases for logistical support, and four military airfields, the most important at Bihac.

The Bihac airfield had five runways, from 7,500 to 10,000 feet long. Electronic state-of-the-art hangar space had been provided in four underground tunnels for about one hundred planes and their maintenance. Its many additional underground facilities placed this airfield among the best-fortified air bases in Europe. A system of thick vertical steel pipes, deeply sunk over every 150 feet of the entire installation, could be filled with explosives if the danger of the base falling to an enemy ever became imminent. When the fighting started in Bosnia-Hercegovina, the army began to fear that the Bihac supermilitary facilities might fall into Croatian or Bosnian hands. On May 16, 1992, the army filled the pipes with explosives and the Bihac airfield and its underground facilities, built at the cost of eight billion dollars, were destroyed in one megaexplosion lasting only minutes.

Earlier that spring, on the eve of international recognition of independent Bosnia, President Alija Izetbegovic asked the commands of army units stationed in Bosnia to remain and help build the armed forces of the new state. The generals responded with disdain and sent a shower of bombs on points alleged to be Ustashe strongholds in western Hercegovina.

Bosnia received international recognition on April 6, 1992, and the Yugoslav army became a foreign force on its territory. The army immediately announced that eighty to ninety percent of its force stationed in Bosnia had been born there and could not be forced to leave the land of their birth. Accordingly, ten percent were withdrawn to Serbia and Montenegro. The withdrawal was supposed to be completed by the end of May but actually was dragged out until the fall. By mid-May Serbian politicians and some generals were claiming that not a single officer or enlisted man of the Yugoslav army was fighting in Bosnia. On May 21, 1993, however, the following notice appeared among the obituaries of *Politika,* the leading official Belgrade newspaper:

> One year has passed since the death of our joyful, our beloved son and brother Marko Hrnjak, born July 5, 1972, a freshman in construction engineering at the University of Belgrade, doing his military service as a parachutist with the Airborne Brigade. He was killed on May 23, 1992, in the vicinity of Mostar, at a time when not a single soldier, citizen of the Republic of Serbia was outside of Serbia. For a year we have been asking generals and politicians why he was killed and who is responsible for Marko's death. We are met by silence or untruths. We will continue to ask. Mother, Budislavka; sister, Ana; and father, Vladimir.

The Serbs of Bosnia-Hercegovina had formed their own parliament back in October 1991, and they had voted overwhelmingly in early November 1991 to remain in Yugoslavia. And the Bosnian Serb recruits and officers of the army who had remained behind formed another army serving the self-proclaimed Serb Republic of Bosnia-Hercegovina whose president is Radovan Karadzic. That army's commander is General Ratko Mladic, a career officer who had made his reputation and earned the rank of full general at Vukovar. Mladic ordered the first shellings of Sarajevo on May 6 and 7 from artillery in the hills surrounding the city, well emplaced a long time before.

The army of the Serb Republic of Bosnia has been financed by paper money whose only cover is the help of every kind received from Serbia. In 1993 it had between seventy thousand and eighty thousand men and women under arms, not counting the multitude of irregular formations or outright extremist bands formed on its own territory or in Serbia. Its striking force includes 400 tanks, 20 armored personnel carriers, and some 500 artillery pieces. Its air force has 20 fighter-trainers, 20 helicopters, and 4 missile systems. It is believed also to have squadron of MiG-21s.

The forces of the Serb Republic of Bosnia, Milosevic's extended arm, were not the only army waging war in Bosnia. The Croatian Defense Council (HVO), a well-armed, fifty-thousand-strong force, acted as the extended arm of Tudjman. In 1993, it rapidly increased its heavy firepower, especially its artillery and armored vehicles. On the territory it held, the HVO was financed by the Croatian regime and by Hercegovinian Croat émigrés living in Western Europe.

The army of Bosnia-Hercegovina is referred to often as the Muslim army or "Alija's army," although it includes, aside from Bosnian Muslims, also Bosnian Croats and Serbs fighting for a unified Bosnia-Hercegovina. Its strength totals two hundred thousand men and women with sidearms but little heavy weaponry. It receives some support in troops and weapons from Iran, along with a trickle of Muslim volunteers, labeled *mujahideen,* and limited financial and moral support from some other Muslim nations. In 1992–93 any serious effort to arm this force was shackled by the arms embargo but especially by the fact that every route for bringing in heavy weapons had to pass through Croatia, and the Croatians were not in the least inclined to allow war material to reach the Muslims. By 1994, however, the Bosnian army emerged much better organized and equipped than before, despite the arms embargo.

The Bosnian Serb army is by far the strongest in manpower and firepower. In 1992–93, it plowed over Bosnian-Hercegovinian territory in all directions with unrestrained use of its firepower and unprecedented brutality until it held seventy percent of the country under its heel.

The new Army of Yugoslavia replaced the Yugoslav People's Army in May 1992. It was formed from the earlier army units stationed in Serbia and Montenegro and withdrawn from Slovenia, Croatia, Bosnia-Hercegovina, and Macedonia (by peaceful agreement with the government of Macedonia). The new army has some 135,000 recruits and officers, FROG, SAM, Neva, and Volhov missile systems, 140 combat helicopters, 1,000 tanks, 950 armored personnel carriers, 1,360 heavy artillery pieces, 5 submarines, and 4 frigates.

The transformation of the former Yugoslav army is said in military quarters to have begun with the "great victory at Vukovar," and the new army is described as having a "new quality" because of the "recovery, revitalization, capacitation, and selection achieved" by Yugoslavia's armed forces in that "battle." Mass purges of top-ranking officers continued after Vukovar. Only Serb and Montenegrin officers were allowed to keep their jobs. Slobodan Milosevic retired sixty-six generals and admirals virtually overnight. Not one non-Serb top-ranking officer remains in the land force, navy, or air force. The purge of the army was extended to cover civilians employed by the army. Non-Serb civilian employees at one point in mid–1992 were given yellow passes for entry into army facilities, in contrast to the blue passes of their Serb colleagues. The parallel with the yellow Star of David was too obvious, and its use shocked both civilian and army employees. A wholesale dismissal of non-Serb civilian employees began.

The epilogue of the "transformation and revitalization" of the former Yugoslav army has been tragic for its many members of all ranks who before the war sincerely believed they were serving in an armed force dedicated to the protection of the whole of Yugoslavia and all the Yugoslav peoples. Many of them find themselves now with no hope in their future, without rank, often without home or income.

SEVEN

Croatia: The First War

Ejub Štitkovac

For the May 1 holiday of 1991, I decided to visit Daruvar, a large town in the eastern Croatian region known as Slavonia. This was just somewhat over a month before the war in Croatia would begin. I had been to Daruvar often. It was a hospitable town, and its people seemed to compete in their efforts to make a guest comfortable. Daruvar was a spa town, its waters especially recommended for the treatment of rheumatic diseases, so it attracted its full quota of visitors year-round. This was also one of the reasons for its exceptional ethnic diversity. Its population was a mixture of twenty-six groups: Croat, Serb, Slovene, Montenegrin, Jewish, Muslim, Albanian, German, Czech, Hungarian, Romani (Gypsy), and a few others, including Italian. Over the years I had met many Daruvarians, and some had become good friends. On my arrival, the town looked unchanged: tranquil, welcoming, the spa full of guests. But from a Croat friend, the first thing I heard was that for several nights tanks of the Yugoslav army had been passing through the town. That did not bode well, he said. I understood the effect of the tanks on the people in Daruvar when my friend refused to join me in visiting a Serb who was a childhood friend of his and in fact had been his best man. When I suggested we go to his friend's together, he said, "Leave that for better times. If the Serbs in Croatia don't wake up and realize that their great leader in Serbia, Slobodan Milosevic, is out to push them into war with us . . . all hell will break loose. I'm sure," he added, "Milosevic will just use them and then leave them high and dry. Mark my words."

In my hotel room that night, trying to sleep, I heard the tanks myself, rumbling through the town, and small-arms fire from the woods around Daruvar. Few were sleeping well that night, I thought. But in the morning, the streets looked normal again, with people going off to work and the marketplace full of goods and buyers. Had the people grown accustomed to tanks in the streets and gunfire from the woods?

At midmorning, I dropped in on the Serb friend. He looked depressed and nervous and said to me, "You journalists are nuts. Instead of sitting quietly in Belgrade, here you are, where the lid's about to blow off. Don't you feel it in the air? Catch the first train back. Later you might not be able to get out." He told me that the Croats were preparing to massacre the Serbs, as they had done during World War II. The Croatian Democratic Union (HDZ) had won the first multiparty elections by a very large majority in Croatia, and my Serb friend said that local HDZ members were drawing up lists of Serbs to be shot. "We'll have to take to the woods again and fight. The army is our big hope, but it's obviously falling apart. Nobody can expect Croatian officers in the Yugoslav army to fight against Croats. The generals will go over to Tudjman, and we'll be like sitting ducks." He was curt when I asked him about his and my friend, the Croat. "We aren't even friends any longer, much less best friends. Whoever kisses the checkerboard [the Croatian flag] is no friend of mine. I wouldn't sit at the same table with him. Don't mention him to me again."

Clearly, the lid had already blown off. My Serb friend did, in fact, take off into the woods a few days later. And he became well known by his war name, Struja (Electric).

The local radio station that day reported a bomb thrown at a gas station in Pakrac, some twelve miles to the west. The incident had taken place half an hour after the Belgrade local, the train connecting Daruvar and Belgrade, had passed through. The majority population in Pakrac was Serb, and graffiti on the walls of the town read, "This is Croatia" and "Serbs get out." In Pakrac and a number of other small towns I visited in Slavonia during that May 1 holiday, the streets were full of police and men in a uniform I had never seen before. The next day, the Belgrade local did not show up in Daruvar. That same day, May 2, 1991, things exploded in Borovo Selo.

Borovo Selo is little more than a village, but it derives importance from the neighboring town of Borovo, the center of the Borovo Rubber Goods Manufacturing Company, in the last fifteen years a major manufacturer of rubber goods as well as fashion shoes. Borovo Selo lies close to the town of Vukovar, itself at the Croatian-Serbian border. As in Daruvar, the Serbs here and in towns and villages throughout Croatia harbored many fears that Slobodan Milosevic had gradually awakened in Serbia and beyond over the past three years. The election of HDZ leader Franjo Tudjman in April 1990 had reinforced the fears, and that April marked the start of a radical change in Croatia. Croatia's Serbs became increasingly sensitive to every development affecting them.

Tudjman had done a number of things to disturb the Serbs. Many could be heard discussing his book *Bespuca* (Wilderness), published the year before his election, in which Tudjman, a historian, asserted that the official death toll given for the World War II Croatian death camp Jasenovac was greatly exaggerated. This allegation had been an unavoidable subject for months among the Serbs because Serbs had been the principal victims of the camp. Jasenovac was the only World War II death camp not established and run by the Germans. Its victims, among whom were many Jews, Gypsies, antifascists, and Communists regardless of ethnic origin, number hundreds of thousands. To the astonishment and revulsion of Serbs, Tudjman placed the figure at well below one hundred thousand.

One of Tudjman's campaign promises and a fundamental of his party's electoral platform was to free Croatians from the "Jasenovac complex" and from their guilt associated with the Croatian fascist party, the Ustashe. Tudjman, once elected, began to fulfill his promise by openly and widely supporting national "reconciliation" with the Ustashe, the wartime police, and the Croat army regular forces, the Domobrani. Because of the postwar Communist government in Yugoslavia, Tudjman claimed the fallen members of Ustashe and Domobrani had been forgotten and remained unmourned.

Ordinary Serbs were horrified when, in the gesture of reconciliation with Croatia's past, the streets and squares across Croatia commemorating victims of fascism and heroes of the liberation war were renamed after the infamous Domobrani figures and when youth organizations being formed under Tudjman began commemorating high officials of the 1941–1945 Independent State of Croatia, the NDH.

Then on July 25, 1990, the Croatian Sabor (parliament) adopted a number of amendments to the Croatian constitution allowing for Croatian state symbols to be changed. The Yugoslav flag with its red star emblem was replaced by the Croatian flag with a white and red checkerboard emblem. Croatians saw the checkerboard as their ancient emblem and insisted that the Serbs had no right to complain about a symbol with such deep historical roots. Some Serbs insisted that the emblem had been defiled by the Ustashe government's policy of genocide. (In actuality, the official Ustashe emblem was an embellished *U* placed above the checkerboard shield.) They felt that the use of symbols that provoked associations of genocide were politically and morally unacceptable. The checkerboard, however, was soon being flown everywhere, on official flagpoles and buildings, on private homes, on shops and cafés. At night, Serbs would remove it, often raising instead the Yugoslav flag; in the morning Croats returned it. Tensions grew.

The checkerboard did not disturb the Serbs only as the flag under which they had suffered during World War II, but also as a symbol of what they saw as Tudjman's current intentions. On February 24, 1990, at the first HDZ party rally, Tudjman had spoken the astonishing words "The NDH was not simply a quisling creation and a fascist crime, it was also an expression of the historical aspirations of the Croatian people." Abroad, there was no reaction. In the mouth of a German politician, Serbs insisted, the same statement would have sounded something like "Hitler's Germany was not simply a fascist crime but an expression also of the historical aspirations of the German people." This was unthinkable. Yet Tudjman got away with his claim. Serbs were outraged. What was to come next?

Reports leaked during 1990, while Croatia was still a part of Yugoslavia, on the rapid formation of a new Croatian army and its massive weapons purchases from Poland, Czechoslovakia, Germany, Uganda, Guinea, and anywhere else they were for sale. This too passed unrecorded by the world media. Not even the Jewish community raised its voice. Gradually, the Serbs became convinced that the world cared little about the specter of fascism in Croatia.

And they felt, as early as 1990, abandoned to their fate, possibly a replay of the Ustashe genocide.

Milosevic's propaganda machine in Serbia was quick to recognize the possibilities opened by the groundswell of fear, and he made much of the West's silence about the true intentions of Croatia. Milosevic was helped by Croatia's obvious success, despite all, in presenting itself before the international community as a country deeply committed to liberal democratic principles, meaning, of course, "free elections."

In December 1990 the new constitution of Croatia, still a member of the Yugoslav federation, changed the meaning of the old socialist constitution. Croatian Serbs were no longer recognized as a "constituent nation" in Croatia, their homeland, but became a "national minority." No one was clear as to what this really meant in practical terms, if anything. But soon after, Serbs began losing their jobs in massive numbers. They were fired not just from the police force, where they had been overrepresented in the past, but also from all levels of education, from medical institutions, the tourist industry, and even private firms. What had been fear among many Croatian Serbs turned to panic.

Belgrade's official television, the key instrument in Milosevic's strategy of fear, gave those events a sinister echo. In the peak viewing hours, for more than a year before the outbreak of fighting, news programs and special TV features were dominated not only by the loud commentary on the moves of the new Croatian government, but also by detailed reports and reruns of attacks by Croatian extremists—routinely referred to as "Ustashe"—on Serb property in Croatia: houses, apartments, restaurants, shops, farms. The screen was full of images of shattered roofs, windows, garages, broken furniture and china, destroyed orchards, and dead pets. Panel discussions orchestrated to warn of the imminent extermination of Serbs in Croatia crammed the programming. *Genocide* became a household word in the offical television vocabulary, and panels of experts and citizens, invited to discuss the events before TV viewers, continuously warned that Serbs faced annihilation similar to that of World War II.

Thus the course of events following Franjo Tudjman's election seemed to be almost tailor-made for Milosevic's propaganda machine. Every new step of the new Croatian president appeared to have been, paradoxically, designed to consolidate Milosevic's main point: that the Serbs in Croatia could never again feel safe. It followed that if Croatia continued insisting on leaving Yugoslavia, all Croatian regions with a significant Serbian population would have to be joined to Serbia. By the spring of 1991, it was no longer relevant that such claims were widely exaggerated. Even some Belgrade intellectuals had embraced them as self-evident.

What was relevant was that the events in Croatia after Tudjman's election easily lent themselves to fueling the collective perception in the Serb community of acute, palpable, and inherent danger hovering like a dark cloud over the home of each individual Serb in Croatia. The absence of police investigation or court action in actual cases of violence against individual Serbs or their property was yet another factor in making the Serb community feel under attack and completely unprotected. The international community maintained its silence. It was during these months that armed extremist groups from Serbia—the Seseljites, Arkanites, Dusan Silni, Beli Orlovi, and others—began to infiltrate the Serb communities in Croatia, fanning the national paranoia already aflame and urging the Serb population to arm.

In those early spring days of 1991 many people in settlements with a Serb majority in Croatia woke up to find armed Serb civilians at the entrance routes to their towns and villages. The barricades placed to prevent the entrance of Croat militias created a cold war atmosphere in Croatia a full six months before the actual fighting began. Borovo Selo, with its Serb majority, was quick to set up its own roadblocks, to elect its own local authorities, and to appoint its own armed guards. An agreement was reached with Croatian authorities officially banning entry to Borovo Selo to any Croat police without the explicit permission of the local Serb authorities.

On May 1, 1991, two Croat police in a marked police car entered Borovo Selo without permission. They were immediately arrested. On May 2, the Croatian authorities sent some twenty police to liberate them. Their vehicle was met by a shower of gunfire from Serb irregulars, some local, some from Serbia. The Croatian authorities then sent in 150 policemen in buses as reinforcements. All the requirements were present for a fierce, armed confrontation. The casualties included seventeen dead.

Three versions were immediately provided of the incident. Totally contradictory interpretations from different sources were to become the rule later. The first version was sent out by the newly formed official Croatian news agency, HINA: Croatian police numbering 150 had come to Borovo Selo for a meeting agreed to by both sides. They encountered a barrage of gunfire from the local population and terrorists from Serbia. Twelve "guardians of law and order" and fifteen residents were killed on the spot.

The second version was put together by journalists from statements by local residents: the police entered the village and began shooting at everything that moved. Thirteen police and one local man were killed. The police took women and children as hostages, but the local people, without any outside help, freed the hostages and defeated the police.

A third version was given live on Belgrade television. It was taped by self-appointed Chetnik commander Vojislav Seselj and shown several times: fourteen of Seselj's men had led the battle against "the Ustashe." Fighting with Seselj's boys were six local men and two members of the National Renewal Party from Nova Pazova, a town just outside Belgrade. According to Seselj, one civilian and one hundred Croatian policemen died.

The number and the identity of the dead are not known to this day in either Croatia or Serbia. But the event, marking the beginning of the Croatian war, projects a nutshell image of the overall scene of war. On the one side, Borovo Selo, like many other predominantly Serb localities in Croatia, had already been flooded by paramilitary, ultranationalist groups from Serbia. These groups had set about organizing and arming local Serb irregulars and raising the temperature in the town to the boiling point. This suited well the authorities in Belgrade. The authentic fears of ordinary Serbs served as the ultimate justification for the true intention of the Milosevic regime—to provoke a war that would lead to the changing of borders between Serbia and Croatia and thus to expand Serbia's territory.

On the other side, a Croatian police patrol entering Borovo Selo in violation of a previously reached agreement may be interpreted as a Croat provocation meant to destroy, in the already heated atmosphere, any remaining trust between the Serb and Croat communities. The loss of mutual trust would be an important asset for Tudjman since it would make the secession of Croatia more acceptable even to those Croats who did not fully agree with secession or accept his policy of "freeing Croatians from the Ustashe complex." Tudjman's propaganda machine had already insistently equated the escalating Serbian nationalism with what it labeled "Bolshevism," and Bolshevism, Tudjman had reiterated many times, was responsible for the subordinated position suffered by Croatia in Yugoslavia since 1945. According to Tudjman, Tito's Bolshevism had cost Croatians their national pride as well as a large part of their national product, which had gone to support the Bolshevik federation dominated by Serbia. Milosevic's Bolshevism had brought roadblocks and guns to peaceful Croatian towns and villages. The only alternative for Croatia was secession. Fully aware that war was the price that would have to be paid for secession, Tudjman, like Milosevic, had no qualms about accepting war. Their objectives converged. After Borovo Selo war seemed inevitable.

The late spring and early summer of 1991 were marked by a series of futile meetings at which both Milosevic and Tudjman were present to discuss "avoiding" war. The last such meeting took place on June 6, 1991. It was a meeting, like so many before it, of the presidents of the remaining Yugoslav federal republics. Kiro Gligorov, president of the republic of Macedonia, and Alija Izetbegovic, president of the republic of Bosnia-Hercegovina, tabled a proposal for forming a community of independent republics of Yugoslavia. Tudjman, Milosevic, and Milan Kucan, president of the republic of Slovenia, rejected it outright. The Serbian leadership had already turned down proposals for a Yugoslav confederation.

In truth, no proposal to save Yugoslavia could have won the support of all the parties. By the summer of 1991 it was entirely clear that Slovenia and Croatia wanted nothing less than independence from Yugoslavia, and they had support abroad, especially from Germany and Austria. It was equally clear that Serbia would not accept their departure peacefully, that is, it would use their departure to advance its own ends.

European leaders did nothing for virtually six months after the Yugoslav crisis had entered its critical stage. When they did finally realize that the crisis was not heading for a resolution, they embarked on diplomacy, but their effort lacked coherence, strategy, and real authority. Most important, their diplomacy never came to grips with the fundamental problem of the Yugoslav situation: the "Serbian question." Of eight million Serbs in former Yugoslavia, three million lived outside Serbia, notably in Croatia and Bosnia-Hercegovina. The only way to resolve the situation in 1990, at the time it was still possible, was for the international community to require that personal, political, cultural, and all other rights of minorities be firmly guranteed in every state seeking secession. Had such guarantees been obtained from Croatia, the wind would have been knocked out of Milosevic's sails. His claim that the breakup of Yugoslavia spelled genocide for the Serbs would have been significantly undermined. And it was this claim that lay at the core of his war ideology.

Milorad Pupovac, a Serb professor of linguistics at Zagreb University and president of the antinationalist Serbian democratic movement in Croatia, tried in every possible way to bring some sanity to the situation and establish dialogue between Croatian Serbs and Croats. His efforts were in vain as official Zagreb and Belgrade vilified him for his conciliatory politics. Both accused him of being the agent of the other side. Belgrade and Zagreb mirrored each other's climate at the dawn of the war. Both did everything to neutralize, or to physically eliminate, all those who stood in the way of war.

On June 25, 1991, the parliament of the republic of Croatia unanimously adopted a declaration proclaiming the independence and full sovereignty of the republic of Croatia and setting in motion procedures for ending its union with Yugoslavia. The unanimity was achieved in the absence of the parliament's Serb representatives, who had walked out of the session in protest.

On June 25, 1991, the republic of Slovenia also declared its independence. To make sure it was understood they meant business, Slovenian leaders promptly ordered a change of signs at the border crossings with Austria and Italy—from "Yugoslavia" to "Slovenia." This was a strong act of defiance, meant as an unequivocal provocation to Yugoslavia.

At that time twenty thousand Yugoslav army troops were stationed in Slovenia. Of that number only one thousand were mobilized after the change of signs at the borders. An additional army contingent was sent from southern Serbia and another one from

Croatia—to demonstrate to Croatia that the Yugoslav People's Army was ready to snap into action whenever necessary. In those last days of June and early July, television satellites transmitted to the world pictures of what essentially was a ten-day war for the borders.

The international community assumed that Milosevic, by sending troops to Slovenia to protect the border crossings, was trying to save Yugoslavia. But as it became clear in retrospect, the oppposite was the case. Far from wanting to force Slovenia to remain in Yugoslavia, Milosevic made sure Slovenia would end up being cut off. He placed on the battleground the troops whose number was strikingly inadequate for the alleged job of keeping the borders intact. Milosevic knew that with Slovenia gone, the balance of forces between the remaining members of the Yugoslav federation would have shifted in his favor. Mobilizing troops in Slovenia in the first place was a game designed to support his rhetoric of preserving Yugoslavia.

The war in Slovenia was televised from the beginning. For public consumption, the Yugoslav People's Army, the fourth strongest in Europe, ended up defeated in ten days by Slovenia's own Territorial Defense Forces. On July 8, 1991, a truce was negotiated between Slovenia and Yugoslavia. Slovenia continued on its way to independence. In the background, unseen on the television screens, armed Serbs and Croats had their sights on each other. The Croatian war, about to begin, would claim twenty thousand lives, in contrast to the Slovenian war, in which the total of eight Slovenian civilians were killed.

The murder of Josip Reichl-Kir on July 1, 1991, the young chief of police in Osijek, the largest town in eastern Croatia, offered another proof that neither Croatia nor Serbia was interested in calming the hysteria of fear among the common citizens in the two republics. Tudjman himself had appointed young Reichl-Kir to this sensitive position in the town with a significant Serb population. But as it turned out, Reichl-Kir, like Pupovac, was one of those people who realized that the final hour had come for people of authority to speak out and make every effort to defuse the tensions. In an attempt to build on the remaining vestiges of trust between the Croats and Serbs, Reichl-Kir visited the smaller towns and villages of his district, meeting with representatives of local

Serbs, reassuring the Serbs that his forces would guarantee their safety, and asking them to remove the roadblocks and allow normal traffic through the region. The murderer of Reichl-Kir, as it turned out, was not a Serb but a Croat, the president, furthermore, of HDZ in Tenja, a village near Osijek to be completely destroyed and abandoned only a few months later. HDZ did not favor Reichl-Kir's pacifism. The murder gave a clear signal to the Croatian community in eastern Slavonia that, as far as HDZ was concerned, there would be no peace with the Serbs. On their part, Serb extremists were strengthening their own nationalist campaign in eastern Slavonia. They made sure to remind everyone who might have forgotten that Serbs in Osijek lost their jobs following the HDZ electoral victory and that, unless they armed themselves, Serbs would now lose their lives too.

For the rank-and-file Serb in eastern Croatia, the idea of a "Greater Serbia" meant nothing. It was their fear for survival that made those Serbs paranoid and bitterly aggressive. The opposition in Belgrade had from the start made a point of this inbred, existential fear among Serbs and the use that the ultranationalists were making of it to achieve their ends. The fear was rooted in the Serbian collective memory of their persecution by Croats during World War II. Until 1990 those memories had remained at bay, but not, as is often claimed in the West, because they were forcibly suppressed. On the contrary, past horrors had lost their edge, precisely because generation after generation had grown up in a Yugoslavia where few believed another genocide was thinkable. In that context the shock of new ultranationalism proved even more deadly, and the fears even greater.

Serb nationalist extremists, brought from the outside into the small towns such as Glina, a town about forty miles south of Zagreb, did everything to shatter the unity of the multinational Croatian Democratic Party, a party with strong support among local Serbs. The people of Glina had particularly terrible memories of World War II. In 1941, the Ustashe massacred eight hundred Glina Serbs in a single day, by locking them up in the town's Orthodox church and setting the church ablaze. Nevertheless, for forty-five years after the war, Serbs and Croats in Glina had lived in harmony as neighbors.

On June 26, 1991, a group of Serb extremists attacked the

police station in Glina. The attack was not carried out by the local Serbs but instead by the "Marticevci," an imported group of Serb extremists from Knin, in the remote south of Croatia. The group had been active for months, infiltrating local institutions, spreading alarming rumors about the plans of the Croatian government, provoking intolerance, and, as always, handing out firearms.

Otherwise, the Knin Serbs had been the first, back in August 1990, to set up roadblocks of fresh-cut trees at the entrances to their towns and villages. Knin is an economically unproductive region, with no agriculture or industry to speak of. Since World War II, the Knin region has lived off its three thousand railroad workers. But the town of Knin gives the region immense strategic importance: it is the railroad junction through which all railroad lines must pass to reach the Dalmatian coast and its important Adriatic port, Split. This geographic advantage has never brought riches to anybody, but Tudjman knew that without Knin, Croatia's tourist industry would be crippled. For this reason, one of his first tasks on getting elected was to bring the Knin region under strict control of Zagreb.

The first organized Serb demonstrations for equality in Croatia had occurred in the summer of 1989 in Knin. This was just after an article recognizing Serbian as the language of the Serbs in Croatia had been deleted, under HDZ pressure, from the draft of the new republican constitution of Croatia within the federation of Yugoslavia. In response to the unrest of that summer, Croatian authorities arrested and threatened the local Serb leadership. The Serbs from the Kninska Krajina in southwestern Croatia, many of whom had joined the nationalist Chetniks in World War II, took the Croatian government's harsh response to their protests as a signal that the government intended to suppress Serbian culture and deny all rights to the Serb community in Croatia. That Tudjman and the HDZ had prevailed in Croatia in 1990 was confirmation for the Knin Serbs of the renewal, right before their eyes, of the Ustashe movement. They felt that that movement had to be stopped, immediately and by all means. A local dentist, Milan Babic, and a local police inspector, Milan Martic, took things into their own hands. These were men closed to compromise, insensitive to finesse and nuance, and bellicose in the extreme. From total anonymity, they shot to the top of the Serbian political scene. Generously supplied with weaponry by Slobodan Milosevic, they soon turned out to be his extended arm in Croatia.

The Knin character has its roots in the seventeenth and eighteenth centuries, when Serbs, invited by the Habsburgs, started settling in the region, then part of the Habsburg Empire. Serbs were offered sanctuary from Turkish persecution and were given land in exchange for military obligations to the Habsburg monarchy. In this way, the Habsburgs built a human fortress, the military frontier, or Vojna Krajina, against encroachment by the Turks, and a local frontier culture developed. The rules of war became the rules of life; honor, dignity, and heroism were measured in military terms. While the Serb peasants in Serbia were on the whole peaceable, the Knin Serbs were armed freemen owing military service and allegiance to the Habsburg monarchy. They could be called to serve anywhere. By the nineteenth century many were stationed permanently as part of the regular forces of the different military districts. The descendants of these Serbs gradually came to speak the Croatian variant of Serbo-Croatian and to accept the customs of the local Croatian population, even though they did not convert to Catholicism, despite the animus of the Catholic church. Today, except in their churches, there is virtually no visible difference between the Krajina Serbs and the Croats with whom they have lived; in language, in dress and behavior, in the internal and external appearance of their homes, and in the way they bring up their children, they are indistinguishable.

But in the nineteenth century, in contrast to the Croats whose loyalty was with their own government, the Krajina Serbs were subjects to three ruling powers: Austrian, Hungarian, and Croatian. What suited the Habsburg monarchy did not always suit the local Croatian viceroy. Scattered throughout Croatia, the Serbs, whose military ethos the Habsburgs encouraged, were viewed as a thorn in the side of the Croatian authorities. The status of an unwelcome minority whose relevance to the Habsburgs was only as a military tool conditioned the emergence in the Krajina of a Serbian culture quick to take offense, intolerant, and bellicose.

The "Martic men," *Marticevci,* as Milan Martic's followers came to be called by 1990, struck terror in the non-Serb population of the Krajina. As their paramilitaries made advances, villages emptied, the villagers not even taking the time to lock their homes before fleeing. And the Martic men robbed the homes, locked or unlocked, from cellar to attic. Most of the booty ended up on a burgeoning black market.

Looting was soon the principal motive for going to war for many irregulars, in the Krajina and elsewhere. A Serb from Miokovici, in eastern Croatia, told me how, first, all sorts of self-proclaimed politicians had appeared in his small village and promised the Serbs everything short of "pie in the sky": "'We will beat the Croats and then wherever Serbs live will be Serbia,' they told us. I don't deny that I myself did some shooting, but the worst crimes were committed by the irregulars who came in from Serbia. First they looted the homes of Croats. When they came back a second time they started looting Serb houses, because the Croat houses had already been robbed clean. Now we are being blamed for the murder of all those Croats. We will never be able to go back home again."

Just as they did not loot only Croats, Serbian irregulars did not strike fear only in Croats. Innumerable Serbs in Croatia were against the war and refused to be mobilized and to be turned against their Croat neighbors. For this, many paid with their lives. Many, under explicit threat that their families would be wiped out, ended up putting on a uniform. They became a part of that tragic panorama of war.

There were instances also of Serbs and Croats fighting side by side against either Croatian or Serbian attacks on their homes. Sometimes they fled together. Another villager from Miokovici told me that in August 1991 the Yugoslav army came to the village, handed out weapons, and left an old tank: "They told us to defend our village and that army officers and soldiers would come to help us. For six months we didn't see one regular army officer or soldier. Some of the villagers were killed. Croats from our village fought with us. They were defending their homes just as we were. For the whole time, we stayed in Miokovici. We didn't fight on any front. After these six months, we were ordered to evacuate the village for resettlement in Bosnia. The fighting hadn't started yet in Bosnia. So we left, in a huge column, and we finally reached Banja Luka. About twenty kilometers before Banja Luka, we were met by Serbian Radicals [members of the party of Vojislav Seselj in Serbia] and they took all our money and anything else of value on us, like our weapons, even hunting rifles. They gave us some sort of worthless receipts. With us were the Croats who had fought alongside us. But in Banja Luka, they separated us. I have never been able to learn where the others were taken, to find even a trace of them. I only know for sure that they didn't dare return to Croatia because they would be shot for fighting for their village on our side."

Vukovar was Croatia's Sarajevo—a town under siege and bombardment by the Yugoslav army and Serbian paratroops for four months. Vukovar lies on the Croatian side of the Danube River. Some of the best restaurants used to be situated on the green banks of the river. Belgrade is about eighty kilometers downstream, and the Hungarian border half as many upstream. From early August to late November 1991, the old baroque center of Vukovar, like the rest of the town, came under constant shelling by the Yugoslav army and the Serbian paramilitary formations. For months, the people of Vukovar lived in cellars. Any attempt to leave their shelters was made at the risk of death. The main hospital was moved into its own cellar. On November 20, with the "liberation"—the Serbs' term for their siege of Vukovar—finally over, its people came out of the cellars and into the light of day. Before them was a scene of total devastation. Out in the streets, their feet sank into the rubble of broken bricks, crumbled plaster, shattered glass. All around were twisted iron, the remnants of wood supports, beams, and decorative elements scorched by the fire of exploding shells. The homes were without roofs, walls, doors, or windows. Vukovar was a ghost town.

Numerous defenders of Vukovar were executed after the town fell. Many others disappeared. Some were deported into Serbia. Many nineteen-year-old Yugoslav army recruits sincerely believed they were risking their lives on the Vukovar front for the true liberation of Vukovar. But in the subsequent wave of attacks and murders, known as "ethnic cleansing," the rest of Vukovar's Croats were forced to leave. In their place, Serbs from eastern Croatia, themselves refugees and homeless, moved in. Many had also lost close family. Others would be invalids for the rest of their lives. In Vukovar, a year after the "liberation," those people were still pushing wheelbarrows through the streets, searching through the rubble for perhaps an unbroken plate or a piece of wire usable to put together an electric heater to get them through the coming winter.

In November 1991, Dubrovnik followed Vukovar. Neither Dubrovnik nor Vukovar was under siege nearly as long as Sarajevo, nor did either suffer comparable death and destruction. But old Dubrovnik was dear to Yugoslavs as their most splendid city, internationally known as the "Pearl of the Adriatic." Yugoslav army artillery inflicted considerable damage on the Old City and was much more destructive in the surrounding newer districts. Konavoski Dvori, a small, agriculturally rich, and culturally distinct strip of about twenty kilometers along the coast toward the nearby border with Montenegro, was the real victim. Here the destruction was total. Serbian and Montenegrin irregulars and Yugoslav army reservists went on a rampage, sparing nothing and nobody. Resistance was out of the question; the predominantly Croat population fled in its entirety. Small villages and farms were plundered, and everything from television sets to cows and chickens was carried off. The pillaged homes and farms were burned to the ground, fire was set to fields and orchard, and livestock were killed in huge numbers. Konavoski Dvori burned for days. Along the coast, luxury hotels were destroyed, and only the ashes remained of one-hundred-year-old palm trees, silver pines, and the bougainvillea that used to fall in cascades down steep banks to the shore.

With Dubrovnik the Croatian war entered a new stage, for which no rational explanation could be furnished. No apparent political or military gains for Serb attacking forces could be discerned. The destruction in Dubrovnik placed the full irrationality and capriciousness of the fighting in the Balkans before the eyes of the world. Television zoomed in on the wanton destruction. Viewers who had visited Dubrovnik years earlier and had photographs of themselves taken beside the walls of its Renaissance palaces could now see the smoke rising out of the Old City and the holes opened in its old fortifications by the Yugoslav army artillery. And the world finally realized that something terrible was happening in the Balkans.

Croatian allegations of Serb primitivism, Bolshevism, and brutality, of Serbia's determination to dominate and of its expansionist ambitions sounded closer and closer to the truth with each shell that hit Dubrovnik. And each shell was a contribution to international support for the recognition of Croatia's independence.

With the December 1991 international recognition of Croatia a done deal, Slobodan Milosevic perhaps realized the extent to which he had helped his archenemy Franjo Tudjman to international victory. Milosevic chose war, convinced it was his best means to consolidate his power as the defender of all Serbs. Yet, as Mirko Klarin, *Borba*'s Brussels correspondent wrote at the time, having chosen war Milosevic became Tudjman's most precious enemy. Wanton violence perpetrated by the Serb forces eclipsed the violence of the Croat side. As the bloodshed in Croatia advanced and the world witnessed the destruction of Vukovar and Dubrovnik, the war increasingly came to resemble an orgy of drunken criminals and insane generals. Tudjman, who had done his share to bring about the war, was acutely aware of the extent to which Serb aggression boosted his chances to gain international recognition. Tudjman stubbornly denied Vukovar any military support, abandoning it to the Serb attacks and, effectively, condemning it to death; he sacrificed the town for the benefit of favorable publicity. His was a high-risk game, the kind of game that made sense only under the condition that for its final objective—independence— no price was considered too high.

The Serb forces behaved according to Tudjman's expectations, to the point of madness. This effectively concealed that Serb towns and villages throughout Croatia were being torched and razed too by the HDZ supporters and other right-wing paratroops; that scores of Serbs were massacred from Gospic, Daruvar, Karlovac, Virovitica, Sisak, Ogulin, and other towns; and that a half million Serb civilians had to abandon their homes to escape Croatian reprisals. Milosevic's ruthless offensive on Croatia consolidated the perception abroad of Serbs as nothing but aggressors. The world public could no longer be expected to see Serb civilians as victims needing protection.

This was Milosevic's stupendous favor to Tudjman. Milosevic created an opportunity for Tudjman to insist—Serbian victims notwithstanding—that only international recognition would save bleeding Croatia. Milosevic indeed made it possible for flagrant human rights violations perpetrated by Tudjman's forces to be disregarded by the international community. Counting that the recognition of Croatia would stop Serb advances, the international community recognized Croatia's sovereignty in violation of its own principle that for recognition the human rights record must be clean. The "Serbian question," the question at the root of the war, however, not only remained unresolved but had been greatly exacerbated with the creation of Serb-held territories in the heart of the independent Croatian state, which now has no control over them. The territories are unviable, politically and economically unsustainable in every respect. And every Serb in Croatia today feels infinitely more threatened than at any time since World War II.

As for the international community, its diplomatic activity had been predicated on its own mythology of the Croatian war as a war between the Communist, Serb side and the democratic, Croat side. Refusing to see this war for what it truly was—a calculated, brutal venture involving two criminal regimes—a venture from which both hoped to profit, the international community itself contributed to the conflagration. Worse, having recognized Croatia, the international community left Bosnia-Hercegovina between a rock and a hard place. Alija Izetbegovic, president of Bosnia-Hercegovina, was faced with only two possibilities: to either seek independence himself or to join Milosevic's Yugoslavia. Both options were fatal.

EIGHT

Bosnia and Hercegovina: The Second War

Ejub Štitkovac and Jasminka Udovički

In the summer of 1991, just before the war with Croatia began, a photograph was published in both the Serbian and Croatian mainstream press. The photograph was of the faintly smiling Slobodan Milosevic and Franjo Tudjman, flanking Bosnia's president Alija Izetbegovic as they walk on an empty, sunny beach on the Adriatic; they are engaged in a conversation. A year later, Guido Pampoldi, a columnist for Rome's *La Repubblica,* wrote that the photograph, when he first saw it, struck him as being almost calming. "But now," Pampoldi added, "as I look at it again, it affects me differently. I now see in it the unsuspecting Bosnian being led towards the sea, by the two others, to be drowned. And as they are are taking him ever closer to the water's edge, they are calming him with their smiles."

In March of that year—four months before the Croatian war was to explode—the Serbian and Croatian leaders were linked in an unpublicized but firm alliance over Bosnia. The alliance was sealed in Karadjordjevo, a small estate north of Belgrade. Tito too had been fond of the place and used it to hold talks with his associates. This time, Milosevic and Tudjman, anticipating the approaching collapse of Yugoslavia, met in Karadjordjevo to discuss the future spoils. At stake was Bosnia-Hercegovina. More than a year earlier, in February 1990, Franjo Tudjman, at the time the head of the Croatian Democratic Union (HDZ), had publicly stated that Bosnia-Hercegovina was also a state of the Croatian people and that his plan for the future included expanding Croatia into Bosnia. Now, in March 1991, red pencils in hand, the Serbian and the Croatian presidents proceeded each to allot his own state a portion of Bosnian territory. For starters, this was a game on paper. Six months later, with the war business in Croatia over, the game of dividing Bosnia could start for real.

That Milosevic and Tudjman had been enemies in the Croatian war in 1991–1992 in no way changed either their intentions or their partnership in 1992 and after with regard to Bosnia. Their last handshake in Karadjordjevo in 1991 marked the beginning of the end of Bosnia, the republic that used to be a Yugoslavia in miniature: a tight amalgam of its different populations. The stability of the multiethnic Bosnia had always been considered the reflection of and the guarantee for the stability of Yugoslavia as a whole. To destabilize Bosnia and incite strife among its Serbs, Muslims, and Croats meant to bring into question Yugoslavia itself—a common person knew it just as well as the leaders did.

That is why by the end of 1991 many Yugoslavs were gripped by a chilling fear: that the Croatian war, still ongoing, could easily turn out to have been a mere dress rehearsal for a much more complicated and bloody conflict in Bosnia-Hercegovina. Alija Izetbegovic knew that with the international recognition of Croatia in January 1992, he was being forced to face a terrible dilemma: to follow in the path of Slovenia and Croatia and seek secession for his republic, or to resign himself to an alliance with Slobodan Milosevic and remain in rump Yugoslavia. The president of Bosnia-Hercegovina, in an interview, compared this choice to the choice between leukemia and a brain tumor.

Still, regarding the likelihood of a war in Bosnia, Izetbegovic saw things his own way. If the Croatian war was a rehearsal, he calculated, it had been a poor one indeed. The Yugoslav army, in service of Serbia, had virtually failed in its efforts to draft troops for the war in 1991. In overwhelming numbers draft-age men emigrated or went into hiding—between 150,000 and 200,000 in all. In addition, Izetbegovic thought, a unanimous world condemnation and the economic sanctions had weakened Serbia. And, he reckoned, under such circumstances Serbia would not dare to venture into an incomparably more difficult and costly adventure in Bosnia-Hercegovina.

Regarding the possibility of a war in Bosnia, other Bosnian figures were much more keenly aware of the imminent danger. Adil Zulfikarpasic, the descendant of an old and distinguished Muslim family and the leader of the Muslim Bosnian Organization (MBO), discerned before many others the full and terrible dimensions of a potential conflict with Serbia. Zulfikarpasic considered an independent Bosnia-Hercegovina a dangerous fiction. He warned before the Bosnian elections were to take place in 1990 that the war in Bosnia-Hercegovina, if it ever broke out, would be a war "to destroy an entire nation and to cleanse the territory of its Muslims ... it is not an exaggeration to say it would lead to their total extermination." To avoid the catastrophe, Zulfikarpasic advocated making some kind of agreement with the Serbs instead of pouring fuel on fire by seeking international recognition for Bosnia.

Zulfikarpasic was aware of the effects of Milosevic's propaganda, successful as it had been in instilling in the Serb population a genuine and haunting fear of being cast adrift from Serbia in the event of the breakup of Yugoslavia. Should Croatia and Bosnia become independent, Milosevic's propaganda machine beamed, the Serbs outside Serbia would find themselves at the mercy of hostile regimes, Croatian and Bosnian. To a common Serb on the street Milosevic's slogan "All Serbs in one state" seemed to express concern for the future of Serbs living outside the borders of Serbia. Zulfikarpasic recognized the power of the appeal to Serbian unity and knew that one should tread very carefully to avoid exacerbating the tensions. He was also aware that while the slogan "All Serbs in one state" appeared patriotic to the frightened Serb masses in Bosnia, once accepted, it gave Milosevic license to seek to fulfill ambitions that had little to do with the genuine concern for the unprotected Serbs or with patriotism. To bring all Serbs into one state after Yugoslavia had fallen apart, Milosevic would have to demand the expansion of Serbia's borders; and since historically few borders had ever been altered by peaceful means, the idea itself of joining all Serbs in the same borders was nothing but a war cry. Zulfikarpasic understood this, but few common Serbs did, and neither did Izetbegovic. That was in part the reason that Zulfikarpasic's group of moderates broke away from the Party of Democratic Action (SDA), Alija Izetbegovic's party, two months before the Bosnian elections.

The ethnic makeup of Bosnia's 4.5 million people made the region a powder keg. It was composed of 43.7 percent Muslims; 31.4 percent Serbs; 17.3 percent Croats; and 5.5 percent of those who considered themselves Yugoslavs. Participating in the elections of November 1990 in Bosnia were numerous mini-parties and five larger ones. Two of the larger parties, Party of Democratic Change and Alliance of Reform Forces, were derived from the liberal wing of the former Communist elite and were multiethnic or "Yugoslav." The other three larger ones—the Muslim Party for Democratic Action, the Serbian Democratic Party (SDS), and the Croatian Democratic Union (HDZ)—were parties advocating nationalistic programs. The Serbian and the Croatian nationalist parties in particular each had its own belligerent and extremist wing warning of the imminent civil war in Bosnia. The Serbian SDS extremists warned of the Muslim-Croat conspiracy, or rather "the Khomeini-Ustashe" conspiracy, as this fiction was referred to, against the Serbs. The Croat HDZ extremists, in turn, warned of the Orthodox Serb designs to swallow up Bosnia and insisted that Muslims and Croats must organize to prevent the disaster. The Muslim SDA for its part was divided between a faction loyal to the center-right Izetbegovic and the moderate one led by Zulfikarpasic. But in contrast to the Serb and Croat extremists, Izetbegovic argued that Bosnia must remain one and proposed that a coalition government in Sarajevo, representing all three parties, would be the answer.

Virulent electoral propaganda of the Serb and Croat extremists proved successful in dividing the Bosnian voters, as reflected in the demographics of the vote: each of the three nationalist parties won wherever their ethnic group was in the majority. This was not so much because the Bosnians—be they Serbs, Croats, or Muslims—supported nationalism. But frightened and disoriented, people believed that unless they voted for the party representing their own nation, the other two would prevail—and that spelled danger in a way few could fully articulate at that point.

After the elections, the three nationalist parties loudly proclaimed their elected members would govern in partnership and in the interest of all. Alija Izetbegovic was elected president of the multiethnic Bosnian presidency, but the pressure from Serbia and Croatia made real partnership impossible. Party flags went up in the centers of towns and villages; graffiti of the party's symbols were painted on private homes and public buildings; loyal party cadre was placed in municipal offices.

National fragmentation in the election was the first step to the tearing apart of Bosnia-Hercegovina. Only thirty percent of its territory had ever been ethnically homogeneous; all the rest was mixed. A striking one-fourth of all marriages in Bosnia-Hercegovina involved people of different nationalities. Trying to convey this to a foreign reporter in 1993, Salim Kovacevic, a Muslim seriously wounded by the Serbs during the evacuation of his small Muslim village of Kotorsko, put it this way: "Here you ask me if hatreds between the Yugoslav peoples are something very old. Let me ask you something first." Kovacevic stared the reporter straight in the eye. "Do you love your wife?" The startled reporter nodded yes, and Salim responded: "And why do you suppose we in Bosnia marry each other? Couldn't be because we hate each other, could it? Have you ever heard of anyone marrying out of hatred? We aren't that different from you, you know."

Religion did not divide the people of Bosnia-Hercegovina either. For centuries, Muslim, Catholic, and Orthodox houses of worship faced each other on the squares of Bosnian towns. The Muslims, especially, were not very devoted. Few had ever read the Koran, fasted for Ramadan, or made pilgrimage to Mecca. Services at the mosques were attended mostly by the elderly. A saying was commonly heard: "There'll be time to go to mosque; wait till you get old." Therefore, in the more recent times, being Muslim used to be more an expression of national identity than a statement of faith. The Turks who had brought Islam to Bosnia during the Ottoman Empire had not been proselytizers. Although they often forbade the construction of new churches and monasteries, they destroyed neither and refrained from persecuting Christians and Jews. Accepting Islam, admittedly, was a requirement for advancement into the higher echelons of the Ottoman society. A great number of Serbs and Croats converted, some of them eventually joining either the military or the administrative elite. And although it was not unusual in former Yugoslavia for a Muslim, by origin most likely a Slav, to be teasingly greeted by a friend on the street with "Hi, Turk," the differences between the Muslims, Croats, and Serbs used to be slight indeed.

But in October 1991, following the elections, the Muslim and Croatian legislators approved the eventual secession of Bosnia-Hercegovina from Yugoslavia—the move that accelerated the dissolution of unity of the three Bosnian ethnic groups. The Serb legislators took no part in the decision and instead walked out of the session in protest. On November 9 and 10, the Serbian leadership organized a plebiscite among the Serb population in the republic; the only question on the referendum was secession. Ill adapted to plebiscites, which had no tradition in Tito's Yugoslavia; frightened by the ongoing war in Croatia; panic-stricken by the news of large-scale firing of Serbs in Muslim and Croat regions of Bosnia (even though the same, in reverse, had taken place in the Serb regions); and, finally, confused by Serb propaganda that Izetbegovic allegedly wanted a fundamentalist Muslim state for Bosnia, the common Serbs in Bosnia overwhelmingly voted to remain in Yugoslavia. Responding to the charge of Muslims and Croats that the plebiscite expressed the will of only one ethnic group in Bosnia, and not of all Bosnians, the Serb leaders defiantly pointed out that the 1990 referendum carried out in Croatia also reflected the will of only the majority Croats and not of the Croatian Serbs. Yet the European Community had recognized that referendum as valid and used it as a basis to grant independence to Croatia. Now then—Karadzic and others around him argued—the precedent had been set, and who dared say the plebiscitary will of the Bosnian Serbs was illegitimate?

On December 24, 1991, ignoring the plebiscite and the strong popular opposition among the Serbs, Alija Izetbegovic applied to the European Community for the recognition of independent Bosnia. Bosnia was to be sovereign, in his words "not a gram less, not a gram more" than Croatia or Serbia. The European Community responded that it would recognize Bosnia if the Bosnian people confirmed in a referendum that it was their will. The SDS leader Radovan Karadzic was livid. "The Muslims had started down the path that led Croatia to a hell," he asserted, "except the hell in Bosnia-Hercegovina will be one hundred times worse and will bring about the disappearance of the Muslim nation."

In insisting on a referendum, the European Community failed to adequately respond to the striking analogy between the situation in Bosnia-Hercegovina and that in Croatia on the eve of its conflagration. The European Community failed to comprehend that the "Serbian question," the question of the status of the Serb minority after secession, was the cardinal issue in Bosnia-Hercegovina, just as it has been in Croatia. In Bosnia-Hercegovina, the "Serbian question" was of course further exacerbated by a demographic factor of great importance: the percentage of Serbs in the total population of the republic was almost two and a half times greater than in Croatia. But acting as though this crucial fact was of no consequence, the European Community effectively encouraged the secession of Bosnia-Hercegovina. The Bosnian Serbs, a full one-third of the Bosnian population, through the plebiscite had already cast their hundred percent vote against secession. What the European Community was now indicating to them, in violation of the Bosnian constitution, was that their will was irrelevant.

Predictably, Radovan Karadzic called on the Bosnian Serbs to boycott the Bosnian referendum for independence, and they did. The Muslims and Croats voted and in February 1992 voiced their overwhelming support for secession. The next step would be, as promised, international recognition, the Trojan Horse of the Bosnian tragedy.

On January 9, 1992, SDS representatives had walked out of the republic's parliament, declared their autonomy, and proclaimed that they considered the laws of Bosnia-Hercegovina nonbinding. The Bosnian government, the Serbs insisted, no longer represented the Bosnian Serbs. The Bosnian Serb leaders had begun in 1991 to form throughout Bosnian territory what they called "Serb autonomous regions"—territories under exclusive jurisdiction of the Serbs. With this a new, important step had been taken toward war. Alija Izetbegovic, curiously, seemed to remain unperturbed and failed to take any action. In his statement to the press in early 1992 Izetbegovic said he believed there would be isolated incidents of hostilities but that "a general armed conflict will not erupt."

Only a week after the vote for independence in Bosnia, the Belgrade antiwar independent weekly *Vreme* reported that the Bosnian Serb leadership had decided to organize armed units in every Serb village and town in Bosnia. The article included details on the origin of arms destined for the towns and villages. The arms flow had begun back in 1990 and continued in 1991, as a part of the secret operation that became known under the acronym RAM, whose prime protagonist was a certain Mihalj Kertes, a Hungarian by origin, later to become chief of Milosevic's secret police. Kertes was a person who liked to say that he "owed everything he had achieved in life to Slobodan Milosevic" and that he was ready to die for the man. Under Kertes's command uncounted camouflaged trucks loaded with arms crossed from Serbia into Bosnia-Hercegovina.

The prime minister of Yugoslavia at the time, Ante Markovic, had publicly revealed the RAM operation as early as September 1991. His information came from a tapped telephone conversation between Milosevic and Karadzic in which RAM, Greater Serbia, and the Yugoslav army had all been mentioned. Having come into the possession of the tape, Markovic, a Croat strongly committed to Yugoslavia, accused the Yugoslav army of having "placed itself directly in the service of one side." Three months later, on December 20, 1991, after the 1992 Yugoslav budget assigned eighty-six percent of its total to the military, Markovic resigned.

This resignation, however, made no dent in Milosevic's hold on Serbia's public opinion. Organized buildup of arms and food reserves in Bosnian Serb towns and villages went on. Reporting in December on the Serb mobilization for war in the town of Banja Luka, *Vreme* described Bosnia-Hercegovina as rapidly becoming quicksand. But Izetbegovic gave no indication of hearing. He reckoned that despite everything, Serbia would have to knuckle under to international pressure and abandon its plan of expansion into Bosnia-Hercegovina. Izetbegovic seemed convinced that Bosnia-Hercegovina could achieve independence despite the war designs of the Serb leadership.

On March 18, 1992, in Lisbon, Serbs, Croats, and Muslims agreed to a draft document, the "Cutilheiro plan," organizing Bosnia-Hercegovina into three territorial units, or cantons, ensuring that all three national groups would partake in the power sharing. Croats, whose President Tudjman held talks in January with the Bosnian Serb leader Nikola Koljevic regarding the partition of

Bosnia between Serbs and Croats, were in favor of cantons. So of course were the Serbs. Yet Alija Izetbegovic, who first said yes, changed his mind shortly after he returned to Sarajevo and reneged on the agreement.

On March 1, 1992, violence had erupted at a Serb wedding party in the predominantly Muslim section of Sarajevo. Serb flags were waved at the wedding, and a gunmen, who remained unidentified, fired at the celebrating crowd, killing the groom's father and wounding a guest. This was a spark that set Bosnia aflame. Immediately, barricades—first Serb, then Muslim—sprang up in Sarajevo and elsewhere in Bosnia. But there was still a great deal of reluctance among the people guarding the barricades to engage in any "real" confrontation. The people, often neighbors, pulled stockings over their heads to hide their identity from one another. The Sarajevo raja—"the common folks" in a local, Turkish-derived colloquialism—even then could not believe that the tension would last. Indeed, it was not long, a mere couple of days in fact, before the barricades came down. "You're better looking without that stocking, believe me!" one neighbor was telling another. A song "A stocking on your face" had popped up during the barricade days, and it was sung for weeks afterward as neighbors from different sides once again sat together in local cafés.

On the first day of the barricades, the somber Karadzic and Izetbegovic both appeared on television informing the people that they, the people, had turned on one another. Shortly after Radovan Karadzic told foreign journalists that if Bosnian Muslims persisted in demanding secession from Yugoslavia, "you'll see blood up to the knees." Karadzic would soon prove he was not joking.

On the barricades shots had been fired, and there were more than ten people dead across the republic. But the Sarajevans found a way to speak out against everything the barricades represented. Throughout the city, neighborhood women set up "barbecue barricades" and "cheese pie barricades." To walk through, everyone had to take a bite, irrespective of nationality. Cigarette peddlers raised their "barricades," hawking their wares as available on credit. And even at the official barricades, Sarajevo's love of burlesque prevailed. When a Muslim barricade received warning of an imminent attack by the Serb Chetniks, and the Serbs failed to arrive, one of the masked barricade guards jumped up suddenly and yelled, provoking a round of hearty laughter: "Rajo, I'm off to make sure nothing's happened to the guys!"

The official barricades were gradually removed in the next two days, and tens of thousands took to the streets of Bosnia's towns shouting, "We want to live together." Similar demonstrations had already taken place in Sarajevo. In November 1991, an antiwar demonstration organized by workers in front of the parliament building in Sarajevo drew tens of thousands from all over Bosnia-Hercegovina. A huge crowd of workers, high school and university students, young women and men, and many elderly carried Tito's picture and banners with the "Brotherhood and Unity" slogan. The crowd was addressed by a miner from Tuzla, Izet Redzic. The workers of Bosnia-Hercegovina, he said, would not allow fratricidal war. "We won't give our sons to die for the purposes of others," he said. "We are workers, not soldiers. Our national identity is 'miner.'" Many people held the banner "Yugo, We Love You!"

This and several other antiwar demonstrations that shook Sarajevo during the last month before the siege fed Izetbegovic's belief that the destructive forces hovering over Bosnia-Hercegovina could not prevail. Yet the forces of the Yugoslav army had been greatly strengthened by a contingent transferred to Bosnia from the battlefields of Croatia. In the spring of 1992 the army, whose greatest contingent was now stationed in Bosnia, surrounded one by one all the larger towns in the republic. The army called the operation "military exercises."

President Izetbegovic visited none of the sites to investigate firsthand the "exercises" taking place throughout his republic. Eight months earlier he had shown greater realism. In September 1991, he had brought to the attention of the European Conference on Security and Cooperation in Europe that sixty percent of Yugoslavia's military industry was located in Bosnia-Hercegovina and that the larger part of the officer corps was stationed there. Izetbegovic had requested that the European Conference on Security and Cooperation in Europe use its influence to aid the dismantling of this military complex and to help start a retirement fund for the army officers, anxious at the prospect of being left without job and income. The retirement fund, he explained, would help prevent the army officers from joining the Serb side for fear of losing their jobs. The European Conference, however, ignored the appeal. The world also remained blind to the rapidly mounting tensions in Bosnia, pushing it over the brink of the abyss on April 6, 1992.

On April 6, the fifty-first anniversary of the day Belgrade was leveled by Hitler's bombardment, the European Community recognized the independence of Bosnia-Hercegovina, in violation of the Bosnian constitutional principle requiring the consent of all three Bosnian nations in far-reaching decisions such as secession. Thus the European Community effectively delivered Karadzic a pretext for war. The Serb leader had been supplied with an argument he could only have dreamt of: Karadzic could now claim to the Bosnian Serbs that foreign powers, in a familiar historical pattern, stood in the way of Serb self-determination. It was a powerful argument, and Karadzic exploited it to the maximum. The argument convinced many Serbs, those in Serbia and those in Bosnia-Hercegovina, for whom self-determination, for historical reasons, had special significance, that the war was legitimate and just. They were now on their own, Karadzic and Milosevic repeatedly proclaimed, and they had to "defend their families and their homes." The international recognition of Bosnia-Hercegovina marked the point of no return. Immediately, the slaughter began.

Radovan Karadzic apparently believed that Bosnia-Hercegovina could be conquered in six days. He had on his side not just Slobodan Milosevic in Belgrade but the fully equipped Yugoslav People's Army and the well-armed paramilitary formations, as a rule closely tied to the Belgrade government. The paramilitary units, such as the Tigers or the White Eagles, were overwhelmingly made up of marginal types, many motivated solely by the possibility of making quick money on the plunder of war. These irregulars were sent, or went on their own, to eastern Hercegovina, in the southeast of the former republic, or to the Krajina, around the northwest town of Banja Luka, which was proclaimed the center of the Serbian Republic of Bosnia and Hercegovina (Republika Srpska) on March 27, 1992.

Gunrunning in Bosnia-Hercegovina had been rampant since almost a year before the war began. In downtown Sarajevo, in front of the Grand Hotel Europa, petty thieves and smugglers offered pistols, small-caliber sniper rifles, Kalashnikovs, and bazookas. The dealing went on freely, as though potatoes and not guns were being traded. In the more conservative heartland the strategy was the following. In a village populated by a Serb majority the arms dealer would gather a group of better-off men and would warn them he had information that the Muslims of a neighboring village were preparing to attack. He would then offer arms for self-defense. The story would spread rapidly through the village. Not knowing what to believe, people would come to check out the sale. Seeing others buy, they would buy themselves. It seemed imprudent not to. Often, all arms would be gone in a day. The dealer would then move on to the neighboring, predominantly Muslim village, telling the same story, this time about the Serbs preparing the attack. Many people were borrowing money or selling livestock to buy a gun.

The dealers' stories could not have been as effective without the shooting and killing that started in Mostar as early as the fall of 1991 and in Bosanski Brod in early spring 1992. The Croatian war had spread to those two strategically important Bosnian towns much before the Bosnian war itself had begun. Bosanski Brod, laying just across the Sava River from the Croatian town of Slavonski Brod, was the first town in Bosnia-Hercegovina to be ruined in the Serb-Croat duels over Bosnia during March 1992.

In Mostar the fighting between the Serbs and Croats had begun even earlier, in the fall of 1991. Dating from Turkish times, Mostar was famous for its picturesque center and for its Old Bridge, built in 1566, joining the eastern and western banks of the Neretva River. In prewar Titoist Yugoslavia, Mostar was a favored site of the summer Olympics, the highlight of which was the daring attempts of local boys to dive from the bridge's eighty-foot-high peak into the green Neretva below. TV cameras traditionally filmed the event, and the whole of Yugoslavia watched. But in 1991, seven months before the actual start of the Bosnian war, the quiet of Mostar was broken by machine gun bursts and bomb explosions.

Mostar was the largest town in Hercegovina, thirty-five percent Muslim, thirty-four percent Croat, and nineteen percent Serb. Its misfortune was to be located on the line of confrontation between the Serb and Croat interests in the south of Bosnia-Hercegovina. The Croats felt that Mostar would eventually become the capital of their own mini-state, which they liked to call

"Herceg-Bosnia." During World War II the region, situated in western Hercegovina, had been a major Ustashe stronghold. In 1991 it again became the home of the most extremist Croat nationalists, providing the Serbs with the pretext to insist that Mostar remain within Yugoslavia. Only the Muslims felt that the town inseparably belonged to Bosnia-Hercegovina.

In late 1991 Serb spokesmen in Mostar had claimed that Croatian military units and their Muslim allies were attacking the Serb population; Serbs allegedly had to organize in self-defense. In December 1991, Mostar's municipal government requested that the city be demilitarized. The situation, however, was not in the hands of the city authorities but of armed and organized Serbs and Croats. Two infantry garrisons, an air force base and flight school, an army factory, and several thousand Serb and Croat reservists brought in from the outside remained entrenched. Machine gun fire and explosions shook the city incessantly, four months before the war in Bosnia-Hercegovina began officially.

The clashes between Serbs and Croats over Mostar was a bitter warning to the ordinary people that peace had become precarious and that Bosnia-Hercegovina was highly vulnerable. The common person's analysis of the situation was deeply conflicted. Intuitively, most Bosnians could not contemplate that an all-out war was possible in their republic. Yet the signs coming from Mostar and Bosanski Brod were alarming. In addition, the Serb areas in Bosnia-Hercegovina (the so-called SAO Krajinas), had proclaimed autonomy in the later half of 1991, and there was a great deal of clamoring about their annexation to Serbia in case of Bosnia's secession. This was deeply worrisome, indicating to many common people that they had to get ready for the worst.

Izetbegovic seemed to believe, by contrast, that Serb leadership would be satisfied with the autonomous territory it achieved without bloodshed and that hence there was little reason to believe there could be war. But if that is what he thought, Izetbegovic was overlooking an essential detail: the SAO Krajina territories were scattered, and what the Serb leaders had in mind was creating a territory with continuous borders. That insane objective, indeed, could not be realized without an armed conflict and without population dislocations. In addition, Milosevic's regime had a firm intention, in the event of the secession of Bosnia-Hercegovina, to capture the 18-mile-wide strip along the Bosnian side of the Drina River, separating Serbia from Bosnia. The strip would include, from north to south, the towns of Bijeljina, Zvornik, Bratunac, Srebrenica, Zepa, Rogatica, Visegrad, Gorazde, and Foca, as well as a number of smaller towns. In all of those towns fierce fighting started immediately after the beginning of the Bosnian war.

In early spring 1992, the fuse in Bosnia-Hercegovina was rapidly burning shorter. Only fear of war itself held Bosnia-Hercegovina together until April 1992.

In the final days of 1991, trenches for multibarrel artillery were discovered on Crepoljsko and Bukovik, hills on the outskirts of Sarajevo. Five months later the shelling of Sarajevo would begin from these hills. Yet no system of defense existed on the republic's or the city's part. Nobody in the Izetbegovic government had been charged with the defense of Sarajevo in case of war. When Serbian General Ratko Mladic ordered the artillery to launch fire on the city from the hills immediately following the international recognition of Bosnia-Hercegovina, Izetbegovic's government was thrown into total confusion.

Even after the outbreak of fighting, the people of Sarajevo could not believe that the war would last for more than a few weeks. That is why Sarajevo's Muslims, Jews, Croats, and Serbs alike resisted for a long time leaving the city. Muslims, Jews, and many Serbs shared the same view of Radovan Karadzic and Slobodan Milosevic, and most were equally horrified at the threat the Serb leadership had aimed at the Muslims: "If you choose war, you will disappear from the face of the earth."

Serb reservists arriving in Sarajevo in April and May 1992 were told that all Serbs had fled the city to "escape the terror of the fundamentalists." But every step of the way the reservists ran into Serbs determined to stay. That provoked much confusion in the minds of some soldiers. But a simple explanation was at hand, provided by the Serbian propaganda machine: the Serbs still in Sarajevo were "traitors to their people." Those "traitors" were treated no better than Muslims or Croats by the Serb commanders in the city. Zeljko Bajic, a Sarajevo Serb who before the war was editor of a magazine for the blind, wrote for *Borba,* the Belgrade independent daily, about his experience in his article "How I Was Liberated," which appeared in the last week of July 1992:

> My part of town, called "Aerodrom," was blocked on May 1. Snipers took up positions on all sides. One was nailed down to wherever one happened to be when the firing began. As of that day, the bread supply was cut off; we made do with whatever stores we had, believing the blockade would last only days.
>
> On May 7, Serb soldiers entered the neighborhood, among them many from the neighboring village. Shooting and shelling began on May 13 at dawn and lasted into late evening. We will remember that day because that's when electricity was cut off for ten days. That put an end to the supplies in our refrigerators and box freezers. From then on, until the day of our "liberation," we lived off flour, pasta, and rice. The telephones still worked and I called up friends to keep up their courage and mine.
>
> On Wednesday, June 17, the shelling and shooting started a little before 5 A.M. An hour later I heard loud swearing at our entry. A spray of machine gun fire broke the glass, and an armed man rushed up the stairwell shouting, "Surrender, or I'm throwing a grenade!" His machine gun burst around our front doors, at the hall walls and ceilings. We hurried out with arms up. We were lined up against our building with bullets flying in all directions. And then we were ordered to run, under the rain of infantry fire, into a building across the street. This scene I have dreamed repeatedly since. In the basement we found some fifty other people, men, women, and children. But it didn't last long: men were all ordered out.
>
> Some thirty of us men were crammed into a neighboring basement. One bearded soldier swore at us, calling us "fundamentalists" and "Turkish bastards." His superior entered and barked in disgust, "Toss 'em a couple of pears!" "Pears" was what they called hand grenades. But a few more soldiers came down and ordered arms up, to conduct a search. They found nothing.
>
> Different soldiers came and went all day. Some seemed nice, some mean. Just before night, two appeared bragging how they had "done in" "six each." In front of those, our guards too were meek.

The next morning my parents were allowed at their own risk to cross to our apartment and bring back what they needed most. They returned with the news that I had been liberated from my foreign currency cash and my reporter's tape recorder. The windows were all smashed, and the walls and furniture machine gunned.

Around noon we were told that nobody was forcing us to leave Aerodrom but that it would be leveled. After six days of constantly changing expectations and the wildest stories, the rumor went around that we would be allowed to return to our apartments. My mother was impatient and rushed home. My father didn't dare for fear he might be drafted. My mother came back on the verge of passing out. Everything, literally everything of any value, had been stolen. What's more, the soldiers threatened and swore at us, because here they were fighting on behalf of us Serbs, while we were having a good time.

If the Serb leaders were waging war for a "Greater Serbia," the irregulars and paramilitaries were fighting for the plunder. Once finished with a Muslim home, armed and often drunk irregulars turned on the Serb homes, terrorizing the occupants and carrying off everything they might later be able to sell. Some Serbs thought their property might be safe if they wrote on the walls fronting the street: "Don't touch. This is a Serb house." They soon understood that the plunderers were ethnically color-blind.

Serbs who did not come over actively to the Serb side, who continued their friendly relations with Muslim neighbors or tried to protect them openly, were "traitors" and targets of attacks of all kinds. Srdjan Aleksic, an actor from Trebinje, was one of those "bad Serbs," trying to defend his friend Alen, a Muslim and orphan since childhood. Not only was he unable to save his friend, but two days later he himself died at the Trebinje hospital from the beating he had received.

The first action for the Serbs on taking a town was to mobilize all the Serb men of draft age. Often this had to be carried out under the threat of liquidating the entire family of anybody who refused. The newly drafted were usually placed in the front line and forced to prove themselves by killing the enemy. In Prijedor, the town under attack by the Serbs in the fall of 1992, a Serb tried to save his

Muslim neighbors by loading four families into his truck and driving them to his father's isolated farm. The families remained there, working the farm to be able to feed themselves. When Prijedor fell to the Serbs, however, the Serb who had saved the families was mobilized. He ended up in a unit sent to "liberate" Kozarac, a village on the slopes of Mt. Kozara, seven miles from Prijedor. Most of the population of Kozarac was slaughtered in the process. Alija Midzic, a Muslim telling this story, who lost his leg when a shell hit his third-floor living room back in Prijedor, never found out what had happened to the Serb, whom he knew personally, and whether his friend himself ended up having to kill in Kozarac. Given the circumstances, it is hard to imagine he did not. Asked why the Serb had not run away when he knew he was sure to be drafted, Alija said, his eyebrows raised: "And where would you have wanted him to run to? Prijedor was completely surrounded. There was no place for either me, or him, to hide when they closed in on us."

Meanwhile, the Serb TV studio in Pale was busy broadcasting pictures of slaughtered Serb families. According to Pale, the Muslim extremists and the Ustashe had drawn up lists for the systematic extermination of everything Serb. Yet in parts of Bosnia-Hercegovina where during World War II Muslims and non-Muslims had protected each other, this propaganda proved insufficient. A more brutal approach was designed for such regions. In Bosanska Krupa, a town in the northwest Cazin region, a story was circulated in the summer of 1992 of a Serb, owner of a dairy farm, who had found his wife murdered among the cows in his barn. Several cows had also been shot in the head. Beside his wife's body a piece of paper was left, with the signature of his neighbor. The neighbor was a Muslim, his farm just across the bridge over the Una River. Whether the signature was authentic or not, the Serb could not tell. There had never been much of an opportunity to study how his neighbor signed his name—the two had had no reason to ever exchange letters and written messages before. The Serb never became fully convinced that his neighbor was the one who murdered his wife. But he could not be entirely sure, either, that he hadn't. All contact between the two ended and news of the murder spread like wildfire through the Cazin region. Among the Serbs, who knew neither men, a belief gradually set in that Muslims could not be trusted. Serb television supported the haunting doubts by featuring Bosnian Serb refugees gathering in the summer and fall of 1992 on the slopes of Mt. Ozren, north of Sarajevo, living under tents, without food or water. Interviews with these lost people, expelled from their homes by the Muslim Green Berets, were aired for hours. Before long, Serbs were calling all Muslims "mujahedin."

In eastern Bosnia, meanwhile, an unsparing war was being waged for "ethnically clean" (or, rather, exclusively Serb-populated) territory. By July 1992, the Serbs firmly held a number of towns in the northeastern strip along the Drina: Visegrad, Cajnice, and Foca. Many other towns, like Modrica, changed hands several times. Every time a town fell to one side, Muslim or Croat civilians were massively killed. To destroy the towns, Serbs used every type of force—infantry, heavy artillery, and aircraft. Modrica was leveled, and one of the casualties was the Institute for the Rehabilitation of the Mentally Ill located in the town. Its 240 patients were transported to a nearby village and put under tents. Only one woman doctor, of the former twenty-six, stayed with the patients; with her remained sixteen nurses and one cook. The *Borba* reporter found the patients in late fall 1992 wandering barefoot in the rain, some naked to the waist. None of them knew which calendar year it was. Some were aware a war was being fought around them but had no idea who was fighting.

Along the Serbian-Bosnian border innumerable towns and villages were laid to waste. From the outlying neighborhoods of Han Pjesak, about fifteen miles from the border, all but two Muslim families fled. One of those who had fled, Sonja Piric, a Muslim, gave the following interview to the press upon her arrival in Belgrade in evacuation convoy on November 13, 1992:

> A neighbor, a Serb, broke into the house one morning early, about three months ago. His son had been killed in Sarajevo, and our house was there, near the cemetery where his son was buried. He didn't speak a word, he just came and shot up a window. He then broke down the door, entered, and started shooting at our furniture. Then he started into our room. We two, Mother and I with the little one, opened the window and started to jump out. Another man, waiting in the street, shot at me and the baby. I got a small wound.

The little one, she was killed. We ran away, I was carrying her, I did not know she had been hit, killed. Mother remained in the window. She was hit by the one in the street. . . . They were telling us to get out, that they were cleansing the place. Yes, that's what they said.

Even when local Muslims, in fear for their lives, put themselves on the Serb side by reporting for mobilization in larger ration than the Serbs themselves, this did not save them from being driven out. Such was the case in Trebinje, a region in eastern Hercegovina, where Muslims and Serbs lived as friends until the end of 1992. In January 1993, the order went out for all Muslims to leave the town within the next few days. Alarmed, the Muslims sent a delegation to speak to the town council and were told that official authorities had nothing to do with the order. However, extremist groups from out of town were breaking into houses unhindered, threatening and taking money and valuables away. Then the torching of houses started, first of the landmark Beg house that had been transformed into a museum-restaurant. The Mosque of Osman Pasha, situated within the old town walls, was next. Then the homes of the old and reputable Muslim families came under attack. After each attack, a larger and larger number of Muslim families made up their minds to leave. Local bus owners made big money. A one-way ticket to Denmark, Sweden, or Turkey cost 280 DM (or close to two hundred U.S. dollars). Those who could not afford the ticket had to seek shelter in some refugee facility, from which they usually had to move on within weeks or months, especially if the area where the facility was located fell into the hands of the other side. As a rule refugees were allowed to take only small hand luggage with them. Their homes and everything in them became the booty of irregular forces. Members of these self-appointed armed forces or Serb refugees from other parts of Bosnia-Hercegovina moved into the homes.

In Banja Luka, the proclaimed capital of the Serb Republic in Bosnia, more than four hundred businesses owned by Muslims were blown up. In the remaining shops that stayed open, thugs would appear just before closing time to bully the owners into handing over the day's receipts. The authorities did nothing to protect the owners. Muslims, stripped of all protection under the law, were frequently attacked in the street and robbed of their money and valuables. "We are only waiting for the day when they will be required to wear something like the Star of David," an officer of the UN corps in Banja Luka told *Le Figaro* in November 1993. The Serb authorities insisted that such actions are perpetrated by the extremists, who could not be controlled. International monitors, however, insisted that terrorist acts were routinely organized by the municipality to force the Muslim minority to leave. Banja Luka, which used to have fifty-four percent Serb population before the war, will soon be almost exclusively Serb. The transport of the forced Muslim exiles, who were allowed one plastic bag as "luggage" and whose empty houses were immediately possessed by the Serb military, turned into a profitable business. "Private travel agencies," closely linked to the local authorities, have been busy. One Boris Prpos, a Serb in his sixties, transports between 200 and 250 Muslims every week from Banja Luka to Croatia. He charges 400 DM (nearly three hundred U.S. dollars) per person, but says he gets only 70 DM of the total. The rest goes to the municipality for "war expenses."

The bombing in May 1993 of two sixteenth-century mosques in Banja Luka, the Ferhadija Mosque from 1574 and the Arnaudija Mosque from 1594, had the same objective: to force the Muslims to leave. The minaret of the Ferhadija Mosque remained standing after the blast, but the order came for it to be blown up the next night "for security reasons." The Serb authorities insisted they were worried it might collapse on passersby. As the Fund for Humanitarian Law, a Belgrade-based organization monitoring war crimes in Yugoslavia, reported, the Islamic community asked that it be allowed to collect the remaining stones. The authorities instead sent two bulldozers to the site and took the rubble away.

According to the Yugoslav Islamic community, between April and August 1992 alone, Serb extremists destroyed no less than 430 mosques. Some of these were shelled and bombed during the fighting, but many, like those in Bjeljina, Trebinje, and Banja Luka, were destroyed by terrorist actions aimed at adding pressure on the Muslims to leave the area. The collusion between extremists and local officials, insisting they have nothing to do with the criminal elements, is clear. The municipal authorities remain deaf to the complaints of the Muslim community; instead of providing protection, the authorities recommend that Muslims would do best to leave town. Dismissals from government jobs became massive and included those with proof that they had answered the Serb mobilization call. In despair, people who are suddenly left with no source of income and who are aware that at any moment they could fall victim to Serb extremists "voluntarily" abandon their homes. Of the forty thousand Muslims living in Banja Luka before the war, more than half had left within a year.

In the villages surrounding the town of Prijedor, thirty miles from Banja Luka, no Muslim dreamed of staying past fall 1992, when the Serbs "liberated" the region. Many homes were destroyed. If they were destroyed, their owners were forced to leave. If they were not destroyed, the owners were too afraid to stay anyway. Muslims would rather move to Trnopolje (until early fall 1992 a notorious concentration camp turned into a refugee center) than stay in their own homes surrounding the infamous camp. As soon as the camp became a refugee center, thirty-five hundred men, women, and children poured in to await resettlement. They all could see their homes, or the remnants of their homes, in the distance.

Most of those people had heard stories about the massacre of about 150 to 200 Muslims just released from Trnopolje camp on August 21, 1992. A group of Bosnian Serb soldiers, led by Dragan Mrdja, stopped the truck with the Muslims in the vicinity of Vlasic village, ordered the men to line up in front of a ravine, and shot them dead. Some were shot more than once as they fell. The chief of security forces in Banja Luka, Stojan Zupljanin, confirmed to the *Washington Post* that the massacre indeed had taken place.

Trnopolje was one of three Serb concentration camps near Prijedor. The other two were Keraterm and Omarska. In mid-August 1993, *Borba* published the account of a fifty-year-old woman from Prijedor who had been imprisoned for three months at the Omarska camp, a site that before the war was an ore mine. The woman spoke at the UN World Congress on Human Rights in Vienna. She said:

> Every day people were being brought to the camp. I knew many of them from before. As far as I know, five thousand men, two hundred forty boys age eleven to fourteen, and

thirty-six women were there. Serb authorities aimed primarily at the intellectuals . . . then at the members of Muslim and Croatian parties, and finally at important townspeople. . . . But there were also ordinary people, and people seventy, eighty years old.

I worked at the restaurant. Prisoners came in once a day in groups of thirty. The meal consisted of one piece of bread and a bit of cooked stuff, mainly beans. Of course that was insufficient; people would faint from physical weakness and hunger, particularly children. But the worst was that the meal had to be gulped up in two minutes; if you did not finish in two minutes you were beaten on the spot. People died in the restaurant, in front of our eyes.

The hardest thing was that in addition to the work in the restaurants, women were required to clean interrogation rooms too. Those were full of blood, and we had to wipe off the blood. . . .

One time we were sitting in the kitchen and a drunken Chetnik came in, took out a knife, and started to carve a Serbian cross on the cheek of one of the younger women. The rest of us kept quiet waiting for the same thing to be done to us. . . . They pressed cigarette butts on our arms. . . . What's worst, we had to watch torture every day. They used large iron objects, wide rubber pipes, special cables. I was desperately hoping I would be killed with a bullet.

One hundred to two hundred people died every day from torture. Trucks took the bodies away every day, we don't know where. Perhaps the bodies were being thrown into the old mining shafts, and the shafts were leveled to get rid of the evidence.

. . . We women slept in the two interrogation rooms, eighteen of us per room. At night anybody could come in. They came in usually drunk. They would call out the one they wanted and did what they wanted with her. We held each other by the hand and waited for our turn. We weren't saying anything. There was nothing to say. Five women, my colleagues, did not survive.

Taking people away to the concentration camps played the same role as did rape, massacres of civilians, disappearances, blowing up of mosques, and burning of houses. Faced with the prospect that the same might happen to them, many Muslims left everything behind and fled. In many parts of Bosnia, the Serbs had almost achieved their goal of expelling all non-Serbs. The fact that the international community had recognized Bosnia as an independent country was of no help whatsoever to the Bosnian civilians, since nothing was done to secure the newly established independence. Major General Lewis MacKenzie, the UN field commander in Bosnia as of May 1992, despaired of the "lousy job," as he called it, that the UN was doing in Bosnia. The civilian logistical support he requested never arrived even though it was promised. In Bosnia, MacKenzie said, "There was no command and control after 5 P.M. New York time." Having recognized independent Bosnia, the international community left it to its own resources.

The Croatian side revealed its real ambitions in Bosnia-Hercegovina immediately after the outbreak of war. The international media noticed those ambitions only a year later. From the outset, the Bosnian Croat leadership was split between a hard line whose goal was the division of Bosnia-Hercegovina and a soft line loyal not to the republic of Croatia but to the goal of an independent and sovereign Bosnia-Hercegovina. And from the outset, Franjo Tudjman, in Croatia, encouraged the hard line. Stjepan Kljujic, a member of the Bosnian presidency and a representative of the Croatian soft line, was replaced in the presidency by Mate Boban, a representative of the Croat Hercegovinians, the most radical and militant Croats in Bosnia-Hercegovina.

Prior to his appearance on the Bosnian political scene, Boban worked as a manager of a supermarket; once the Croatian war started, he made a name for himself as one of the most successful arms merchants. Under his direction, and with abundant help from the Tudjman regime and the Croatian expatriate lobby in the West, the Croats conducted preparations for war in Bosnia-Hercegovina and, in contrast to the Muslims, were ready when the war broke out. Martin Spegelj, a former Yugoslav army general and retired general of the Croatian army, in an interview in the summer of 1993 stated that Croatia had sent more of its weaponry into Bosnia-Hercegovina than it had retained in Croatia. From 1991 to 1993 Croatia had purchased three hundred million dollars worth of weapons from arms dealers all over the world. A large part of the funds was funneled in by the many Croat emigrants in Canada, the United States, Latin America, Austria, and Germany. A wide variety of weapons were supplied by Russia and its former satellites, Czechoslovakia, Poland, East Germany, and Hungary, the countries which after the cold war found themselves with large arsenals and little money for food. The major part of the arms brought in from these countries, as well as from countries like Uganda and Guinea, ended up under Boban's control in Bosnia-Hercegovina.

In the townships where the HDZ, the Croat nationalist party, had won a majority, men loyal to the Hercegovinian hard line were immediately assigned to start building a Bosnian-Croat military force. Aware of his military superiority over the Muslims, Mate Boban, on July 5, 1992, proclaimed an independent republic of Herceg-Bosnia, just as Karadzic had done in proclaiming the Serbian Republic of Bosnia and Hercegovina one year earlier. The European Community threatened Croatia with sanctions. Franjo Tudjman proclaimed his innocence and called the affair "adventurism" on the part of Boban. Many in Bosnia-Hercegovina expected Boban's political fortunes to suffer a quick reversal, until it became clear that the attempt to proclaim the republic of Herceg-Bosnia had been a trial balloon launched by Tudjman himself to test worldwide reaction to the division of the country. If anything, the influence of Boban and the Croatian hard liners in Zagreb only grew. The international community hardly noticed. It preferred to believe Tudjman and accepted his assurances that Croatia had nothing to do with the Bosnian war—that is, that no Croatian units were active in Bosnia-Hercegovina. But by the summer of 1992 there could be no doubt that Boban's war machine was running on Tudjman's power supply.

From the moment Boban took over the HDZ, Serbia and Croatia were in league with regard to Bosnia-Hercegovina. That Croatia had recognized the independence of Bosnia-Hercegovina and Serbia had not was of no consequence. Zarko Puhovski, a renowned Zagreb professor of political philosophy, had this to say in a May 1993 interview in the European edition of the Sarajevo weekly *Oslobodjenje:*

> Allow me to cite from personal knowledge that the recognition of Bosnia-Hercegovina by Croatia was the result of the

U.S. chargé d'affaires having clearly told Tudjman that Croatia could not count on U.S. recognition unless it first recognized the independence of Bosnia. . . . That is why I consider it inappropriate for Croatian recognition of Bosnia to be used to prove the good will of Croatia toward Bosnia. . . . On the contrary, the U.S. representatives had demanded to hear by 9 A.M. on the radio that the Croatian recognition of Bosnia had been proclaimed, so New York could be informed. They held their breath until Mr. Bush had woken up, in order to report the big news.

Otherwise, Croatia from the first moment gave military, political, and financial support to its own forces in Herceg-Bosnia. . . . Croatian policy in Bosnia has been very intelligent. . . . The goals set have been reached with relative discretion, without an exaggerated use of force and without provoking the kind of scandals that have cost the Serbian side dearly.

Croatia was able to achieve its goals in Bosnia-Hercegovina with "relative discretion" and "without provoking scandals" owing to two sets of circumstances. The first was the tolerance shown by Western media for Croatia as a "democratic country" enjoying strong German support, that is, a country where democratic elections had been held—its flagrant violations of democratic rights notwithstanding. The second was the undisguised brutality of the Serb offensive in Bosnia and the media spotlight attracted to it as a result. This second circumstance provided a thick smoke screen for Croatian advances. Behind the smoke screen, Boban succeeded in taking over and, virtually unobserved, expelling Serbs from the areas considered "Croat ethnic territory," "the heart of the Croat nation." Having established himself, Mate Boban began ruling things as though Herceg-Bosnia were part of Croatia. His people came to completely control the police, the schools, and the economy in the occupied territory. Croat propaganda meanwhile insisted that "Muslims should be grateful to Boban for having liberated them from the Serbs."

Even before the Croats got a firm hold on "their territory," it was not rare for Serbs and Croats to loan each other an artillery piece or a tank for the afternoon, to be used against the Muslims. Regarding their strategy in Bosnia, Serbs and Croats had been allies before the Bosnian war and during the war. Mate Boban and

Radovan Karadzic were in regular contact with each other. In early May 1992 they met in Graz, Austria, and signed a document outlining how they imagined Bosnia should be divided between them. There is little doubt that the two were acting under the direction of Milosevic and Tudjman, as the division of Bosnia between Serbs and Croats remained the enduring goal of both sides.

Boban's moves, like those of Karadzic, were guided exclusively by the objective of an ethnically Croatian Herceg-Bosnia. Boban had little interest in the defense of the Muslims, alleged Croatian allies. In addition, the Hercegovinian lobby in Zagreb did everything it could to prevent weapons sent in 1992–1993 by Iran from reaching the Bosnian Muslims. Most of the weapons ended up in Croatian hands.

Following two months of extensive meetings with all sides, the Vance-Owen plan, first drafted in October 1992 in Geneva, offered an outline of the political organization of Bosnia-Hercegovina and of a cessation of hostilities. The plan did not mention cantons, the concept the Muslim side considered unacceptable, and called instead for the regionalization of Bosnia into seven to ten regions, with the central government, composed of representatives from every region, based in Sarajevo. The territories captured by the Serbs could not be linked and were to remain discrete administrative units. Karadzic responded with a resolute "Enough of breaking the Serbs apart!" and left no doubt he was dead set on preserving "our people's unity." He insisted on three states in Bosnia, based on ethnic and religious principles. The Vance-Owen team rejected his response because it implied enforced transfer of populations.

In January 1993 the Vance-Owen team brought together the warring sides again in Geneva and presented them with a ten-point plan calling for the establishment of a "highly decentralized state" of three constitutive units made up of ten provinces. The state would be demilitarized, and the UN, European Community, and Conference for Security and Cooperation in Europe would be directly involved in constitutional elections, the court, and the formation of a multiethnic army and police forces. The Muslims objected to the three-way division of Bosnia. Slobodan Milosevic, present in Geneva and weakened at home despite having won the rigged elections in Serbia in December 1992, seemed to have undergone a change of heart. He told Karadzic that if Bosnian Serbs wanted to fight the whole world, they shouldn't count on him for supplies. Karadzic signed the Vance-Owen plan but said that the Serb parliament in the Serbian Republic of Bosnia and Hercegovina had to ratify his signature. On January 20, 1993, the day of Bill Clinton's inauguration, the Bosnian Serb parliament ratified the agreement 55 to 15. Karadzic called the agreement "hell," adding that "it will force us to live together with our greatest enemies, people who attack our homes, our innocent civilians, even our cradles."

But before the details of the plan could be worked out in Geneva, on January 22, 1993, Croatian forces attacked Serb-controlled territories near the port of Zadar in Croatia. Tudjman pledged to "liberate every inch of Croatia from the Serbs." The Muslims, no longer sure they still wanted the Vance-Owen plan, began looking to Clinton for military assistance. The Vance-Owen plan broke down on January 30, 1993. At that point Muslim and Croat clashes in the area of Gornji Vakuf started in earnest. Both Cyrus Vance and Lord Owen insisted that Clinton should put American troops on the ground. In February 1993, however, George Stephanopoulos, the White House communications director, made it clear that the president did not "specifically embrace or reject the Vance-Owen plan." Instead of forming any kind of policy on Bosnia, Clinton started his air drops of food to eastern Bosnia, besieged by the Serb forces, in February 1993.

In April and May 1993, as a full-scale war between Croats and Muslims was raging north and west of Sarajevo, with masked Croats killing Muslims house by house in Vitez and Mostar, the pressure to accept the Vance-Owen plan was renewed. Meanwhile, many civilians were losing their lives in the Serb offensive on the eastern Bosnian enclave of Zepa. The renewed Vance-Owen plan allotted Bosnian Croats territory equal in share to that allotted to Muslims, although the Croat population in Bosnia-Hercegovina was two and a half times smaller than the Muslim population. Croats were to receive not only the territory they had occupied, but additional territory where Muslims were in the majority. Predictably, the Croat representatives signed the plan immediately and without complaint.

The Vance-Owen plan met total failure, however, when on May 5 the Bosnian Serb parliament rejected it in defiance of the strong words Milosevic delivered on Mt. Jahorina, where he traveled to urge the parliament to accept the plan. According to the plan, the Serbs were required to give back a greater portion of the land they had captured in the war. The plan gave them pastures, the Serb leaders claimed, leaving Muslims and Croats the natural resources, industrial regions, and electrical plants. After voting no on such a plan, the Bosnian Serb parliament told its guests—Serb president Slobodan Milosevic, president of rump Yugoslavia Dobrica Cosic, and president of Montenegro Momir Bulatovic—they had better take a good breath of Jahorina mountain air because it was probably the last time they would be allowed on Bosnian territory.

In the May 15–16 referendum Karadzic had organized hoping to avert the Vance-Owen proposed peace, the plan was rejected. No one could quite understand how it was possible to conduct a referendum in a war-torn area such as Bosnia in the first place. In any case, judging by the vote, many ordinary Serbs in Bosnia seem to have still been convinced that the Bosnian war was fought to defend Serbian homes from the fundamentalists and the Ustashe. To have implanted and sustained this conviction among the ordinary Serb population was the veritable feat of Karadzic's and Milosevic's social engineering.

The collapse of the Vance-Owen plan left the international community with no coherent policy on Bosnia. The next year would go by with Washington and the European powers trying to figure out whether or not to use force in Bosnia and whether to lift the arms embargo on the Muslims.

The threat of NATO air strikes following the slaughter on the Markale marketplace in the center of Sarajevo in February 1994 and the siege of Gorazde that lasted until March 1994 forced the withdrawal of Serb weapons from the hills surrounding both cities. This, however, failed to enhance a comprehensive settlement in Bosnia. By spring 1994 the Serbs had achieved all their objectives in Bosnia: they held more than seventy percent of the territory, and they wanted this ratified through some kind of a peace treaty. But the Muslims, who meanwhile had entered a federation with Croatia, hardened their position toward the Serbs. In view of the great loss of their territories and of the full-scale genocide of Muslim civilians, Izetbegovic was more than reluctant to sign any peace treaty. In May 1994 he seemed to be even more committed than he had been a year earlier—when he was saying insistently that he was interested in territories, not peace—to winning back the land militarily. Radovan Karadzic and other Bosnian Serb leaders also remained entrenched despite the pressures put on them in the summer of 1994 by the Contact Group, which includes the United States, and despite the decision reached by Slobodan Milosevic to seal the borders between Serbia and Bosnia to prevent any transfer of arms and ammunition in exchange for lifting sanctions against Serbia. So, at the brink of another winter, the Bosnian war entered its "low-level phase," bringing new waves of terror on the Bosnian civilians and new cycles of expulsions of Muslim populations from their towns and villages.

NINE

The Serbian Resistance

Ivan Torov

That there is a Serbian resistance will come as a surprise to many. The resistance, both in the media and within the anti-war movement, goes largely unreported abroad. True, it has proved unable to mobilize a massive grassroots challenge to the regime of Slobodan Milosevic and to war. Yet it represents the voice of conscience in Serbia, the voice without which the overall picture remains incomplete.

The road from nationalism to war divided journalists in Serbia, sweeping most into the service of the official propaganda machine. A few, however, recognized early on the dangerous direction Serbia was taking. Their only resort was to sever themselves from the regime by starting independent, privately owned, alternative media. They succeeded at great personal risk and founded the weekly newsmagazine *Vreme,* the biweekly *Republika,* and two broadcast media, independent TV Studio B and radio Studio B-92, all openly and vigorously opposed to the war. They also transformed *Borba* from an official daily into an independent daily.

The opposition media face two kinds of obstacles: political, having to do with the personal risk for each independent media reporter and member of the staff, and economic. The latter turned out to be much harder to surmount. International sanctions imposed on Serbia caused quite quickly a drastic drop in the standard of living of the general population, and consequently a precipitous drop in the circulation of the press. Yugoslavs have always been avid readers of newspapers. But in 1991 and 1992 people started buying the papers—independent and official alike—every other day. Soon, however, as salaries and pensions turned insufficient even for bread and vegetables, most readers were buying just the Sunday edition if they hadn't given up the daily press altogether. The official press is much less affected by this trend because it is state-subsidized. But the independent press found itself unable to purchase paper, printing ink, film, and other supplies and to pay its journalists and staff viable salaries. It is also barely able to finance the costs of investigative reporting, its reason for being. Nevertheless, all three—*Borba, Vreme,* and *Republika*—have continued publication, although no one working for them can ever be sure how stable their enterprises are from one issue to the next.

The three publications have different backgrounds and different editorial policies. *Republika* and *Vreme* are new, dating from 1989 and 1990. *Borba* is one of the two oldest dailies in the country; only *Politika,* the semi-official Belgrade daily, has a longer tradition. *Borba* started out as an opposition paper in 1922, when it was the mouthpiece of the illegal Yugoslav Communist Party. Until World War II, the paper appeared irregularly. During the war, however, it was published with remarkable regularity at the front, among the partisans, as the paper of the National Liberation Movement. In 1945, *Borba* entered the least exciting chapter of its history: it became the establishment daily of the ruling Communist Party. Its top management and editors of the first postwar years were people close to Tito. In 1948 especially, at the time of Tito's break with Stalin, *Borba* reached an incredible daily circulation of 800,000. It was obligatory daily reading for party members. They carried it in jacket or coat pocket and made sure to fold it so that its logo was visible: to read *Borba* was a demonstration of party loyalty. Later, in the 1950s, 1960s, and beyond, circulation was kept high by free subscriptions, especially to higher-echelon party members.

When Stanislav Marinkovic, a prestigious Belgrade journalist and *Borba*'s new editor-in-chief, decided in the mid–1980s to turn *Borba* into an independent paper, the first problem he faced was expanding the readership by ridding *Borba* of its party connection. It worked in his favor that by then Yugoslavia had become a rather weak federation and that the republics had little interest in a federal paper like *Borba.* With the all-out support of most of his staff, Marinkovic turned the paper around in a few months. Immediately, *Borba* opened itself to critical reporting in the politically most sensitive areas. It addressed the effects of the 1974 constitution, the nationalist friction brewing in Kosova, the economy, and cover-ups in political quarters. Its new image was consolidated with its uncompromising reporting of the Serbian Eighth Party Session in 1987, when Milosevic made his grab for power, replacing Serb President Ivan Stambolic with his own man before taking over the office himself. *Slobodna Dalmacija,* a Croatian paper with a similar attitude, voted *Borba* Newspaper of the Year for 1987.

Milosevic immediately realized the threat *Borba* posed to his regime. The paper repeatedly warned of the danger of rising nationalism and pointed to the manipulations of national pride on the part of the regime. In 1990 Milosevic tried in various ways to choke off the paper, but at the time the republic of Serbia had no power over it: it was still nominally a "federal" publication. Eventually, that same year, after Yugoslav Prime Minister Ante Markovic had made room in the Yugoslav economy for the private sector, *Borba* was able to save itself by putting its shares up for public sale and by going private. The thousands of readers *Borba* had won and others who wanted to show their support for an independent press bought up most of the shares in only a few months, despite the novelty of such a privatization effort and an already galloping inflation. A number of private and socialist-sector firms and banks also became important shareholders.

At this point, many of the top journalists moved from other Belgrade media (TV Belgrade, *Politika,* and most of the evening papers) to *Borba.* It was not an easy decision for any of them, considering the strong official pressure *Borba* had been under since 1987. The paper was accused of being "on the payrolls of the Vatican, Germany, and the CIA"; it was proclaimed a "destroyer of Yugoslavia," "out to revive capitalism." When propaganda did not work, Milosevic imposed higher taxes and created artificial shortages of newsprint and other supplies, hoping to break *Borba* financially. When that had no effect, word was leaked of the regime's plans to annul the already completed privatization and confiscate all the paper's property. In 1992, new pressure was added, this time on *Borba*'s printers, who in the end were talked into refusing to run the presses for *Borba* for "patriotic reasons." For the first time since 1945, *Borba* disappeared from the newsstands for a week.

All this created great financial difficulties for the paper. Before the Croatian war broke out in 1991, *Borba* had resident correspondents in Zagreb, Sarajevo, Split, Osijek, and many other important towns throughout Yugoslavia. But when the telephone connections and postal services between Serbia and Croatia were cut off in 1991, *Borba* was severed from its network of correspondents. The international sanctions made automobile fuel impossible to buy, and it became increasingly difficult to send staff members out on special assignments. The services of the international news agencies were beyond reach because the paper had no foreign currency to pay for them. *Borba* turned for help to the ham radio network. It made a cautious selection from the Serbian news agency dispatches and, whenever money permitted, sent its correspondents by public transportation on longer assignments to war areas. With time, *Borba* was able to send a few resident correspondents to Hercegovina, Knin, and even Sarajevo. Because of their unbiased reporting, these reporters often became targets of all three warring sides. The Serb side in Sarajevo kidnapped Zeljko Vukovic and Natka Buturovic, correspondents who were unknown before they were sent to Sarajevo but who quickly gained great respect in Belgrade for their objective reporting. The two were kept incommunicado and, despite repeated protests from *Borba*, for months nothing could be learned about them. Finally they were released and returned to Belgrade, but the Serb side captured another correspondent from Sarajevo, Aleksandar Srebrov, and sentenced him in Sarajevo to five years in jail for "anti-Serb reporting." Despite all pressures, however, *Borba* remains the only independent daily in Serbia reporting news reliably.

In October 1990, *Borba* was joined by the weekly *Vreme*, founded with limited initial capital from a well-known Belgrade liberal lawyer, Srdja Popovic. The idea of starting a weekly newsmagazine came from a group of his journalist friends who felt that at the time when the collapse of Yugoslavia was all but imminent, a weekly was necessary to represent a liberal, pro-Yugoslav viewpoint. The idea attracted some of the best journalists still working for the official media. They took the risk with a magazine that at the outset could not even be registered in Serbia, because Serbia still had no legislation in the area of private-sector news and information companies. *Vreme* started by registering in Croatia; it moved to Serbia only six months later, when the law allowing the registration of privately owned media was finally passed. By leaving the official media for a private, independent weekly, journalists who joined *Vreme* were gambling their entire careers. Nevertheless, the original staff grew to twenty-three full-time journalists and forty additional staff, an overwhelming number of whom are non-Serbs.

At the outset *Vreme* was conceived of as a news weekly, but it has meanwhile become a news and opinion magazine covering in depth Milosevic's war policy, as well as the policies of Tudjman and Izetbegovic. The point has been to lay bare the realities behind the scenes and at the front, the war crimes, the role played by the Yugoslav army in the destruction of Croatia and Bosnia, and the human and material cost of war to the civilian populations on all sides. The magazine also features critical coverage of the economy that cannot be found in any other domestic source. Its tone is deliberately restrained and cool, in contrast to the often hysterical tone of the official media. Its graphic design is modeled on some prominent world weeklies, such as *Newsweek* and *Time*. *Vreme* considers even these formal factors to be a sort of active opposition to the regime.

High school students wearing *Vreme* T-shirts sell the magazine on Saturdays and Sundays at open markets, in front of supermarkets, at bus and tram stops, and next to the newsstands too. For these young people, selling *Vreme* and, more recently, *Borba* is a way of earning some money, but it is also a statement of personal antiregime protest. In Zagreb *Vreme* is distributed clandestinely, in doorways, or delivered directly to the home addresses of secret subscribers. Tudjman's regime had banned its sale in Croatia, maintaining that "were it not for *Vreme*, Croatia's international standing would be much better." Twenty-five hundred copies of each issue are sent monthly to Slovenia, nine hundred copies to Macedonia, and two hundred fifty to Banja Luka, the Serb capital in Bosnia-Hercegovina. Whole issues, or photocopies of particular articles, crop up even at the front lines in Bosnia.

Vreme has become a major source of independent and unbiased information not only internally but also for the foreign news agencies, including the BBC, who often request interviews and analysis. Housed in a space the size of a large private apartment in downtown Belgrade, *Vreme* had only ten computers, and many journalists had to work on old manual typewriters. In 1993 the newsstand price of each issue was lower than the cost of producing it. The sanctions have depleted circulation and reduced earnings to a fraction of what they were when the weekly was founded in 1990.

The regime has never moved directly against the magazine, but the relentless official propaganda has succeeded at making the public at large suspicious of it. Its main target group for readership turned out to be the generation that came of age in the late 1960s. The magazine is regularly attacked by state television, in government statements, and in the parliament. Its accounting books once had to be rendered to tax inspectors. Two members of the editorial staff have been taken to court but were acquitted. Journalists occasionally receive anonymous letters and phone calls, frequently alluding to information about their families or themselves that is private and would be hard to obtain by regularly available channels. Even though *Vreme* has no proof of the government's involvement in this kind of harassment, it seems clear that some of the threatening information used against its journalists cannot be obtained without official cooperation.

Like many other antiwar organizations and groups in Serbia, *Vreme* has received help from the Soros Foundation, a private organization for the advancement of open societies in Eastern Europe. Soros bailed out the magazine with financial assistance at the magazine's most difficult moment in 1993.

Republika, the first periodical of the civil opposition in Yugoslavia, was founded in March 1989, eighteen months before *Vreme.* From the first issue to spring 1993, this small-circulation journal received most of its funds from Rudi Supek, a Croat and one of the most distinguished philosophers of former Yugoslavia. Supek donated his whole pension—coming from the French government for his service as a French Resistance fighter and a Buchenwald concentration camp prisoner—to *Republika.* Supek died in the spring of 1993 and from then on the journal has depended on the voluntary contributions of its supporters and, for paper costs, on the Soros Foundation.

Republika is devoted to political commentary and analysis, not news, and to the active support of the individuals and movements resisting the war. In the first half of 1990 it published as a separate book the only comprehensive study of the Kosova problem available in Serbia, covering all relevant dimensions of the issue, legal, political, and cultural. Publication of the study was financed by the editor of *Republika*, Nebojsa Popov, with money from the sale of a house he had just inherited from his parents. In the spring of 1991, four months before the outbreak of war in Croatia, *Republika* was the first among the journals to warn of the dangers of fascism in Serbia and Croatia. It was the first also to feature criticism of the Serbian authoritarian regime and to promote antiwar ideas, groups, and movements. From the start of the war, the journal encouraged and supported draft resisters and war deserters. It also found lawyers willing to offer resisters legal counsel and emigration advice. In a special 1992 issue it published valuable documentation on antiwar activity in Belgrade. It has continuously worked to bring together the various antiwar groups, organizing a number of round tables and publishing several special studies on acute problems related to political issues and the war. *Republika* was the first to report in 1992 on the expulsions of Croats from Hrtkovci, in the north of Serbia, and the first, in 1993, to write on the disappearance of a group of twenty-one Muslims (who were most likely killed) from a Belgrade-Bar train. To this day *Republika* runs a support group for the families of the disappeared and pays for their lawyers.

Because of its limited financial resources, the journal publishes only between five thousand and fifteen thousand copies per issue. Yet it has subscribers in all the countries of Western Europe, in the United States, and even in Japan. The subscribers often photocopy the issue and send it on to friends. Both in Belgrade and abroad, each issue is circulated hand to hand. *Borba,* in its daily column "What Others Write," regularly carries lead articles from *Republika.*

Independent TV Studio B (NTV Studio B) began broadcasting in November 1990 with only one direct transmitter and four relays, reaching no more than 3.5 million viewers living about sixty miles beyond Belgrade. For NTV to be able to broadcast across Serbia, three or four additional relays would be necessary, since satellite transmission is financially beyond reach. But because of its independent policies and its determination to offer objective coverage, the station was labeled the "enemy channel" from the very outset. In 1991 at the time of antiwar demonstrations, its studios were raided by the police and its broadcasting was interrupted. Its tapes of the war demonstrations were confiscated.

Like the other independent media, NTV has revealed war criminals, provided a louder voice for the protests of the civil opposition, and exposed the machinations of the regime. One of the most popular of its programs has been "Viewers' Interview," in which a well-known personality directly answers called-in questions. On this program NTV was first to bring face to face Milosevic's party and the opposition. It also reruns daily the news and information reports carried by the international television networks—an important source of information for an audience cut off from the world. On a few occasions World Net used a satellite to link NTV's journalists and guests with analysts and reporters in Washington, Philadelphia, Paris, and London. The shows were broadcast live.

With a great deal of effort, in late 1991 NTV was able to collect the necessary funds to buy equipment to slightly increase its broadcasting range. Although the equipment had already been paid for in London, it could not be imported because sanctions had been imposed before the shipment was made. Appeals to the UN Security Council, stating the obvious importance of an independent TV channel for Serbia, were to no avail for a long time. The equipment was allowed to cross the border into Serbia only ten days before the 1992 Serbian elections were to take place. It was too late to alter the impact that state-controlled television had on the voters. In any case, immediately after the truck carrying the equipment entered Serbia, it was kidnapped on the open road by a band of masked, armed men. NTV suspects the operation was run by the Serbian police.

As with all the other independent media, maintaining sources of information has been the most serious professional problem for NTV. Direct communication with the correspondents in Croatia and Bosnia-Hecegovina is impossible; all communication must go through Hungary. Lack of automobile fuel is another serious obstacle. Gasoline and diesel fuel have been rationed under the sanctions, and NTV has to cover all its needs with only about thirteen gallons a month.

In the summer of 1993, NTV was forced to drastically reduce its programming because of financial difficulties. The government quickly reacted by providing abundant financing to its own spin-off channel, TV Politika, which was able to obtain some recent U.S. films despite the sanctions and to produce a quantity of new entertainment programs. Milosevic thus scored a new success. TV Politika's viewer ratings jumped, whereas ratings for NTV dropped. In 1993 NTV lost many of its advertising clients, and the financial crunch affected its programming. It is now much less significant as an opposition TV channel than it was in the past.

Radio B-92 is still going strong, even though its general manager, Sasa Vucinic, complains that the station, which broadcasts without a license, has no tapes, no cassettes, and no parts to repair its technical equipment. The station is run by young people, whose motto is "Believe no one, not even us." Their programming is a mixture of information and entertainment, good music, above all, and a great deal of sharp satire. The news analysis is in-depth and scathing, intentionally rendered in the style of an *enfant terrible*. The reporters rely on humor and surprise as their method of delivery, even though their investigative and analytical work is extremely serious. At one point in 1993 the station announced that its regular team had gone on vacation and that it had been temporarily replaced by a new bunch who changed the name of the station. "From now on," the announcer said, "we are the SPS Radio." Listeners started calling in disbelief: SPS is the initials of Milosevic's Socialist Party. Suddenly, on Studio B-92, sympathetic things were said about the government, and criticism was launched on antiwar groups. More and more phone calls came in. There were about six hundred in all in a single day. The main message of the listeners was "What do you think you are doing!? You think we'll let you do this to us? Shape up or get off the air now." B-92 taped every call and broadcast the gems the next day to protest repeated denials of its requests for a frequency license.

The listeners of B-92 are mainly the young and middle-aged. Without B-92, many say, life in Serbia would be nothing but an exercise in self-degradation.

The independent media have given coverage to all the manifestations of the civil opposition: the Civil Resistance Movement, the Center for Antiwar Action, the student movement, Women against War, the Women's Antiwar Caucus, Women in Black, the Women's Parliament, the Belgrade Circle, the Belgrade branch of the Helsinki Civil Parliament, and other peace groups outside of Belgrade in Novi Sad, Pristina, Becej, Pancevo, Ada, as well as in Zagreb, Ljubljana, and Skopje. Without the wide and up-to-date coverage provided by the Belgrade independent media, the antiwar movement would be unknown even in Serbia.

Some antiwar demonstrations have brought out large crowds, others only small groups of fifty to one hundred people. In former Yugoslavia there was no tradition of independent public protest and civil disobedience, and this has been a major handicap. The absence of experience in grassroots political organizing and the absence of practice of public demonstrations has had its toll: the antiwar movement has remained quite isolated and proved unable to inspire the support of a wider stratum of the population.

On July 15, 1991, immediately following the start of the war in Slovenia, the Center for Antiwar Action, founded earlier that month, called a press conference to set out its position of "negotiations instead of war and violence" and to call for desertion from the army. To help deserters, the center organized assistance by a small number of Belgrade's best lawyers. The call for desertion spread throughout Serbia, and the center opened branches even in out-of-the-way villages.

The Civil Resistance Movement joined the call for desertion and in late 1991 launched the Civil Campaign against War, with the goal of collecting the hundred thousand signatures necessary to force the government to hold a referendum on the draft. In the very tense atmosphere, a few months after the fighting began in Croatia, *Borba* published on ten separate days the call of the Civil Resistance Movement for signatures. NTV aired several special spots with the message that nobody may be drafted against his will for a war that is fratricidal; every individual, the message read, has the right to make a decision according to his own conscience.

In many towns, people went out on their own initiative to collect signatures requesting that a referendum be held. In Belgrade, a number of public personalities joined in the street campaign to collect signatures. But instead of the required one hundred thousand signatures, only seventy thousand were collected. The referendum was not held, but this first mass campaign with its message "We demand to be asked!" found a wide echo in the Serbian public and encouraged over more than one hundred thousand men in Serbia and Montenegro to avoid the draft by escaping across the border or by going into hiding with friends or relatives.

Every evening from October 1, 1991, to February 1, 1992, the Civil Resistance Movement and Center for Antiwar Action organized the lighting of candles in front of the presidency building in the heart of Belgrade. The candles were lit in memory of all those, regardless of nationality, who had died and would still die in the war, and in solidarity with Serbia's growing number of war deserters. Among others, Cyrus Vance lit one candle himself on New Year's Eve 1991. *Borba* gave daily coverage to the campaign in pictures and words throughout the four months of its nightly duration.

At the end of the candle-lighting campaign, in February 1992, two months before the fighting began in Bosnia-Hercegovina, *Borba* allowed the main force behind the Civil Resistance Movement, Natasa Kandic, to organize a daily column under the heading "The Civil Antiwar Campaign." She invited prominent people in public life and many others to write for the column. Not one of the persons she asked refused, and the column appeared daily for two and a half months.

On April 22, 1992, a rock concert organized by the Center for Antiwar Action was held in Belgrade. "Don't Count on Us!" was the song-message against being sent to fight in the war in Bosnia. On May 4, the Civil Resistance Movement organized a public "black ribbon" demonstration in support of and solidarity with the people of Sarajevo. A column of 150,000 people carried a black paper ribbon (cloth turned out to be unavailable in the empty stores) 1,400 yards long in total silence through the downtown center of Belgrade. The ribbon arrived intact at the final destination after many hours of march.

In May 1992, Belgrade composers and actors protested the distortions of nationalism in culture by kneeling in silence in the park across the street from the Yugoslav parliament building. On June 30, the "Tolling Bells" protest was held, organized by the Civil Resistance Movement together with other antiwar groups, demanding an immediate end to the regime's politics of war and Milosevic's immediate resignation. Bell towers were built on trucks borrowed from the town's theaters with the intention of driving through the center of downtown with the bells ringing. However, at the start of the demonstration, police blocked the passage of the trucks, claiming that, as theatrical decorations, they required special transit permits. Having anticipated that the police would find a way to sabotage the demonstration, its organizers had asked ahead of time that participants bring bells as well as pots and pans of their own. The marchers circled through the city, ringing their small, hand-held noisemakers to the presidency building.

In July 1992, a long student protest began, including a series of partial strikes and ending with a peace march of several thousand students through the city. That summer also, the Center for Antiwar Action held a number of open panel discussions and talks on topics such as "Bosnia Today," "Fascism at the End of the Twentieth Century," "A Peaceful Bosnia," "Bosnian Vukovars," and "Open Society Parties in Serbia and Montenegro." The practice of open discussions and talks was established by the Belgrade Circle, founded in January 1992. The discussions are still held every Saturday morning in a centrally located small theater. Several hundred people regularly attend to hear the voice of civil protest raised by writers, university professors, artists, architects, journalists, and stage and screen personalities. Some of the topics have been "Life with the Monstrosity," "Is Another Serbia Possible?," "Manufacturers of National Hate," "The Murderers of Cities," and "How Far We Have Fallen." A guest from one or another European country is an occasional speaker. At the end of 1992, with the financial assistance of *Borba,* the Belgrade Circle published *The Other Serbia,* a collection of articles featuring the existence in Serbia of many different voices against the Milosevic regime and in favor of an end to the wars and an affirmation of an antinationalist, pluralist society. The book was translated into English, German, and French. During 1993, the Belgrade Circle spread its activity to other towns in Serbia and also to Skopje in Macedonia and Ljubljana in Slovenia.

The Civil Resistance Movement, followed by the Belgrade Circle and Center for Antiwar Action, reacted quickly and forcefully to threats and expulsions in 1992 and later against non-Serb families of the northern Vojvodina province. The Civil Resistance Movement also brought to the attention of *Borba, Vreme,* and NTV Studio B the details of the pressures and outright persecution of some old Croat families in the village of Hrtkovci to force them to leave their village. A highly vocal campaign followed in the independent media against attacks on Croat and Hungarian villagers in Vojvodina. In July 1992, the "yellow ribbon" protest took place in front of the parliament building with a crowd of some two thousand, all wearing yellow ribbons around their upper arms. The reference was to the Star of David that Jews were forced to wear during World War II. At the end of the protest, the yellow ribbons were tied to the ropes of the flag poles in front of the parliament, raised, and left fluttering in the air. Protesters also wore cardboard signs around their necks with a bull's-eye over the heart. Written on one sign was "I am Orthodox, and Catholic, and Muslim, and Jewish, and Buddhist, and atheist."

In the second half of 1993, the Center for Antiwar Action, which by that time had received important funding from the Soros Foundation, UNICEF, and the UN High Commission for Refugees (UNHCR), undertook a series of interrelated projects aimed at reinforcing the traditional spirit of tolerance in Serbia's multinational communities. It sent teams of about ten specialists into towns and villages of Vojvodina to hold three-week conflict resolution meetings with the local populations. The center ran a similar program in Belgrade and outlying schools, especially in those where enrollment includes a large proportion of children of mixed ethnic descent. Center specialists taught teachers, school counselors, and psychologists the basics of conflict resolution so they could apply them in the classroom and with children individually. The center also sent teams, reinforced with clinical psychologists and social workers, to refugee camps for mothers and children in Serbia and Montenegro to help the refugees adjust to their new circumstances.

Women's groups sent a number of organizations of their own, among others the SOS hotline for battered women and children and an aid center for war victims of rape. One group, Women in Black, has held a regular weekly antiwar protest since 1991 in Belgrade. Independent women's groups work with other antiwar groups in Belgrade, Novi Sad, Pristina, Becej, Ada, Pancevo, as well as in Skopje, Zagreb, and Ljubljana.

In late 1992, with the help of the Soros Foundation, the Fund for Humanitarian Law was founded in Belgrade. The fund is a collection center for documentation of war crimes and violations of human rights throughout the territory of former Yugoslavia. It does field investigations by tracing witnesses to crimes both in Yugoslavia and abroad; the purpose is to corroborate every story with at least three or four independent sources. The fund issues regular "Spotlight Reports" on specific instances of war crimes, expulsions of local populations, massacres, rape, as well as every other category of human rights violations. The fund has gained high regard among the international organizations and agencies working in this field. Its reports are prepared in Serbo-Croatian and English and sent to a long mailing list of organizations and individuals within Yugoslavia and abroad. The purpose is to keep the public at home and abroad informed and to maintain constant pressure on the governments throughout former Yugoslavia against violations of human rights. An important goal of the fund is to identify the criminals and crimes and thus work against the tendency in former Yugoslavia and abroad to attach collective guilt to entire populations.

Taking an active and public antiwar position in Serbia has meant accepting exposure to many risks. Not only are the activists being attacked, but the Soros Foundation is too. It is today officially considered the principal "anti-Yugoslav" organization to be avoided by patriots, despite the fact that, in addition to its aid to resistance organizations, it also has sent aid to those in need in Serbia: in 1993 alone, it sent $9.3 million worth of medicines and medical supplies to Serbia alone, provided substantial aid to its refugees, and given basic necessities to a number of its children's camps. The antiwar movement Soros supports is now threatened by exhaustion and haunted by the awareness of how minimal its results have been over three years of protest. The movement and the independent press have kept the principles of human rights and democracy alive in extremely trying times, but they have not significantly affected the course of events. That is, for many, a source of despair in the war that appears to be without end.

TEN

Voices of Opposition in Croatia

Sven Balas

In the spring of 1984, I was sitting with a friend in a Dubrovnik bar. On the wall over the bar hung a picture of Marshal Tito in a snow-white uniform, dead four years but yet immortal, proving his health by playing the piano. Looking at Tito through his beer glass, my friend cried out, "Don't play it again, Sam!"

Unfortunately, however, my friend was unclear in his vision. The icon remained silent, but Croatia today must suffer through an endless and unentertaining spectacle, offered by one of the most ridiculous and inept performers on the stage of contemporary history. I refer to the president of the Croatian Republic, General Doctor Franjo Tudjman, the new "Father of the Nation," the self-appointed "Arch-Croat," aspiring "SuperCroat."

Much about Tudjman, the leader of Croatia since 1990, is reminiscent of Tito. Like Tito, Tudjman travels in a private jet, rides in a bulletproof limousine, resides in a variety of castles, enjoys handmade suits and shoes, sails a yacht, and maintains his own personal vacation miniparadise in the islands of Brioni off the northern Adriatic coast—precisely where Tito also disported himself.

Every year, Tudjman picks, with his own hands, a basket of tangerines from an orchard that was Tito's own, on the isle of Vanga at Brioni. The fruit is then mailed to selected orphans. Tito nursed the same habit; the parents of his peacetime orphans were unknown, but alive, while the fathers of Tudjman's orphans are

Croatian soldiers who died in the recent war. In both cases, the gift of tangerines suggests the wise Father of the Nation concerned and caring for his children.

Tudjman also has characteristics in common with Slobodan Milosevic, his Serbian counterpart in the resurrection of extremist nationalism. Although Tudjman is a generation older than Milosevic, both are authentic products of the Yugoslav Communist apparatus: Milosevic of the party, Tudjman of the army. Tudjman, born in 1922, joined the Partisan movement during World War II as a convinced Marxist and rose to become the youngest general in Tito's armed forces. Milosevic and Tudjman were also, of course, both educated in the Tito state's system of professional training: Milosevic learned business—the art of manipulating Western finance for the short-term benefit of Yugoslav institutional borrowers, while Tudjman studied history and philosophy.

Today Tudjman exercises a near-dictatorial power over the hungry and humiliated citizens of Croatia, many thousands of whom are now refugees, and plays a determining role in the fate of Bosnia-Hercegovina. The blame for the war must be placed squrely on the plate of Slobodan Milosevic and his murderous partners in ideology, Radovan Karadzic, Ratko Mladic, Vojislav Seselj, and others. But the Croatian people now must survive, day after day, under Tudjman, whose four years in power already have made Tito look good to many and make many others wonder if a Pinochet or some other Third World dictator would not have wanted, after all, to be more like Tudjman.

Tudjman and his new mass party, the Croatian Democratic Union (HDZ), were elected to office in 1990. The election was fair. HDZ was mainly opposed by the crumbling remnants of the Croatian Communist bureaucracy, which did not lack talented personalities but which was profoundly discredited among the mass of Croats, and by a coalition of small social democratic and liberal parties headed by intellectuals who were widely respected and admired but whom few Croats thought could lead the country through the difficult transition from Yugoslav socialism. Most important, neither the Croatian Communists nor the opposition coalition projected an image of martial strength in the face of the Milosevic threat, which Tudjman brought with him thanks to his military background. In addition, Tudjman, who had been imprisoned during the Tito regime for Croat nationalism, enjoyed the halo of a martyr. HDZ won handily.

But doubts about Tudjman were also expressed, from the beginning, by Croat liberals, based on Tudjman's revisionist views of Croatian history as expressed in his writings, as well as his apparent authoritarian leanings, which many saw as a continuation of his Communist past. Nevertheless, like other post-Communist states, Croatia in 1990 basked in the celebration of what all took for granted would be a new regime of basic democratic rights.

One such right was the principle of a free press. Croatia enjoyed broad literacy and a profound commitment by its intelligentsia to literary excellence as well as to the protection of the Croat language. In addition, its media were proud of their professionalism, rare enough in Tito's Yugoslavia but offering a staggering contrast to the press even in such literate socialist countries as the former Czechoslovakia. Nearly all Croatian intellectuals and journalists believed that the fall of the Communist regime would bring about an enormous expansion of free and competitive Croatian media, such as has been seen in such countries as the Czech Republic. However, it was not to be.

From the beginning of his administration Tudjman acted aggressively toward the media. Television, a state agency, was almost immediately made an HDZ fiefdom. One by one, print journals and reporting teams known for their objectivity and independence fell under his control. Tudjman attempted to justify his restrictions on the media by citing the management difficulties inherent in the transfer of former Communist media properties to new owners. In addition, he asserted that virtually the whole Croatian media class were nothing but the hirelings of the former regime.

But these pretexts did not address certain other, interrelated questions: why issues of management or, for that matter, ideology should impinge on editorial and reportorial professionalism; why it proved nearly impossible for liberal Croat intellectuals who had never been associated with the regime to set up new, serious organs of opinion; and why, by contrast, it was so easy for Ustashe nostalgics to suddenly flood the country with their printed propaganda.

The cases of the Zagreb weekly *Danas* (Today) and the Split daily *Slobodna Dalmacija* (Free Dalmatia)—considered the highest-quality news organs in former Yugoslavia—are illustrative.

"Liberated" from Communist supervision, they came under attack from the HDZ, whose hard-line wing, based on a layer of ultranationalists from Hercegovina, interpreted any variation from the new party line as treason to the Croat cause. Once the 1991 war began in earnest, HDZ criticism of journalists who had not surrendered to Tudjman's "coordination" became annoyed with the claim of betrayal in wartime. But the basic theme continued: experienced, professionally capable reporters and editors were denounced as Chetniks, Yugoslavists, Communists.

Danas attempted to resist the onslaught. However, its publisher was the Zagreb daily *Vjesnik* (Courier), which became the mouthpiece of Tudjman's regime and which decided to stop printing *Danas*. The *Danas* team went to Slovenia for printing, but the magazine's distribution was then outlawed in Croatia. Newsstands and individuals selling *Danas* in Croatia ran the risk of court action. *Danas* expired.

The history of *Slobodna Dalmacija* was more difficult and complex. Published in the port of Split, this daily had a circulation of one hundred thousand in the 1980s and was read all over Croatia as well as in the diaspora. It was open to all sides. In 1991, it denounced Croat violations of the human rights of Serbs, something no other Croat media would touch. But Tudjman's government decided to privatize the paper through issuance of stock, while barring the journalists, who were labeled along with the former managers as holdovers from the Communist era, from becoming majority stockholders. Its best editors and reporters quit in protest, and *Slobodna Dalmacija* came under direct government supervision, through bank control of the stock majority. Its editorial policies were redefined and it became yet another nationalist organ.

Still, through the transition and war, some opposition voices established themselves in Croatia. They include the daily *Novi List* (New Journal), published in the northern Adriatic port city of Rijeka, which also issues the political-satirical weekly *Feral Tribune* as a supplement edited by former *Slobodna Dalmacija* journalists. Other independent mass media include Radio 101 in Zagreb and Omladinska Televizija (Youth Television). The most consistent and forceful expression of opposition to Tudjman's Croatia has come from two intellectual journals issued in Zagreb, *Erasmus* and *Vi-*

jenac (The Wreath). But *Feral Tribune* represents the loudest and most spirited protest.

Erasmus and *Vijenac* are serious, highbrow journals, handsomely designed and printed, profoundly opposed to the Tudjman regime although with an audience limited to the educated classes both in Croatia and the diaspora. The editor in chief of *Erasmus* is Slavko Goldstein, one of the most remarkable figures in the history of postwar Croatia. Born in the old Habsburg garrison town of Karlovac, and among a group of fifty-five Jews protected during the early period of the Holocaust by a village of Croatian peasants, Goldstein had served as president of the Zagreb Jewish community in the last decades of the Tito regime but was better known as a publisher and a prominent defender of Croat culture. In this context, he became something of an idol for the pre–1990 Croatian public and even cooperated with Tudjman during the latter's dissident period. However, in the 1990 election Goldstein was seen by many as the architect of the liberal coalition that presented itself as an alternative both to the old Communist bureaucracy and to the HDZ.

The contributors to *Erasmus* include poets, politicians, philosophers, artists, authors, and professors as well as the acclaimed intellectual leaders of the Croat diaspora. *Vijenac* is published by Matica Hrvatska (The Croatian Hive), one of the most noble and significant institutions in Croat cultural history. Established in 1842 to advance Croatian culture and paralleled by Matica Srpska (The Serbian Hive) and other Slav entities of the same character, Matica Hrvatska was suppressed, its branches throughout Croatia shut down, by Tito in 1972 for its defense of what was alleged to be "Croat nationalism." It is viewed as above reproach by many Croats, and its values have always been rational and liberal. Like *Erasmus*, *Vijenac* publishes the outstanding Croat intellectuals of the present time.

The leading group of opposition intellectuals includes Ivan Supek, physicist, essayist, philosopher, dramatist, historian, and rector of Zagreb University, a true Renaissance man with a long and valiant career defending the freedom of the mind against Hitlerism, Stalinism, and Titoism as well as Tudjmanism. Supek is perhaps the most representative Croatian intellectual of this century, like his brother Rudi Supek, who financed, until his death, the antiwar monthly *Republika* in Belgrade. As a scientist, Ivan Supek studied under Werner Heisenberg at the University of Leipzig where, upon receipt of his degree, he was arrested by the Gestapo and deported from Nazi Germany as a Communist. A Communist he was, but of the remarkable, now forgotten kind once so common in central Europe who equated revolution with a challenge to human limits, as much at home in a discussion of modern art or psychoanalysis as of physics or Croatian history. His lightly fictionalized treatment of Tito's repression of Croat Communists directly after World War II, *Krunski Svjedok Protiv Hebranga* (Crown Witness against Hebrang), is a central document of contemporary Croat history.

While Supek resides in Zagreb, another member of this group whose talents, achievements, and high principles are widely admired is a professor of history at Yale University, Ivo Banac. Banac, the youngest of the group, is the author of two major historical works, *The National Question in Yugoslavia* and *With Stalin against Tito*. Both works have established him as a leading Slavic scholar in the United States and the acknowledged moral leader of the democratic Croatians. A brilliant stylist in English scholarly prose as well as a researcher without peer, a popular lecturer and mentor to students, Banac, all the way from New Haven, is a considerable thorn in Tudjman's side.

Another leading figure in this group is the poet Vlado Gotovac (b. 1930), the guiding spirit behind the post–1990 resurrection of Matica Hrvatska, a writer of great literary gifts and a man of unbreakable honesty and morality who was imprisoned and nearly murdered in Tito's prisons after the 1972 purge of Croat intellectuals. His book *Moj Slucaj* (My Case) is a genuine classic of the antitotalitarian dissident experience; it is no surprise, therefore, that Gotovac is an exceptionally articulate critic of Tudjman's authoritarian pretensions. The saddest aspect of Croatian life today is that men like Supek, Gotovac, and Goldstein, once so highly esteemed for their brave actions in defense of Croat liberty, are now freely subjected to the cheap attacks of Tudjman's sycophants and that Croats who should know better remain silent.

Vijenac and *Erasmus* share this group of contributors, although *Vijenac* is perhaps more reader-friendly than the rigorous *Erasmus*. Both, however, are mainly aimed at a specialized, intellectual audience.

A point that should not be omitted is that these intellectuals have been the most prominent Croat critics not only of Tudjman's abuses of power but also of his clear propensity to strike a rotten deal with Milosevic, mainly to the disadvantage of independent Bosnia-Hercegovina. Tudjman has indicated he would favor a carve-up of Bosnia-Hercegovina that would grant Milosevic much of the Great Serbia for which he launched his wars, so long as Croatian ambitions in western Hercegovina are satisfied. For Banac and other oppositional figures, any such deal with Milosevic represents a moral disaster for the Croat nation as well as a real possibility of national suicide, since a Milosevic appeased will clearly be a Milosevic encouraged to pursue further gains.

Novi List, published in Rijeka, draws on different resources in its pursuit of an independent democratic line. It is by no means so aggressively critical as the intellectual organs, although it issues *Feral Tribune* in a print run of fifty thousand weekly copies, distributed throughout Croatia. *Novi List* reflects long-established suspicions on the part of the communities living on the northern Adriatic coast, including Istria, the communities closer to the real West in Italy, cosmopolitan and relatively well off, toward the centralizing powers in Zagreb, the Croatian capital. Istria has a small Italian minority and also has its own dialect of Croatian, known as *cakavica,* which has largely fallen into neglect. *Novi List*'s columns regularly express Istrian regional concerns in undiluted language. One of its most prominent and entertaining contributors is the author and journalist Roman Latkovic, whose comments on the latest manifestations of insanity in Croat national economic and political life are discussed for days in cafés, on the streets and in the parks, at work or in class, with friends and around the family dinner table.

Feral Tribune is in a class by itself. It is the real "people's voice"; as its masthead says, it is "the property of those who write and read it." *Feral* journalists have a simple message, repeated again and again: not all Croats are the same, out to massacre Serbs and Muslims; not all Serbs want to cut the throats of Croats. All Croats, Serbs, and Muslims are victims of a madness fostered by the army and the police, a madness nourished by fear. This message, simple enough on its face but in Croatia as elsewhere in former Yugoslavia now extremely complicated and challenging, is conveyed through sharp, hilarious irony, through a native and delicious malice, and through satire. *Feral* seeks not only to point out the individuals and events that brought Croatia to its present nightmare, but also to be funny. *Feral,* created by *Slobodna Dalmacija* journalists, reflects the sophisticated Mediterranean mentality of Dalmatia, which like Istria is suspicious of Croat centralists but which is also known for the prevalence of an unsparing, quick wit, cultivated in the streets of cities like Sibenik, Zadar, Split, and Dubrovnik, where an inability to take a joke is considered a major character flaw.

Feral applies that wit, deeply ingrained in the local culture, to the analysis of public policy. Early every Monday, after *Feral* arrives on the newsstands, people are seen with their faces buried in its pages, stopping to giggle, often roaring with laughter, alone on the street. A stir of anticipation is felt throughout the weekend, as people await Monday and the arrival of *Feral Tribune.* After three years of shameless propaganda and lies from the "coordinated" media, it is quite remarkable that *Feral* can still make people want to read and believe what they read. It says, in cold print, in black and white collages and cartoons, and typically in the vernacular of the streets, the truths the mass of people themselves dare not express. It also gives the average person the vicarious satisfaction of seeing the regime they hate torn to shreds, if only verbally.

The paper's title and nameplate are a modified version of the *International Herald Tribune* logo, poking fun at the paper's limited, local interest but also hinting at ambitions transcending regional concerns. In the Dalmatian dialect of Croatian, *feral* means street lamp or, simply, a light. Between the words *Feral* and *Tribune* in the logo appears an old miniature engraving of a goddess surrounded by butterflies, rising from a floating banner that reads, in Italian, "Pazzia, Regina di Mondo" (Madness, the Queen of the World), a takeoff on "Pax, Regina Mundi" (Peace, the Queen of the World). Peace is indeed the main concern of *Feral Tribune.* Beneath the logo the paper defines itself as "The weekly magazine of Croatian Anarchists, Protestants, and Heretics, dear to God but not unpopular with the Devil, either."

Feral's editors are Viktor Ivancic, Predrag Lucic, and Boris Dezulovic. The first syllables of their names have been merged to form the paper's slogan: *Viva Ludez. Ludez* is *Feral*'s term for insanity, a word that does not appear in any Croatian slang dictionary but that is easily recognized, and not only in Crotia, to mean craziness, lunacy, creative madness. It means, in loose translation, "All power to the mad!" In times of murderous nationalist pathology, only a surrealist creative madness offers a way out.

Yet *Feral Tribune* is not simply a humor weekly. It is also a serious political journal. Divided into two sections, it entertains but also interprets the Yugoslav tragedy. In the front lampoon section, computer graphics are used to create collages bringing together absurd composites in a single image. The favorite subject is, of course, Franjo Tudjman, who, like the British politicians who are seen in *Private Eye* or the French ones seen in *Canard Enchainé* (The Bound Duck), has appeared naked in *Feral* many times. The cover of the still remembered winter 1993 issue shows a composite photograph of fat and naked Tudjman enjoying a postsex pillow chat with an equally naked Milosevic. In another, a naked Milosevic, posing as the proud father, shows off an infant with the head of Radovan Karadzic, the deranged leader of the Bosnian Serb extremists. Two pages further, the Croat prime minister Nikica Valentic is shown on the toilet.

Tudjman's government has sought to exploit *Feral's* use of sexual or other scandalous graphics. On June 18, 1994, a "pornography" tax was slapped on the paper. This measure, in effect a tax on images, aimed at the destruction of *Feral Tribune* while disguising what was, in truth, an act of brutal censorship. Tudjman has always wanted his government to appear Western and democratic along German or Austrian lines. But the voice of the opposition irritates him; it irritates him intolerably. A tax on "pornographic" publishing allows him to get out of the accusation of censorship while still killing off *Feral Tribune*.

After the imposition of the fine, the editors of *Feral* called various public figures in Croatia for comment. Nenad Popovic, a leading publisher, said that the Croatian government was attempting to cripple, to incapacitate, the most important opposition forum in the country. Popovic stressed that Croatia finds itself marginalized in Europe and the world at large as a natural result of such official policies. The presence of foreign ambassadors in Zagreb prevents the Croatian sovereign from holding a public book burning to which all newspapers and books he dislikes would be consigned. He has to do it behind the scenes. Secretly, clumsily, Tudjman is murdering *Feral Tribune.*

It is, of course, more than a matter of personal irritation on the part of Tudjman at a media source beyond his control. *Feral Tribune* calls things by their real names; it denounces Croat racism and anti-Semitism as well as the intrigues and mutual back scratching within the new establishment. It addresses the greatest of all taboos: Croat war crimes. It even publishes Serbian opposition journalists, such as Petar Lukovic of *Vreme,* the independent Belgrade weekly. Worst of all, from the perspective of the HDZ hard-liners, *Feral Tribune* is in high demand in Serbia, where its articles are reprinted both in *Vreme* and in the daily *Borba.* It must therefore be part of a Chetnik-Communist conspiracy against Croatia. Many impressionable folk are swayed by such arguments; in the spring of 1994 seven private suits were filed against *Feral Tribune,* demanding damages that would have totaled half a million dollars. Nevertheless, *Feral Tribune* remains untamed.

In the summer of 1994, *Feral Tribune,* in its wild manner, addressed a symbolic action by Tudjman involving another kind of animal behavior and referring to the most negative aspect of Croatian history. Tudjman ordered the name of the Croatian currency changed from the dinar to the kuna. The kuna takes its name from animal skins, weasel or mink, used in the far past as money. But the kuna was also the name of the Croatian currency under the so-called Independent State of Croatia—the infamous pro-Nazi puppet regime of the Ustashe, headed by Ante Pavelic during World War II.

Slavko Goldstein has accurately described Tudjman and his party as seeking "to combine national radicalism with proclamations of tolerance, threats of war with a policy of appeasement, the partisan antifascist tradition with some of the Ustashe . . . ideas and symbols." The latter trend was visible in a number of highly controversial actions in which Tudjman flirted with the Ustashe constituency, of which the adoption of the kuna was the worst example. Instead of doing everything he could to distance himself from Pavelic, Tudjman reinstated Pavelic's currency.

Ivo Banac wrote (as cited in *Vreme* in June 1994), "We who have dedicated our lives to struggling, abroad, for the defense of

Croatia from kunaism may now thank political commissar Tudjman for this gesture of historical reconciliation. . . . Unfortunately, the cost of his adventure with the kuna will be paid by others, not least by the [Croatian] refugees . . . presented by Serbian propaganda as coauthors, wrapped in kuna pelts, of Tudjman's book *Wilderness.*"

Feral Tribune pointed out that the worst aspect of the whole kuna matter was that the decision was made in defiance of the Croatian parliament, which has never been known for its powers of resistance to Tudjman's inveiglements but which did not vote for the kuna. Rather, it voted for the title *kruna,* or crown, a name without any historical blemish. However, Tudjman acted by decree, giving the money the name he preferred. One might ask what significance the name of the Croatian currency has when most Croatians' pockets are empty. Who cares? Nevertheless, this imposed decision humiliated the haves as well as the have-nots, since money is a feature of life few if any can completely ignore. If you are lucky, you have to look at it every day.

Beyond the disgust and condemnation provoked by the kuna, there is the worry felt by the average Croat, both at home and abroad, at the image it perpetuates. The world recalls Ante Pavelic as a demented, vampiric criminal and the Ustashe as sadistic monsters. Liberal and democratic Croats, of whom there are many, as well as those who felt some pride at Tito's partial Croat heritage, have gravitated between outrage and profound depression about the labeling of all Croats as genocidal neo-Nazis. But such unfair and prejudiced judgment of a whole people is not easily alleviated when the world press accurately reports that Croat troops inside the country as well as in Bosnia-Hercegovina revel in displaying swastikas and real, as opposed to figurative, Ustashe symbols, while giving the fascist salute and singing Ustashe songs.

Tudjman simply does not care about such trifles. Asked to explain his decision regarding the kuna, he declared, according to *Feral Tribune,* "What's going on here? Some people don't like the kuna? Who are they? Why didn't the Germans change the name of the deutsche mark, the Italians the lira, the French the franc? They were also occupied by Hitler, weren't they?" But, of course, francs, lire, and marks existed before Petain, Mussolini, or Hitler took power, whereas the kuna has existed only under Ante Pavelic and Franjo Tudjman; a tragedy the first time, a farce this time.

Tudjman sees in the kuna an expression of Croat national sovereignty and the stability of the Croat dominion. When asked why outstanding Croats such as Ljudevit Gaj or Josip Juraj Strosmajer, leaders of the Croat national revival in the nineteenth century, as well as of the movements for South Slavic unity, were not pictured on the new currency (which also lacked any portraits of women), Tudjman burst out, "Who says we should have put Gaj and Strosmajer on the currency? Are you saying we should advocate Illyrianism or Yugoslavism all over again?" For Tudjman, these movements are best forgotten, notwithstanding their achievements, while the Ustashe are better memorialized.

Under the Ustashe regime, fewer than ten percent of the Croatian populace supported Pavelic. The same is true today, with about the same percentage supporting Tudjman. If he prefers such historical company, so does *Feral Tribune* take pleasure in the company of his enemies, who love *Feral* for strengthening their community of belief.

Unperturbed by his isolation, even from his own parliament, Tudjman, in another interview soon after the introduction of the new currency, compared himself to Christ. *Feral Tribune* quoted him as saying "Jesus had problems also" and explaining that, like Tudjman's own followers, some of Christ's disciples had failed to accompany the martyr in his crucifixion. More such was to come.

In April 1994, two of Tudjman's closest disciples, Stipe Mesic and Josip Manolic, who joined with him to found the HDZ in 1990, were purged—just as in the old days of Tito and, even, of Stalin. For two months, *Feral* reported the story. Mesic and Manolic, who had been trusted by Tudjman with the highest governmental responsibilities, had committed a simple crime: they disagreed with Tudjman too often. Tudjman, who sees himself as the state, decided to be rid of them—the two most valuable and reasonable politicians with whom he was associated. In response to an interviewer's mention that Mesic and Manolic had created the HDZ, Tudjman said he was tired of seeing credit go to those who did not deserve it. Without me, he said, HDZ would not exist. Not only that, Croatia would not exist, he added. And once more he

compared himself with Christ. "The withdrawal of Mesic and Manolic is no surprise," he said. "I have said before and I will repeat:
Christ had twelve disciples. One betrayed him, another denied
him." Tudjman clearly has arrived at a point where he feels confident in blurting out whatever inanity occurs to him at any moment.
Unfortunately, behind him stands a formidable state and military
power. This makes him feel secure, while it makes *Feral Tribune,*
the independent intellectuals and journalists, as well as a great
many hardy, patriotic Croats very anxious, very often.

In the spring of 1994, *Feral* editor Viktor Ivancic was suddenly drafted into the Croatian army—the only Croat editor in
chief to whom this happened. His conscription represented a violation of law in that, as defined constitutionally, the role of journalists in wartime is to remain with their publication and keep its
editorial board together. It was only because of reaction abroad,
especially from Italy and France, that Ivancic was released from
military service.

Today, faced with all the troubles before him, including the
pornography tax that even a wealthy newspaper could not afford
to pay, Ivancic stands firm: "We have no doubt that an attempt is
being made to liquidate *Feral Tribune*. . . . But we shall continue
to appear, printed on toilet paper if necessary." His spirit, not Tudjman's, is the true expression of the best in the history of the
Croat nation.

Conclusion

Jasminka Udovički and James Ridgeway

T here may be nothing more symbolic of the cruelty and destructiveness of the Yugoslav wars than the final demolition, in November 1993, of the Stari Most, or Old Bridge, in Mostar, the capital of Hercegovina. Completed in 1566 by Hajrudin, a contemporary of the great Ottoman architect Sinan (who was himself of Balkan Christian origin), the bridge was considered by many to be the most beautiful Ottoman structure in the entire Balkan region. Its complete leveling was carried out by Croat militia—members of the so-called Croatian Defense Council (HVO), especially avid in the display of symbols from the Ustashe era, who sought to "ethnically cleanse" Muslims from Hercegovina and who aimed their artillery at the Stari Most in a catharsis of ultranationalist rage. Similar brutalities, first by the Serbian irregulars who seized Mostar at the beginning of the Bosnian war, then by the Croat forces who retook it, resulted in the obliteration of the town's old Turkish quarter, on the left bank of the River Neretva, with its seventeen historic mosques.

During the Tito era, Mostar, the Turkish quarter, the mosques, and the great bridge, as well as the local youths who competed in diving from it into the Neretva, were a major attraction for foreign and domestic tourists. In August 1994 the first diving contest was held in Mostar since the beginning of the fighting. A makeshift bridge was constructed to replace the Old Bridge. In late July 1994 an old crane was hauled in from somewhere to test the waters of the Neretva and establish if the pieces of the Old Bridge had sunk deep enough in the riverbed to allow for a risk-free dive

225

from the improvised structure that replaced it. Amidst the ruins, the summer brought memories of old local rituals, and once again, as before, preparations for the diving contest drew a cheering crowd.

Mostar was a ruin, but it was quiet, while central Bosnia and the Bosnian Muslim enclave around Bihac were not. It could be argued that by midsummer 1994 a low-intensity war had begun its first year in Bosnia. The forging of a tenuous federation of Bosnia and Croatia in the spring had helped end hostilities between Bosnian Muslims and Bosnian Croats. The new merger was presented to media abroad as an act of reconciliation between two of the three warring parties in the Bosnian cockpit, which would bring Bosnia one step closer to peace.

In reality, the federation was viewed by many among both Croatians and Bosnian Muslims as nothing more than a pragmatic, temporary move. "Federation," said Mehmed Aligic, a general in the new Army of Bosnia-Hercegovina, "means opening the roads into Bosnia, and opening the roads means more arms." In early summer 1994, in the old Bosnian town of Travnik, Sir Michael Rose, British commander of the United Nations (UNPROFOR) troops in Bosnia, tried to argue with Aligic, declaring that the Muslim-led forces loyal to a Bosnian republic were not strong enough to regain the lost territories by force. But Aligic was not convinced. Since the Bosnian loyalists were not winning in Geneva, their only choice was to continue fighting on the ground.

The formation of a shaky federation between a Croatia ruled by Franjo Tudjman and a Bosnian republic fighting for its life did not mark an end to the war but, merely, a new phase. Some believed that in this period fighting would become even more intense and argued that fighting would increase if, as the United States began to advocate, the United Nations embargo on arms supplies to the former Yugoslavia, which had been extended to independent Bosnia-Hercegovina, was lifted.

In some respects, the Croatian-Bosnian federation provided an alternative to lifting the embargo, since Iran and other Muslim powers were able to keep a limited stream of weapons flowing into Bosnia through Croatia. Croatia permitted the arms to move under its supervision, often confiscating a share for itself. Removal of the embargo would simply open the process to chaos, as was seen on the international arms markets, both public and clandestine, in 1990 and 1991 when Croatia scrambled to find weapons everywhere from former East Germany to Panama and beyond.

In any event, the traffic of arms via Croatia, as well as seizures of arms from Yugoslav and Serbian forces, local manufacturing, progress in the organization and training of Bosnian loyalist troops, and some territorial gains, as well as the promise of backup from Washington, had become disincentives for the Bosnian government to seek peace. Bosnian politicians frequently indicated that they had acceded to peace proposals advanced by such entities as the international Contact Group, composed of the main global powers and countries with troops in Bosnia, only because they knew that the Bosnian Serb leaders would reject them.

Some observers doubted that the Bosnia-Hercegovinian army could reconquer much territory from the Serbs without significant help from the Croatian army. But the Croats, as noted in the Belgrade opposition weekly *Vreme,* have demonstrated little enthusiasm for such an outcome. The federation itself met with scant support from Croats living in western Hercegovina, or Herceg-Bosna, as that area came to be known. For two years, in a situation much like that experienced among Serbs, the Bosnian Croats were exposed to a propaganda campaign that insisted on the impossibility of a common life with the Muslims and the necessity of a separate Croatian Republic of Herceg-Bosna that would, of course, eventually be absorbed into Croatia. And then, suddenly, they and the Muslims found themselves, once again, in a common state. Western Hercegovina became a Croatian canton within the Bosnian republic, but a rather small one. Medjugorje, the Catholic place of pilgrimage near Mostar that had been a major prewar tourist attraction, was included in a Bosnian Muslim canton rather than a Croatian one. So were Mostar, which Hercegovinian Croats consider inalienably theirs, and the enchanting resort of Neum, which provides Bosnia with its only outlet to the sea, on the Adriatic coast.

Among the Hercegovinian Croats, the proclamation of the federation came close to provoking an armed rebellion. One tabloid in Serbia even reported that members of the Croatian army in Hercegovina had put the Serbian Chetnik cockade on their hats as a protest. As one sop to such feelings, Herceg-Bosna adopted the new Croatian currency, the kuna, regardless of what the future currency in Bosnia may turn out to be. Even under the umbrella of a federation, then, Croats had carved their own territory out of Bosnia-Hercegovina. To further appease them, Tudjman promoted to the rank of general Croatian army commander Praljak, the officer responsible for the final destruction of Mostar's Old Bridge.

Some powerful Croats clearly did not see the federation as a desirable end in itself; for them, the real virtue of a federation would rest in the opportunities it created for the final annexation of a share of Bosnia by Croatia. Tudjman's minister of defense, Gojko Susak, was another among those who admitted from the beginning that the federation was only a temporary measure. According to Susak, Croatia had to agree to the Vienna accords in which the federation was established, but about the eventual disposition of matters, he said, "We'll see." In any case, the Croats were ill inclined to fight alongside the Muslims against the Serbs, fearing that Muslims would gain strength, which could induce them to abandon any alliance with the Croats.

Two overall tendencies have become visible in the Bosnian war. The new army of Bosnia-Hercegovina has increased its strength and proficiency. The morale of its troops is high. "They are like the Vietcong," one Western observer remarked. The Serbian side, meanwhile, is growing perceptibly weaker. Its greatest advantage, its assets in arms and ammunition, which helped keep its morale high, had in large part melted away during twenty-eight months of war. Numerous Bosnian Serb refugees in Serbia and Montenegro, ordered in July 1994 to report for military service, failed to show up. Out of 850 draft-age refugees in the Montenegrin coastal town of Herceg Novi, for example, only two reported to the army command.

To continue the war, Radovan Karadzic, leader of the Bosnian Serb rebels, would have to impose a forced mobilization, as he frequently has in the past. Many Bosnian refugees confirm something that the world media tend to ignore: a considerable number of the Bosnian Serb civilians fighting on the rebel or "Chetnik" side in the war did so against their will; many were coerced into service by threats to their lives and the lives of their families. Such an army, left without energy supplies and ammunition and now abandoned by their creator, Slobodan Milosevic, could hardly be expected to sustain anything but a sluggish, low-intensity war. The war drive, to continue, would have to depend increasingly on local warlords and the criminal underworld.

In an open letter to the Bosnian Serb leadership, dated July 31, 1994, and following their rejection of the Contact Group peace plan, Milosevic charged that leadership with seeking to realize private ambitions by sacrificing the lives of Serbian youth, placing their interests above those of Serbs as a whole, demonstrating a cruel indifference to the interests of Serbs in Serbia, and, finally, with deceiving Belgrade. To underscore this turn against his proxies, Milosevic sealed the border with Bosnia and agreed to allow international monitors to be placed along the Drina River.

Milosevic's showdown with Karadzic and Company and his decision to leave the Bosnian Serbs high and dry confirmed the analysis of those in Belgrade who claimed that Milosevic had no particular attachment to any idea or program as such, including his pledge of "protection of the Serbs," that his only aim was personal power, and that he would change his course in midstream if it proved useful for his political survival. In a bitterly ironic reversal, Milosevic, in effect, freed the antiwar opposition in Serbia from its state of isolation: apparently effortlessly, he crossed the barricades and aligned himself not only with the antiwar groups within the country but also with the West. It was unclear how much support he could expect from the army, but, if need be, he could remove the top army command. Milosevic staked his future on the economic survival of Serbia, for which a lifting of the international sanctions imposed in the wake of the Bosnian atrocities was absolutely necessary. Let the Bosnian Serbs fend for themselves. Both they and the Croatian Serbs seem to have vastly overestimated the stability of their alliance with Milosevic.

It is unlikely that Milosevic will fly to the aid of the Croatian Serbs anytime in the future. Tudjman gave the impression of weighing his options, trying to decide on and prepare an attack on the self-proclaimed Serb "republics" in the Croatian Krajinas, so as to reintegrate them under Croatian authority, if such would prove advantageous for him in the elections set for Croatia in December 1994. The Croatian Krajinas, notwithstanding the blood that has been spilled over them, are of exceptionally limited viability as regional entities, politically, economically, and, even, without Milosevic's help, militarily. Of about 430,000 people living in the Lika region of Dalmatia, the heart of the Krajinas, only eight percent are employed, less than one half of arable land is being cultivated, livestock has been almost thoroughly destroyed, business activity and industrial production have ground to a halt, tourism is nonexistent—in short, the Krajinas are fully dependent on Belgrade and could soon be threatened with starvation. Milosevic, who created the problem, will, when he needs to, charge the Serbian leadership in the Croatian Krajinas with selfishness and will cut them off.

The Krajinas are Croatia's equivalent of the Kosova problem in Serbia. If Milosevic can wash his hands of the Croatian Serbs with ease, he will find it considerably more difficult to so handle Kosova. He has barred Amnesty International from Kosova; he has prevented Tadeusz Mazowiecki, the UN Special Rapporteur for Human Rights for former Yugoslavia, from setting up an office in Belgrade to watch Kosova; he expelled monitors from the Conference for Security and Cooperation in Europe from the region in July 1993. In winter 1993, he ordered the Albanian Academy of Arts and Sciences in Kosova closed. The Kosova economy, which between the mid–1960s and 1990 absorbed over ten billion dollars in Yugoslav federal aid, is now at a total standstill. Kosova is full of boarded-up enterprises and rusted machinery. The mines at Trepca, producing lead, zinc, silver, and other metals, are closed, losing the economy between one hundred and one hundred fifty million dollars annually. Some one hundred thousand workers from other industries have been laid off.

A whole generation of Kosovar Albanians has come of age under the Belgrade-imposed siege, which has been answered with a boycott of Serbian institutions by the Albanians and the proclamation of a Kosova Republic (recognized only by Albania, and at the lowest level). The new generation has been educated in private, underground, and illegal Albanian schools and has grown used to a parallel life in the Kosova Republic. Most of the youth are unemployed, and, according to the Belgrade-based Humanitarian Law Fund, as well as Helsinki Watch and Human Rights Watch, they are beaten, tortured, and killed by the Serbian police on the slightest pretexts. Even if Milosevic does nothing to further aggravate conflict in Kosova, violence could erupt as a response to the brutality of daily life.

However, the Democratic League of Kosova (LDK), the main party of the Kosovar Albanians, led by Ibrahim Rugova, has successfully maintained a policy of nonviolent resistance, although the LDK is plagued with internal unrest. The international community has endorsed the need for Kosova to regain its prior autonomy within Serbia but has made it clear it would not support independence for Kosova. In May 1994, Rugova and Albanian President Sali Berisha met in Tirana and agreed to work toward dialogue between Kosovar Albanians and the Serbian authorities. Milan Panic, the prime minister (briefly) of rump Yugoslavia, had initiated negotiations with Rugova in 1992.

Had Panic won the Serbian elections against Milosevic that December, tensions in Kosova might have been somewhat eased. Kosovar Albanians knew that without their support, Panic would lose in the elections. In spite of it, they boycotted the elections and refused to support Panic. This signaled to many in Belgrade, supportive of the autonomy of Kosova, that autonomy itself was not the ultimate Albanian objective. With Panic the Albanians could have won autonomy but would have given up the efforts of achieving independence. With the reestablishment of their former autonomy, such as the Kosovar Albanians enjoyed between 1974 and 1987, the international community would have considered the Kosova problem solved. Little understanding would have remained for Kosova's secession. Two prominent Albanian leaders, Adem Demaçi and Veton Surroi, have argued that Albanians should accept a high level of autonomy within Serbia. But Demaçi, in particular, has grown isolated from Kosovar Albanian opinion, which remains wary of any compromise with Serbs.

Most Serbs remain touchy, to put it very mildly, about their belief in their "historical right" to Kosova. The medieval Orthodox monasteries in Kosova, which Serbs consider their greatest cultural treasure and which would, should Kosova secede, end up in a foreign country, are always brought up as a justification for Serbian fears of Kosovar Albanian secession. Veton Surroi has suggested a creative solution: partition of Kosova and an extraterritorial status for the monasteries, with free access to the monasteries guaranteed. This proposal, however, has met with little approval.

Although the Kosovar Albanian leadership today believes that Albanian interests in Kosova can be defended only by nonviolent means, the ethnic partition of Bosnia would establish the basis for the same policy to be implemented in Kosova. If and when the partition of Bosnia is carried out, Kosova Albanians might demand that the international community follow its own principles in Kosova. But rather than bringing a true Balkan settlement, this sort of development would more likely open up yet another chapter of war, spreading it south.

Whatever happens in Kosova will reverberate in Macedonia, which, with Slovenia, is the only region of former Yugoslavia spared from nationalist hysteria, although its own ethnic strains are by no means negligible. "Our country exemplifies the possibility of multiethnic existence," said its president, Kiro Gligorov, in a February 1994 interview. Macedonia, for a time, appeared to be doing quite well, certainly when compared with the parts of former Yugoslavia wracked by the war. To ameliorate the impact of sanctions imposed on neighboring Serbia, a major trading partner, Macedonia redirected much of its commerce through the Greek port of Salonika. People from Serbia who visited Lake Ohrid in the summer of 1992 reported that in comparison to Serbia under sanctions, Macedonia looked "like California." Everything seemed lush and abundant, the stores were full, and the prices were reasonable. And the Macedonians were mellow and hospitable, genuinely uninterested in taking sides or pursuing political agendas.

But on February 16, 1994, Greece, swept with a demagogic campaign against Macedonia, cut the Salonika lifeline. It declared its own trade embargo, so long as the state continued to be named Macedonia. That name alone, a purely geographical appellation that also applies to areas in Bulgaria and northern Greece, became the pretext for Greek politicians and a hypnotized Greek public to demand imposition of a blockade that has cost Macedonia sixty million dollars per month. Macedonian President Kiro Gligorov insists that the problem is imaginary and has tried to reason with Greece by offering assurances that Macedonia has no intention whatever of claiming any part of presently Greek territory. Yet because of the blockade, Macedonian trade has again been redirected, this time through Bulgaria and Albania. Traffic, both commercial and tourist, has run from Belgrade south to Athens via Macedonia for most of this century; the backward condition of the transport and commerce infrastructure along the alternative, long-neglected West-to-East route has made the cost of Macedonian exports and imports rise fourfold. Above all, the blockade has deprived Macedonia of its energy resources. Businesses in Macedonia, large and small, have closed. People are laid off, factories have been forced to suspend two-thirds or more of production, and farmers have stopped raising crops for export. Unemployment is rising, and even those who still work have not seen a paycheck for months. Finally, Macedonian currency and financial institutions are by no means stable.

With economic hardship came the aggravation of ethnic tensions. The composition of Macedonia's population is a subject of considerable debate. A 1991 census recorded a population of about two million, of which 425,000, or something like one-fifth, were Albanian. The Albanians themselves insist that their numbers in Macedonia run closer to forty percent of the total, or 800,000. In that census about 44,000 Serbs were also listed. Some Serbs, apparently carried away by past claims to Macedonia as "South Serbia," assert that their numbers in the country may reach 180,000 and even 400,000, but this is a hallucination. The Albanians, for their part, have threatened to boycott further voting in Macedonia if what they consider to be an officially sanctioned but demographically invalid undercount of their community is not rectified.

The main Albanian party in Macedonia is the Party of Democratic Prosperity (PDP), from which a radical wing has emerged, headed by Mendu Thaci. Thaci is opposed to any collaboration with the Macedonian state authorities, including participation in the legislature, unless Albanians are guaranteed a higher number of parliamentary representatives and more posts in the state bureaucracy.

Albanian militancy has fostered anti-Albanian resentment among Macedonian Slavs and even a certain pro-Serb sentiment. In the beginning of 1994, President Gligorov denied that Serbia represented a threat to Macedonia. He pointed out that the Yugoslav army evacuated Macedonia without incident. Nevertheless, and despite Gligorov's optimism, Milosevic has so far refused to recognize the independence of Macedonia—a move that would have scored points with the international community because it would indicate that Serbia has no intention of spreading the Yugo-slav war south.

Gligorov has tried to argue with Milosevic that recognition would prevent the spread of Albanian unrest into Macedonia. Milosevic has not budged. He may believe that the dynamics of ethnic rivalry in Macedonia will, in the end, favor him. If the Slavic Macedonians perceive the Albanians as the source of their principal problem, Serbia may try to intervene as Macedonia's ally and protector. In that case, Macedonia might end up returning to some form of union with Serbia—another triumph for Milosevic.

Genuine peace in Macedonia cannot be assured as long as the tensions in Kosova are running high and as long as Macedonia's own economy continues to decline at its current rate. Neither the European countries nor the United States, however, seem to have fully grasped the gravity of the situation. They have not helped Macedonia offset the colossal losses its economy incurred because of the sanctions against Serbia under Milosevic; worse, the international community has failed to put significant pressure on Greece to abandon its illegal and provocative assault on the well-being of the Macedonians, using the fictitious excuse of the country's name. Some among Macedonia's Slav nationalists have heightened their rhetoric against the wise and moderate government of Kiro Gligorov.

The inept handling of Macedonia by the international community parallels, of course, the scandalously incompetent response to the horrors of the war in Bosnia. The July 1994 Bosnian peace proposal, presented as the "ultimate" plan by the Contact Group, had one rather inconvenient flaw: nobody really wanted it. Not the Bosnian Serbs, who thought the plan would require them to surrender the most valuable parts of territory they had seized, and too much of it at that; not the Bosnian Muslims and their loyalist allies, who did not believe that the Serbs would honor the agreement but who also felt that their military fortunes were improving; not the Croats, because the deal guaranteed the Serbs a corridor to the areas they occupied in Croatia; and, finally, not Bill Clinton, for had the plan been adopted, the United States would have been expected to send up to thirty thousand ground troops to maintain peace.

The rejection of the proposal by the Bosnian Serb leaders led President Clinton back to the idea of lifting the arms embargo; but in September Bosnian President Alija Izetbegovic backed off even from that request. Of course, lifting the embargo would not end the war; it would only "level the playing field," something demanded by a significant sector of Western opinion in order to show that action had been taken. The war would continue, and its momentum would probably be restored. The UN and international observers would, presumably, leave, with the civilian population more than ever at the mercy of the armed powers. The Bosnia-Hercegovinian army might in the end recapture some, even perhaps most, of the Serb-held territory. "Great Serbia" might be crippled, its territories outside Serbia itself amputated. The war for the conquest of territory would have come to a just end. But meanwhile, tens, perhaps hundreds, of thousands more Bosnian Muslim civilians, along with high numbers of Croatian and Bosnian Serb civilians, would have lost their homes, their loved ones, their future, and their lives. "Peace?" said one Bosnian woman to a Western reporter, "in ten years, perhaps. I'll be forty-five, if things go well."

The war did not begin as her war—a people's war. The hatred that astounded the world was engineered, not innate. Today, three and a half years after the war began, hatred has become quite real. Yet it is safe to assume that in the long run, after the carnage and "ethnic cleansing" are ended, some form of cooperation, beginning with the economy, will be restored between the former Yugoslav republics. Without such cooperation, the successor states face insurmountable obstacles to development. Not ideology or mutual affinity but economic reality will render ethnically pure fiefdoms or reservations obsolete, once they resume functioning in peacetime, as normal political entities. The bonds broken for the sake of a territorial redivision will tend to form anew, not because anyone has forgotten the horrors of war but because a common household will prove to be the least costly and economically most rational outcome—indeed the only viable one. Everyday life will compel the populations to intermix and blend once again. And whatever the borders, the states will again become nationally mixed. All this may take time, perhaps a great deal of time. But for durable peace and stability in the Balkans, nothing less will do.

About the Authors

Sven Balas is the pseudonym for a young Croatian writer and broadcaster who wishes to remain anonymous.

Slavko Ćuruvija (Serb), born in 1949 in Belgrade, Serbia, was named Yugoslavia's Journalist of the Year in 1989. Until 1993 he worked as a political commentator for *Borba,* the Belgrade independent daily, after which he briefly served as the paper's temporary executive editor. In 1994 he left *Borba* to become the producer of a political program of the independent television station Studio B.

Branka Prpa-Jovanović (Croatian), born in 1953 in Split, Croatia, is a historian married to a Serb and works at the Institute of the History of Modern Serbia in Belgrade.

Milan Milošević (Serb), born in 1945 in Belgrade, Serbia, is the political commentator for the independent weekly *Vreme.*

James Ridgeway, born in 1936 in Auburn, New York, is the Washington, D.C., correspondent for *The Village Voice,* where he has worked for more than twenty years. He traveled to the former Yugoslavia for the *Voice* in 1991. He is the author of more than a dozen books, including *Blood in the Face: The Ku Klux Klan, Aryan Nations, Nazi Skinheads, and the Rise of a New White Culture; March to War;* and *The Haiti Files.* With Kevin Rafferty, he has produced and directed two films: *Blood in the Face* and *Feed.*

Stipe Sikavica (Croatian), born in 1936 in Split, Croatia, was a journalist for *The People's Army* and *Front,* two principal Yugoslav army periodicals. He was forced to retire in 1991 after publishing in *NIN,* the leading Belgrade weekly at the time, an article on the role of the military establishment in helping Milosevic consolidate his power. He has been a freelance writer since 1989 for *Borba,* the Belgrade independent daily, and, more recently, *Republika,* the independent monthly.

Ejub Štitkovac (Muslim), born in 1947 in Zepa, eastern Bosnia, graduated from Gazi Husrevbeg, Sarajevo's Islamic theological school, and worked as an imam for two years near Mostar. He is currently a commentator on the Islamic and Arab world for the independent daily *Borba.*

Mirko Tepavac (mixed Serb and Croat origin), born in 1922 in Zemun, was the minister of foreign affairs in former Yugoslavia from the 1960s until he resigned in 1972. He is now the main contributor to the independent oppositional Belgrade monthly *Republika.*

Ivan Torov (Macedonian), born in 1945 in Stip, Macedonia, is a political commentator for the independent Belgrade daily *Borba.* In 1987 he received *Borba's* annual award for journalism. He was a correspondent for a number of journals and magazines in former Yugoslavia, including *Danas* (Zagreb) and *Oslobodjenje* (Sarajevo).

Jasminka Udovički (Serb), born in 1945 in Belgrade, is a professor of social science at the Massachusetts College of Art in Boston, where she has taught since 1979. She travels frequently to the former Yugoslavia, and her reports on the Balkan crisis have appeared in *The Village Voice, Radical America,* and *In These Times.*

Selected Bibliography

Banac, Ivo. *National Question in Yugoslavia: Origin, History, Politics.* Ithaca: Cornell University Press, 1984.

Cohen, Leonard. *Broken Bonds: The Disintegration of Yugoslavia.* Boulder, Colo.: Westview Press, 1993.

Cohen, Leonard, and Warwick, Paul. *Political Cohesion in a Fragile Mosaic: The Yugoslav Experience.* Boulder, Colo.: Westview Press, 1983.

Djordjević, Dimitrije, ed. *The Creation of Yugoslavia, 1914–1918.* Santa Barbara: Clio Books, 1980.

Glenny, Misha. *The Fall of Yugoslavia.* New York: Penguin Books, 1992.

Hobsbawm, E. J. *Nations and Nationalism since 1780.* Cambridge: Cambridge University Press, 1990.

Jelavich, Barbara. *History of the Balkans.* Cambridge: Cambridge University Press, 1983.

Jelavich, Charles. *The Establishment of the Balkan National States, 1804–1920.* Seattle: University of Washington Press, 1977.

Lydall, Harold. *Yugoslavia in Crisis.* New York: Clarendon Press, 1989.

Rusinow, Denison. *The Yugoslav Experiment, 1948–1974.* Stanford: Stanford University Press, 1977.

Singleton, Fred. *A Short History of the Yugoslav Peoples.* London: Cambridge University Press, 1985.

Taylor, A. J. P. *The Habsburg Monarchy, 1809–1918.* London, 1941.

Thompson, Mark. *A Paper House.* New York: Pantheon Books, 1992.

Vucinich, Wayne S. *Serbia between East and West.* Stanford: Stanford University Press, 1954.

West, Rebecca. *Black Lamb and Gray Falcon: A Journey through Yugoslavia.* New York: Viking Press, 1941.

Index